DISCARD

PRAISE FOR *WE ARE CHARLESTON*

"Emotional, careful, and rich, *We Are Charleston* makes sense of the senseless, the Charleston, South Carolina, massacre of June 2015. From one abominable event the book shapes a testament, an investigation, and a history. *We Are Charleston* sets the crime within the flow of race, church life, and Southern history and offers moving portraits of the victims. It does the near impossible, which is to redeem tragedy on behalf of hope."

—Edward Ball, author, *Slaves in the Family*

"This is a beautifully woven story, rich in history and narrative detail, that describes how the Mother Emanuel AME Church turned hate into forgiveness, and an act of brutality into a lesson that has inspired the nation and the world."

—Erik Calonius, former *Wall Street Journal* writer and author, *The Wanderer: The Last American Slave Ship and the Conspiracy That Set Its Sails*

"The authors intensely probe the sanctified character of African Methodism and reveal how the members of Mother Emanuel in Charleston and other AME churches stress personal holiness that undergirds forgiveness and social holiness that mandates militant opposition to the social sin of racism. These attributes, deeply embedded in African American religion, have shown the nation and the world a sure route to healing and reconciliation."

—Dennis C. Dickerson, retired AME Church historiographer; and James M. Lawson, Jr. Professor of History, Vanderbilt University

"In *We Are Charleston* a sharp investigative reporter, a distinguished historian, and a gifted poet have blended their skills, their knowledge, and their humanity in order to craft a probing account of and an insightful meditation on what happened to nine people who got caught being black and trying to be Christian on a warm night in Charleston. This unsentimental yet sensitive book will become a very important part of the way that we remember and honor those nine unique individuals. It will also become an indispensable part of the way that we try to understand the spiritual, racial, social, and political meanings of a tragic moment in a long history that we all share."

—Reginald F. Hildebrand, associate professor, African American
Studies & History, University of North Carolina at Chapel Hill

WE ARE
CHARLESTON

WE ARE
CHARLESTON

Tragedy and Triumph at Mother Emanuel

Herb Frazier

Bernard Edward Powers Jr., PhD

Marjory Wentworth

W Publishing Group

An Imprint of Thomas Nelson

Published in Nashville, Tennessee, by W Publishing Group, an imprint of Thomas Nelson.

Thomas Nelson titles may be purchased in bulk for educational, business, fund-raising, or sales promotional use. For information, please e-mail SpecialMarkets@ ThomasNelson.com.

The personal stories told in this book are based on true events, and permission has been granted for the use of the real names of and correspondence from individuals interviewed for the writing of this book.

All historic newspapers quoted were transcribed by Dr. Bernard Edward Powers Jr., and, unless otherwise noted, were viewed on microfilm, the *Christian Recorder, Essex Patriot,* and *New York Freeman* at the College of Charleston Addlestone Library and the *Charleston Courier* (also sometimes known as the *Charleston News and Courier* and *Post and Courier*) at the downtown branch of the Charleston County Public Library and the College of Charleston Addlestone Library.

Scripture quotations marked NRSV are from the New Revised Standard Version Bible. © 1989 National Council of the Churches of Christ in the United States of America. Used by permission. All rights reserved.

Scripture quotations marked KJV are from the King James Version. Public domain.

Library of Congress Control Number: 2016930186

ISBN 978-0-7180-7731-0

Printed in the United States of America

16 17 18 19 20 RRD 6 5 4 3 2 1

In memory of Sharonda Coleman-Singleton, Cynthia Graham Hurd, Susie Jackson, Ethel Lance, DePayne Middleton-Doctor, Clementa Carlos Pinckney, Tywanza Sanders, Daniel L. Simmons Sr., and Myra Thompson. For Jennifer and Malana Pinckney, Felicia Sanders and her granddaughter, and Polly Sheppard.

*

Herb Frazier dedicates this book to his father, the late Benjamin Frazier. He also extends a special dedication to his mother, Albertha Nelson Frazier, and to the next generation: his grandchildren, Lauryn, Nicholas, Kinsley, and Connor Thomas; Nathaniel Hamilton; and Roman Lee Frazier.

Dr. Bernard Edward Powers Jr. dedicates this book to John Burkett, his maternal grandfather, who never attended school beyond the fourth grade but whose lifelong example of self-education inspired his grandson's love of reading.

Marjory Wentworth dedicates this book to the memory of her father, John Heath, whose love and knowledge of history and literature are still her greatest inspiration. Special thanks to her family: Peter, Mary, Hunter, Alice, Oliver, and Taylor.

Forgiveness is nothing less than the way we heal the world.

—Bishop Desmond Tutu and Mpho
Tutu, *The Book of Forgiving*

CONTENTS

INTRODUCTION

The flash of the assailant's pistol on the evening of June 17, 2015, touched off a series of events that shook the foundation of Charleston's already beleaguered Mother Emanuel AME Church, reverberating back to its very beginnings. Comparatively few people knew anything about this congregation before the heartrending news stories emerged, but it is a church that through the years has experienced the trials of the biblical Job. More than once, the hands of man or the raw forces of nature have shaken the church to its core, threatening its very existence. Now, in the aftermath of more recent events, Mother Emanuel is faced once again with having to find a way to heal and rebuild, both literally and metaphorically.

Like the rest of the community and, indeed, the nation, we were deeply saddened and unnerved that such an unspeakable crime could be committed in the place we love and call our own. We were also captivated by the tremendous outpouring of sympathy emanating from around the world for our fair city by the sea. Everyone wanted to do something to relieve the pain, to somehow right the wrong or even assuage personal guilt for failing to challenge the racist forces still extant in America. None of us was a stranger to Mother Emanuel; to the contrary, we each had close friends or relatives in the church, and, in fact, Herb grew up in the congregation where his grandmother and father were members.

Although each of us was in the midst of other projects, what had occurred could not be ignored; we, too, desired to act by pooling our collective professional resources to explore the tragedy. Using the tools of the investigative reporter to find the central stories, the historian's grasp of the past as context, and the poet's ability to plumb the depths of the human condition, we began this new project together. We soon discovered that to be successful, it would take our combined abilities to achieve a task that not one of us could have accomplished alone. And it's this unique combination of backgrounds and experiences united by our shared passion for our home that enables us to tell this story in one voice, speaking to and for many others. The title addresses who we are as writers while suggesting the universality of what happened in Charleston. What happened on June 17 was an assault on humanity, and what has happened since has implications that echo far beyond South Carolina.

The summer that Emanuel's walls were scarred by bullets and the floors stained with blood also witnessed a renewed wave of church burnings and shots fired into Southern black churches—all of which were painful reminders of the long history of violence perpetrated against African Americans and their sanctuaries. The Charleston church shooting was the most recent in a series of events that further shattered the myth that President Barack Obama's election had ushered in a post-racial America. And if there was any doubt, the events of the previous year—in Ferguson, Baltimore, and North Charleston—clearly showed that race still mattered in America, but black lives seemed not to. Reverend Clementa Pinckney, the late pastor of Mother Emanuel, once put it this way: "I think South Carolina has—and across the South we have—a deep appreciation of history. We haven't always had a deep appreciation of each other's histories."[1]

What follows is an attempt to use the tragedy that occurred in

Charleston as a way to explore the racialized history of the city and our nation that made such a crime possible. Known as the Holy City, Charleston is, ironically, the cradle of slavery. This inherent contradiction has led to tension in the region. Yet Charleston, rated several times as the number-one United States city to visit by *Conde Nast Traveler* and *Travel and Leisure* magazines,[2] remained immune from racial unrest. North Charleston, the adjoining city where unarmed Walter Scott was shot in the back multiple times by a white policeman on April 4, 2015, seemed worlds away from Charleston's charming cobblestone streets lined with horse-drawn carriages filled with tourists. It seems even farther from where Carnival Cruise ships unload at the end of North Market Street, not far from Gadsden's Wharf, where ships carrying thousands of Africans to be sold into slavery once docked. These elements of Charleston's history represent the other side of the city so well known for its preservation ethic and colonial-era and antebellum mansions. Racist attitudes rooted in the dark past have sometimes been preserved in the present.

We also want to explain the origins and nature of the African Methodist Episcopal Church (AME) and the position of Mother Emanuel in the denomination and in Charleston. As symbols they are important, and without this understanding a visitor or casual news reader can't fully grasp the meaning of what happened on June 17.

African Methodism grew out of the struggle against slavery and institutional racism as black people sought physical, financial, and cultural autonomy. Emanuel's roots are found among Charleston's largely enslaved population before the Civil War. While efforts to build a congregation were initially thwarted by a determined racist persecution, after the war Emanuel's congregants experienced a resurrection that enabled them to forge ahead in the struggle for racial justice. In that regard, Emanuel and other AME churches remained true to the principles of the denominational founder, Richard Allen. Their efforts, along with those of other denominations, were also prominent in the civil rights movement, and the struggle continues to the present time to embody the meaning of Martin Luther King Jr.'s "Beloved Community," a term he popularized that "captured the imagination of people of goodwill all over the world." For Dr. King, the Beloved Community was "a realistic, achievable goal that could be attained by a critical mass of people committed to and trained in the philosophy and methods of nonviolence."[3]

Last, and certainly not least, this work explores the boundless gift of grace—exemplified by the forgiveness that family members have demonstrated—which emanates from the spiritual philosophy of the church. We know those teachings because we have had the opportunity to commune at Emanuel Church and interact with the family members in intimate settings so we could tell their stories. The Emanuel Nine, along with the five who survived this tragedy and their extended families, lived the word of the gospel; their spirit of forgiveness was in keeping with those whose lives were built around Christ's teachings. They practiced what they preached, and they will serve as a model for what is possible.

When President Obama gave the eulogy for Rev. Pinckney, he referenced the racist attack on Charleston's original AME church and the scattering of its congregation—as well as the church's capacity to rise up again, like a phoenix from the ashes. Emanuel's families have consistently demonstrated this ability. This capacity for resurrection is central to the story that unfolds in the following pages.

ONE

WRONG CHURCH, WRONG PEOPLE, WRONG DAY

Wednesday night is church night in the South, and it is no different at Mother Emanuel African Methodist Episcopal Church. The white stucco church stands near the heart of downtown Charleston along Calhoun Street, an east-west thoroughfare that spans the city. This particular Wednesday evening fell during a series of steamy, hot summer days, when the temperature reached almost one hundred degrees, and as the sun set, about fifty dedicated members of Mother Emanuel gathered for the Quarterly Conference. Six o'clock is normally the time set aside for Bible study at the church, but this evening it was delayed for the earlier business meeting. Budget items were discussed, and plans for the long-overdue elevator, still under construction, were hashed out. Fifty-nine-year-old Myra Thompson received a license renewal, and Reverend DePayne Middleton-Doctor, forty-nine, and Dr. Brenda Nelson received their local licenses to minister from Presiding Elder Norvel Goff. After the meeting most folks went home, but a dozen of the most devout parishioners stayed for the Bible study, which started around eight o'clock.

Polly Sheppard, a seventy-year-old retired nurse, was going to leave after the business meeting, but she ran into Thompson in the ladies' room and decided to stay since Thompson was leading the night's Bible study. Nelson, a Bible study regular, went home to check on her sputtering air conditioner, to make sure it had been repaired and was blowing cold air again.

At exactly 8:16 p.m., a skinny young white man with a classic bowl haircut, wearing a sweatshirt and a small fanny pack, entered the back door of the church and joined the small group gathered in the large central room on the lower level of the church, below the sanctuary. Surrounded by smaller meeting rooms and offices, this room is used for church dinners and similar social gatherings. Thirteen participants sat around tables covered with white cloths to study passages from the fourth chapter of Mark. In verses 13 to 20, Jesus explains to his followers the parable of the sower that he had just finished teaching to the multitude by the sea. He warned against those who only half-heartedly embrace God's teaching. Among them the word is "sown on rocky ground. . . . But they have no root, and endure only for a while; then, when trouble or persecution arises on account of the word, immediately they fall away" (vv. 16–17 NRSV). This passage continues to describe the way "the cares of the world, and the lure of wealth . . . choke the word, and it yields nothing" (v. 19 NRSV). Hauntingly, in verse 15, Satan is described as coming and taking away "the word that is sown in them."

The young man asked to sit next to the church's pastor, Clementa Pinckney, and for a time the visitor remained quiet. Though a stranger to the group, he was welcomed and included as anyone would have been in this house of worship. Toward the end of the Bible study, Myra Thompson started to say the benediction. As eyes were closed and heads were bowed, the young man with the child's haircut pulled a handgun from his fanny pack and started shooting.

He shot Pinckney point-blank. Reverend Daniel L. Simmons Sr.

immediately lunged at the shooter, crying out for his pastor; the young man fired at Simmons multiple times. There is some speculation that the killer may have panicked when Simmons reacted. But there is no question that the young man fired seventy-seven bullets, leaving eight people dead and one mortally wounded. Felicia Sanders had grabbed her eleven-year-old granddaughter and pushed her face against her body so the child wouldn't cry out, telling her to play dead. Her twenty-six-year-old son, Tywanza, had been shot and was beside her and his eighty-seven-year-old aunt, Susie Jackson.

Tywanza tried to convince the gunman to stop firing during one of the five times the killer reloaded. Tywanza pleaded with him not to do it, but the gunman had a racial agenda: "I have to do this. You rape our women, and you're taking over our country. And you have to go," he shouted. "It don't matter, I'm going to shoot you all."[1] Tywanza had posted a Snapchat video of the Bible class minutes before the gunman opened fire. The gunman is seen in the video.

Tywanza and Pinckney were among those who died in the room, in addition to Tywanza's aunt, Susie Jackson, and her cousin, Ethel Lance, the church's sexton. Also among the dead were Cynthia Graham Hurd, a librarian; Myra Thompson, a minister; and Reverend Sharonda Coleman-Singleton, a mother of three. Rev. DePayne Middleton-Doctor, a mother of four, lay dead too. Vietnam veteran Daniel L. Simmons Sr. was rushed to a hospital, where he died.

The killer walked past Polly Sheppard, who was cowering under a table praying.[2] He asked her if she had been shot, and she answered no. Some have said he spared her life. The gunman kept walking, and although he tried firing his gun, he'd run out of bullets. He then left through the door he'd entered less than one hour before, got in his car, and drove away into the night.

Jennifer Pinckney, the pastor's wife, and their youngest daughter, Malana, were in the church office. They heard everything that was going on. During the rounds of gunfire, Malana asked her mother, "Mama, is Daddy going to die?" Jennifer called 911.[3] Sheppard could hear the sirens approaching and immediately went into nurse mode, checking on Felicia's son, Tywanza.[4] She checked Pinckney's pulse, and she knew he was dead. Miraculously, both Felicia Sanders and her granddaughter were survivors too.

Soon Calhoun Street, ironically named for pro-slavery senator and vice president John C. Calhoun, was swarming with police cruisers and ambulances. The street was sealed at the cross streets on either end of the block. Police armed with assault weapons were on patrol as a helicopter hovered overhead. When WCSC television anchorman Raphael James arrived on the scene with another reporter and two videographers around 9:20 p.m., he didn't know many details about the shooting, but when the coroner arrived, his worst fears were confirmed. James knew Pinckney and hoped that he was still at the Hillary Clinton presidential campaign event elsewhere in the city that evening. As James and his crew were stationed at Calhoun and Meeting streets, *Post and Courier* reporter Andrew Knapp was arriving from the east side of the church. He had grabbed his cameras and other gear from his car and begun to walk toward the church. Before any official announcement, Knapp knew the magnitude of the tragedy. He heard on his smartphone app, which monitors emergency channels, that eight were dead inside the church.[5]

A crowd had already gathered at the edge of the barrier west of the church, and Raphael James was at the center of it. An acquaintance approached and said his aunt, Susie Jackson, was in the church. Apart from that, there was no clear sense of who was inside Mother Emanuel, who the victims were, and whether or not there were any survivors. Church and community leaders and more journalists began to arrive. According to James, "the atmosphere was electric, and tension was in the air."[6] For all they knew, the shooter was nearby. Those tense times were heightened when James and others heard a loud bang that sounded like a gunshot. The sound seemed to have come from a corner gas station. James saw that police had grabbed a young white man wearing dark pants and a light gray sweatshirt. The man matched the description of the gunman, but as James points out, this description would fit "85 percent of the thousands of male College of Charleston students living within a quarter-mile radius of Mother Emanuel AME Church."[7] The man was soon released. He was a local photographer who was taking pictures of the people who had gathered nearby.

It hadn't taken long for authorities to see a clear image of the killer from church security cameras, and that image was circulated among police nationwide. Fear was palpable; could there be more shootings? "In that moment, we could believe anything," James later said.[8] News crews were moved another block west of the church. Soon there were bomb threats at nearby hotels. Although no one was evacuated, traffic was diverted. Additional vehicles from the coroner's office pulled up to the church. Was at least one of the bomb scares a ruse to clear journalists and others away from the scene when the bodies were being removed? Hundreds had gathered in Marion Square, a large open space west of the church. While clergy tried to calm people, activists and others were seething with rage and threatening, "We're going to get this guy."[9] Peace prevailed, however, and around 11:30 p.m. at a press conference, Charleston mayor Joseph P. Riley Jr. was adamant about referring to the shootings as a hate crime. Charleston police chief Greg Mullen confirmed the worst: eight people were found dead in the church. (Authorities would later confirm Simmons had died at the Medical University Hospital.) At that time no names were released, but word circulated that Pinckney had left the Clinton event for the Bible study.

Meanwhile, the families were notified, and they gathered at two nearby hotels. Church elders and pastors, ten chaplains, and a number of community leaders were there to comfort them. People initially gathered in the Courtyard Marriott, which is located almost across the street from the church, but it was decided the hotel was too close to the crime scene, so everyone was moved farther away, to the Embassy Suites hotel on Meeting Street. According to the Coastal Crisis Chaplaincy's senior chaplain on the scene, Rob Dewey Sr., within an hour of the shooting, approximately three hundred relatives, friends, and members of the church were gathered in the ballroom of the Embassy Suites. They ranged in age from toddlers to the elderly. Once the facts emerged, the coroner's office met with family members of the nine who were killed in two of the smaller side rooms. Once Presiding Elder Norvel Goff and other AME pastors arrived, they prayed together, and Goff led the group in the old hymn "What a Friend We Have in Jesus."[10] According to Black Lives Matter activist Muhiyidin d'Baha—who was one of the people who wanted to shut down the city in hopes of finding the killer—elder James Johnson of the National Action Network told him to let the police do their job and go comfort the grieving relatives. When d'Baha met with family members, grief and fear, not anger, were palpable.[11] People stayed at the hotel until 4:30 a.m. The city was on high alert, and few slept that long, hot night in June.

The Federal Bureau of Investigation joined the investigation almost immediately, releasing a photograph of a black 2000 Hyundai sedan. By Thursday morning, Dylann Roof, a twenty-one-year-old from Eastover, South Carolina, was identified as the suspect. Authorities discovered that his ATM card was used in Charlotte, North Carolina, a little before six o'clock that morning. Around the same time, Roof's father phoned the authorities and identified him from the security footage, according to a court affidavit from Charleston police. Later that morning Deborah Dills, who worked at a florist shop in Kings Mountain, North Carolina, was on her way to work when she recognized Roof's Hyundai and his distinct haircut from newspaper photos. She called her boss, who notified local police. A minister of music at her own church, Dills was devastated by the news of the church shooting and told the *Post and Courier* that she had been at her own church Wednesday night and felt that it could easily have been her that was murdered.[12] At 10:40 a.m. on June 18, police pulled Roof's car over onto a dirt driveway along US Highway 74 in Shelby, North Carolina. Officers slowly approached the vehicle, and Roof was cooperative. He was searched for weapons, handcuffed, and arrested in a surprisingly calm manner.

Back in Charleston, leaders, community activists, clergy, and caring citizens were called together for a prayer vigil at Morris Brown, another historic AME church, by Presiding Elder Joseph Darby. Hundreds filled the pews, including Mayor Riley, South Carolina governor Nikki R. Haley, US representative James Clyburn, South Carolina senator Tim Scott, and dozens of other officials. Hundreds more gathered outside to sing hymns and pray, to hold one another up in the midday sun. Police handed out bottles of water, and nearby, a furniture store opened its air-conditioned showrooms. The crowd was both black and white, and no one seemed to notice or care.

It became immediately clear that the community was joined together in grief and support, but the day after the prayer vigil, numerous bomb threats were reported in and around Charleston, and at least three buildings were evacuated, including a church. Still, the community continued to come together across racial lines, and a Friday night prayer vigil was planned at the College of Charleston basketball arena. Thousands attended, and the stage was filled with clergy, local and state officials, and police. This came to the attention of Reverend Nelson Rivers III, who also noticed US Republican senators Tim Scott and Lindsey Graham and Republican congressman Mark Sanford in the audience. It was an opportunity for him to call for the removal of the Confederate flag from the statehouse. He knew "they need[ed] to hear this now,"[13] and when he spoke, the mostly white crowd jumped to its feet in thunderous applause. He was astounded.

Mayor Riley, an active supporter of taking down the flag, spoke about dedicating the planned International African American Museum to the victims and in addressing the community's collective grief, stated, "In our broken hearts, we realize we love each other more."[14] Local leaders called for unity and peace. There were prayers and hymns, and everyone was handed a rose when they walked through the doors. Most of the attendees carried their roses to Calhoun Street, past Anderson Cooper and other recognizable media personalities reporting from platforms assembled on the sidewalks, to join the throng of people paying respects in front of Mother Emanuel. One block east of the church, a wreath hung on the door of Charleston County Public Library in honor of long-serving librarian Cynthia Graham Hurd.

The day after the shooting, President Obama spoke about his confidence in "the outpouring of unity and strength and fellowship and love across Charleston . . . from all races, from all faiths, from all places of worship."[15] The president's grim face showed his sadness over yet another episode of gun violence. He and Vice President Joe Biden had met Pinckney, who was also a South Carolina state senator. The president came to Charleston within days to eulogize Pinckney. The city of Charleston quickly established the Mother Emanuel Hope Fund to help families of the victims; and the aircraft maker Boeing, which has a plant in North Charleston, immediately donated $100,000. Similar donations would soon follow from other companies with South Carolina ties, including Volvo Cars of North America, Benefitfocus, Google, and Starbucks. The Carolina Panthers football team offered to pay for all of the funerals. Benefit concerts were planned, and more than fifty restaurants joined forces for a fund-raising event called "A Community United." People gathered to form a giant heart in Marion Square; numerous church prayer vigils were held. So many community events were happening that the Post and Courier featured a daily listing. Everyone wanted to do something to help in whatever capacity they could. And every day thousands of people filed past Mother Emanuel to lay flowers and cards, to light candles, to openly weep and pray.

On Sunday morning Mother Emanuel opened its doors, and people passed by the white media tents to attend church. Every church in Charleston rang bells at 10:00 a.m. in a show of solidarity. Churches all across the country did the same. The Bridge to Peace unity chain, a march across the two-mile Arthur Ravenel Jr. Bridge, was planned on Facebook for that evening. (Ironically, the bridge is named for former federal and state legislator Arthur Ravenel, a segregationist who once called the NAACP the "National Association for the Advancement of Retarded People"[16]—just another contradiction in Charleston's conflicted history of race relations.) The march was led by relatives of those who were slain. A few thousand people were expected, but more than twenty-five thousand joined in. As people reached the bridge, they held hands and continued marching. Charleston-area resident and comedian Stephen Colbert and his family participated. Line after line of families with children waved American flags and carried homemade signs of support and gratitude for local leaders. The Red Cross and local police handed out thousands of bottles of water. There were nine minutes of silence, spontaneous singing, and prayers—always prayers.

TWO

FORGIVENESS

An air of fear that had hung over Charleston for a day was blown out to sea with the quick arrest of a suspect. Behind it rushed in the urgent curiosity to discover who Dylann Roof was and why he had committed this shocking deed that was quickly labeled a hate crime. Fate had handed the church such a horrific tragedy—not just for the nine souls who died but also for the five who were destined to survive it—and everyone wanted, *needed*, answers.

Roof had been named a suspect before noon on the day after the shooting. A nationwide police bulletin warned the suspect was armed, dangerous, and should be approached with caution. Later that day Roof was captured in Shelby, North Carolina, a three-and-a-half-hour drive northwest of Charleston. His older sister, Amber Roof, lived there with her fiancé. Roof was cooperative as he was searched, handcuffed, and arrested. A gun was found in the car. Roof was allowed to exit his vehicle before he was frisked. He was also casually escorted to a police cruiser and allowed to step into the backseat of the vehicle under his own power. After police took him to a local lockup, he announced he was hungry. Police got him a Burger King meal. Social media reacted to a perceived double standard in Roof's treatment that was in stark contrast to the rough handling of numerous black suspects, particularly twenty-five-year-old Freddie Gray in Baltimore, Maryland, who was unrestrained in a fast-moving police van in April 2015, during which he suffered a fatal spinal cord injury.

Roof did not challenge his return to South Carolina. He was flown back to Charleston on a state-owned plane that evening under very tight security, then placed in the Charleston County Detention Center in North Charleston. He was confined in a cell near Michael Slager, the former North Charleston police officer who was charged with murder in the April 4, 2015, death of fifty-four-year-old Walter Scott, an unarmed black North Charleston resident who was shot in the back. The day after Roof's arrest, nine families were preparing to get their first answers about the tragedy that had been visited upon them.

✳

Ethel Lance fussed over the appearance of the historic Emanuel sanctuary. For three decades as the church's custodian, she'd taken pride in keeping the church spotless. Lance's daughter Esther said that if her mother "saw a scuff on the floor she'd say, 'Oh no, don't ya'll mess up my floor.'"[1] At one time her duties even extended a block down Calhoun Street, where she'd worked as a custodian at the Gaillard Municipal Auditorium from its opening in 1968 until her retirement in 2002.

Ethel Lance's personality mirrored her attention to detail in everything, especially her family. She was a doting but no-nonsense protector of seven grandchildren and four great-grandchildren. Esther Lance said her seventy-year-old mother was a "strong" woman. "If she saw something wrong, she'll tell you. When you right, you're right. But if you're wrong, she will let you know. She's not going to sugar-coat anything."[2]

Ethel Lance and her husband, Nathaniel Lance, raised their family in Charleston's West Ashley suburb. Following his death in 1988, Ethel took over as matriarch. Of her five children, all but one is alive; cancer claimed her daughter Terrie Washington at age fifty-three in 2013. At Ethel's funeral, Terrie's daughter, Najee Washington, said her mother's and grandmother's reunion in heaven filled her with "pure joy."[3]

Ethel was the cousin of Susie Jackson, also slain at the church. Eighty-seven years old, Susie was a church trustee and choir member. She had two children of her own, but she opened her Alexander Street home, located not far from the church, to everyone who needed a meal or shelter. Like Ethel, Susie also was the matriarch of her family. "She was a loving person, she never had no animosity toward nobody," said Susie's son, Walter Jackson of Cleveland, Ohio. Susie Jackson had raised her son in a government-funded housing project on the city's east side, near the church. When Walter moved away, she opened the bedroom to two youngsters who needed a home. "She took in others," Walter Jackson said of his mother. "She was just that type of person."[4]

In a single flash of gun violence, Susie was one of three people snatched from her family. The other was twenty-six-year-old Tywanza Sanders, Susie Jackson's nephew. He tried to save his aunt's life, but was instead gunned down too. Sanders was a barber in North Charleston, an aspiring rapper and actor, poet, motivational speaker, and entrepreneur. In 2014, he earned a business administration degree from Allen University, an AME-supported, four-year institution in Columbia, South Carolina.

A regular at Columbia's open-mic poetry night, Mind Gravy, Sanders would skateboard down to the Five Points neighborhood almost every Wednesday night from the Allen campus. He was known for his humility and was well-liked and respected in poetry circles. Unlike many young people's work, full of anger, his performance poems were always thoughtful. According to Mind Gravy director Al Black, "Tywanza was almost like a sixties poet" in terms of tone and subject matter.[5]

The tall Sanders had a captivating smile that placed those around him at ease and snagged him a role in a play being rehearsed at a local Baptist church, recalled North Charleston cast member Nowa Fludd. Sanders had been teased by female members of the cast for not dating regularly. Playwright Hortense Mitchell, who recruited Sanders for her play *Life*, was surprised by his response. He didn't want a relationship until he had something to offer.[6]

Emanuel's property committee was guided by its chairwoman, Myra Thompson. She was in the midst of restoring church-owned properties, and with a smaller project completed, her attention was turning to the structural needs of the church. The fifty-nine-year-old mother, retired schoolteacher, and pastor's wife had her license to preach in the AME Church renewed the night she died in her house of faith. As a teacher, Thompson worked up to the end in the church where she'd grown up. She led the Bible study session where a stranger among them was welcomed to sit and listen.

Rev. Simmons may have been in the best position to stop the shooter. The veteran had a license to carry a gun, but the weapon was in his car. Simmons had returned decades before from Vietnam with a Purple Heart. Soon he entered another service, the ministry, and led three AME churches in the Mount Pleasant community east of Charleston. After three decades in those pulpits, he joined Emanuel's ministerial staff, its spiritual heart. He was a regular at Bible study.

Simmons was as tough as a drill sergeant though he had a smile that could be seen a mile away. He was born in Clarendon County, one of the counties that make up South Carolina's impoverished stretch of communities along Interstate 95 dubbed the "Corridor of Shame." He was a fourth-generation preacher. After serving in the US Army, Simmons graduated from Allen University and later earned master's degrees in social work from the University of South Carolina and divinity from Lutheran Seminary. During the shooting, he was wounded, then rushed to the Medical University Hospital, where he died. He was the last of the victims to be laid to rest.

Rev. DePayne Middleton-Doctor sang in the church choir and had preached at AME and Baptist churches in the Charleston area. This forty-nine-year-old mother of four girls had retired in 2005, as director of the Charleston County Community Development Block Grant Program. The year before her death, she had become an admissions coordinator for the Charleston learning center of Southern Wesleyan University.[7] Middleton-Doctor's best friend and kindred spirit, Jackie Starks, will never forget her friend's voice. "So angelic it could move the very depth of your heart . . . How do you describe an angel?"[8]

Rev. Sharonda Coleman-Singleton, a speech pathologist, was also the girls' track coach at Goose Creek High School, a campus in Berkeley County, South Carolina. She encouraged her runners to give their best with sweet endearments, such as "suga' pie" or just plain "suga." She was on Emanuel's ministerial staff. Coleman-Singleton, a New Jersey native, was the forty-five-year-old mother of three, including her eldest son, Chris Singleton, a baseball player at Charleston Southern University. At a prayer vigil on the CSU campus, Chris Singleton said, "My mom was a God-fearing woman. And she loved everybody with all her heart."[9]

In the block east of Emanuel stands the main branch of the Charleston County Public Library (CCPL). The death of fellow librarian Cynthia Graham Hurd shook her colleagues deeply. A Charleston native, Hurd was a lover of books who enjoyed a thirty-one-year career with the library system; her life was divided between the church and the library. For more than two decades, beginning in 1990, she had been branch manager of the John L. Dart Branch, located in a predominantly African American community on Charleston's peninsula. Later she was promoted to manager of a regional branch in the St. Andrews community west of Charleston. The CCPL has voted to rename that branch in her honor.

Hurd, who had five siblings, grew up in Mother Emanuel. Her

brother, former North Carolina state senator Malcolm Graham, said, "The church is home to us," adding that when their mother passed away fifteen years ago, Cynthia "took over the role of mother. She was the one who brought us together."[10] She died four days shy of her fifty-fifth birthday. She is survived by her husband, Arthur Stephen Hurd, a merchant seaman who was at sea near Saudi Arabia when his wife was murdered.

At age thirteen, Clementa Carlos Pinckney was called to preach in the AME Church. At age eighteen, he was named pastor of his own church. At twenty-three, he was elected (in 1996) to the South Carolina House of Representatives from Jasper County, becoming the youngest African American elected to the legislature. Four years later he was elected to the South Carolina Senate. In 2010, he was appointed Emanuel's pastor. The forty-one-year-old Pinckney had fought hard for the people from his senatorial district on several issues, including Medicaid funding, voting rights access, and police body cameras.

In the late 1990s, when Pinckney was pursuing a master's in public administration at the University of South Carolina, he interned at the Department of Mental Health's division of quality improvement with Mary Catherine Adams, a trained nurse. That was during the time Pinckney was elected to the House of Representatives. Adams and others from the office attended his swearing-in ceremony. "I've had a lot of interns, but he stood out," she remembers. "At such a young age, Clementa was mature, kind, and genuine, and professional without being pretentious." Pinckney chose to intern at the mental health agency because it was a subject he didn't know enough about. Adams continues, "When he died, it was disbelief. It was sickening—and to find out how it happened. But to know, people were so forgiving. For me, as a Southern woman, it is difficult to understand how someone could have that much racial hatred. I have seen it before, but to think someone would enter a church and take lives like that. For a mental illness, we have medications. You can't medicate for someone's hatred."[11]

Pinckney was a quiet, humble man with a rich baritone voice that boomed across a room; it drew people to his side. His associate and friend Sen. Vincent Sheheen referred to him as the voice for the voiceless.[12] Others called him the Senate's moral compass. Pinckney's district includes parts of six counties, about the size of Rhode Island, that touch the southern portion of the "Corridor of Shame," a zone where social and political issues set the tone for his legislative agenda. In a 2010 interview, Pinckney said, "Loving God is never separate from loving our brothers and sisters. It's always the same."[13]

Those killed by the assailant's gunfire have come to be known as the Emanuel Nine. However, five other members of the congregation were in the church the night bullets riddled the room where they held Bible study. One bullet pierced the wall of the pastor's office, where Pinckney's wife, Jennifer Pinckney, and the couple's youngest daughter, Malana, were hiding. In the Bible study room, the killer was unaware Felicia Sanders and her granddaughter were alive on the hard tile floor in pools of warm blood. As the gunman prepared to leave, he paused at Polly Sheppard's feet, where she was hiding under a long folding table. He told her, "I am going to let you live so you can tell the story of what happened."[14]

※

The gray-block detention center where Roof was being held is adjacent to a courtroom where he appeared for a bond hearing on nine counts of murder and one charge of possession of a weapon during the commission of a violent crime.[15] Roof was wrapped in a bulletproof vest as two sheriff's department deputies, also wearing body protection, escorted him to a tiny room equipped with a video camera and monitor. On the screen Roof could see and hear Charleston County chief magistrate James Gosnell. Roof may have unknowingly found a kindred spirit in the judge, who was a Civil War reenactor and who had once used the word *nigger* in the courtroom.[16]

Before the hearing began, Gosnell announced he wanted to read a statement to the audience in the packed courtroom and those who watched the live news coverage. "Charleston is a very strong community. We have big hearts. We are a very loving community, and we are going to reach out to everyone, all victims, and will touch them. We have victims; nine of them. But we also have victims on the other side. There are victims on this young man's side of the family," he said, gesturing for emphasis. "Nobody would have thrown them into the whirlwind of events that they have been thrown into. We must find it in our heart at some point in time not only to help those that are victims but to also help his family as well."[17] The judge's remarks received criticisms as unwarranted and bordering on grandstanding during a high-profile court case.

Roof's family had a response to the tragedy. Through his attorneys, public defender Ashley Pennington of Charleston and Boyd Young of Columbia, they offered their sympathies with hopes and prayers for healing nationwide.[18]

Some of the relatives of the nine people who died spoke at the bond hearing, offering surprising and unexpected sentiment. They spoke directly to the suspect. Roof stood motionless and silent through the thirteen-minute hearing. He answered, "Yes, sir," to questions from the judge about his address, age, and to affirm he was unemployed. Roof could not see the relatives of those who died, but he could hear their voices shake with emotion and rise with emphasis.

Nadine Collier, Ethel Lance's daughter, spoke with a quivering voice. "I just want everybody to know, to you [Roof], I forgive you. You took something really precious away from me." Her voice rose in tone and emphasis as she said, "I will never talk to her ever again. I will never be able to hold her again, but I forgive you and have mercy on your soul. You hurt me. You hurt a lot of people, but I forgive you."[19]

Myra Thompson's husband, Anthony Thompson, vicar of Holy Trinity Reformed Episcopal Church in downtown Charleston, told the defendant: "I forgive you, my family forgives you, but we would like for you to take this opportunity to repent, repent, confess and give your life to the one who matters the most—Christ—so he can change it, he can change your ways no matter what happens to you and you will be okay. Do that and you will be better off than you are right now."[20]

Felicia Sanders, Tywanza Sanders's mother, added similar sentiments. "We welcomed you Wednesday night in our Bible study with open arms." Those who died, she told Roof, were some of the most beautiful people she knew. Some sobbed softly as she spoke. "Every fiber in my body hurts, and I will never be the same. Tywanza Sanders was my son, but Tywanza was my hero . . . May God have mercy on you."[21]

Simmons's granddaughter, Alana Simmons, said, "Although my grandfather and the other victims died at the hands of hate, this is proof—everyone's plea for your soul is proof that they lived and loved, and their legacies will live and love so hate won't win. And I just want to thank the court for making sure that hate does not win."[22]

Bethane Middleton-Brown, Middleton-Doctor's sister, expressed a similar thought. "For me I am a work in progress, and I acknowledge that I am very angry," she said with heavy emotion. "But one thing that DePayne has always joined in our family with is that she taught me that we are the family that love built. We have no room for hate so we have to forgive. I pray God on your soul, and I also thank God that I won't be around when your judgment day comes with him."[23]

The judge's invitation to speak on behalf of Coleman-Singleton, Hurd, and Pinckney was not taken up.

※

Church member Marguerite Michel didn't attend the bond hearing but watched it on television from her modest home two miles north of the city's thriving historic district. Each Sunday Michel headed in that direction for service at Emanuel, which she joined at age sixteen, just two years before a Wall Street crash triggered the Great Depression. She was the church's oldest member at age 104. Marguerite Michel died February 13, 2016. She was buried in the Emanuel cemetery.

Michel was in the audience for the televised eulogistic service of Emanuel's beloved pastor, Clementa Pinckney, attended by President Obama, who delivered a rousing and emotional eulogy and warmed the nation's heart with his rendition of "Amazing Grace."

"I love my God. Look how he brought me through. He didn't have to bring me this far," Michel said. "I ask him every day, if I have done anything [wrong], please forgive. Please forgive me." Although she sought forgiveness from the Creator for unbeknownst transgressions, she would be hard-pressed to forgive the suspect who took the life of nine people she loved. "I don't know about that [forgiveness]. Nine people gone. I am trying to figure it out. You don't come to church to hurt people. You come to church to help and to love one another. How can you say you love God and hate the people you see in the church?"[24]

Michel said she was close to those who were slain, but perhaps she was closest to Ethel Lance and Susie Jackson through their shared experiences with the church's senior citizens program.

After Sunday services Myra Thompson sometimes tested Michel's memory.

"She would tease her all the time," Michel's youngest daughter, Ferrel Greene, recalled.

"Do you remember me?" Thompson would ask.

Michel would counter, "Who are you?"[25]

Michel not only appreciated the span of her existence on earth but Emanuel's existence as a church. On the wall behind her chair hangs a painting of Emanuel, labeled with milestone dates: 1818 and 1891.[26] She witnessed some of the church's most historic moments. She was in the dimly lit sanctuary the night Martin Luther King Jr. preached to an overflowing audience swaying side to side with arms linked as they sang "We Shall Overcome."[27]

Michel remembered fondly Reverend Benjamin James Glover, who had led the young people in the church during sit-in demonstrations to break segregated lunch counters in the city's business district. While she didn't participate in those marches, years later in 1969, she joined with striking black nurses at the then Medical College of South Carolina, who were protesting for more than just higher wages. They were demanding to be treated with the respect that was afforded to white nurses.[28]

Now Emanuel is at another historic crossroads. The church has been a target of hate before, dating back to its burning following Denmark Vesey's failed slave conspiracy in 1822 (see chapter 6). Church members say hate will not win over evil, but it is difficult to understand the source of this modern-day hatred from a suspect who is only twenty-one years old. Surely he has not lived long enough to harbor so much deep-seated hatred. This white man, who sought to ignite a race war, is now accused of killing nine black people at a prominent and historic AME church in Charleston, the cradle of slavery. Several factors seem to have aligned to suggest the suspect was an astute and deranged student of history or, perhaps, just an unfortunate and unwitting agent of fate.

Following Roof's arrest authorities learned more about him. A racist manifesto that authorities said was written by Roof was released to the media. It had appeared on a website that purportedly belonged to him. In it he said, "I have no choice. I am not in the position to, alone, go into the ghetto and fight. I chose Charleston because it is [*sic*] most historic city in my state and at one time had the highest ratio of blacks to Whites in the country. We have no skinheads, no real KKK, no one doing anything but talking on the internet [*sic*]. Well someone has to have the bravery to take it to the real world, and I guess that has to be me."[29]

Roof is remembered by some former neighbors as the strange, bug-eyed boy with a bowl haircut who helped with yard work in rural

Lexington County. Some can't fathom how he learned to have such deep resentment toward people of African descent. Weeks before his arrest Roof had told friends he wanted to do "something big," and he had plans to commit a mass shooting at the College of Charleston. Another friend remembered that Roof wasn't mean, but he had "a darkness to his life."[30] These are contrary statements about a young man with no record of violence, who has remained largely silent aside from the website.

In 1994, Dylann Roof was born to Amelia "Amy" Cowles Roof and Franklin Bennett "Benn" Roof, who had divorced three years earlier. They attempted to rebuild their marriage, but it failed. Dylann lived with his mother.

In November 1999, when Dylann was five, his father, a construction contractor, married Paige Mann (they would file for divorce a decade later). Paige and Benn had a comfortable life, with expensive vehicles and a three-thousand-square-foot, custom-built home in the Earlewood area of Columbia. They had four other properties—one of which was a house in the Florida Keys, where they lived for a time, but Dylann Roof apparently never attended school there. Neighbors did not see him often, but they do recall he was small for his age.[31]

Paige Mann, Dylann's stepmother, cared for him while his father was away from home for as many as four days a week. Her stepson, she says, was "a loner and quiet and very smart—too smart. He was locked in his room looking up bad stuff on the computer. Something on the computer drew him in—this is Internet evil."[32]

After the Roofs returned separately to South Carolina in late 2008, a foreclosure claimed the house in the Keys; then Benn Roof's construction business failed. Paige alleged that abuse led her to leave her husband; meanwhile a private detective gave Benn proof that his wife was cheating on him. The breakup of his father's marriage occurred as Dylann Roof was entering the ninth grade in Lexington, South Carolina, where he had previously attended fourth and eighth grades. School officials there described him as a "very transient student." His home life was just as transient. Dylann Roof often alternated living in Lexington—a rural, mostly white community west of Columbia—where his mother lived, to Columbia, where his father owned real estate.[33]

But what happened to shape Dylann Roof's attitudes about race? As a shy fifth grader in Columbia, Roof was in school with black students, but he was not able to click with the "in" crowd. Two years later, in the seventh grade, Roof showed little evidence of racial hatred, Caleb Brown, a childhood friend, remembered. Roof had a close relationship with Brown, a mixed-race boy, at the urging of the boys' mothers. Brown and Roof met as part of a class project that required students to ask their parents about their heritage. Roof asked the curly-haired and dark-skinned Brown about his lineage, and he was told that Brown's father was black. It didn't change the way Roof treated Brown. While they were pals, Roof didn't have a wide circle of friends.[34]

As a middle schooler Roof began losing interest in academics, which had become boring. Roof also frequently complained that his father put him to work landscaping—probably to keep him busy and out of trouble—but in an interview with the *New York Times*, Roof's friends said he had become more interested in smoking grass than cutting it. By the time he got to high school, his father's marriage had imploded, and Roof was distracted from school, a pursuit he'd already lost interest in; he repeated the ninth grade. In 2010, he finished the last three months of his second chance at the ninth grade in Columbia, but from that point no records for Roof were found at schools in Columbia or Lexington.[35]

Years later Roof does show up in criminal records. At a local shopping mall in February 2015, he unsettled employees of a business by asking store employees about the number of people working in the business and what time they would leave. The fact that he was dressed in black contributed to the feeling of unease, and the police were called. A police officer searched Roof and found a prescription drug, Suboxone, which treats opiate addiction. He was charged with a misdemeanor and was barred from the mall for a year. Another police officer questioned Roof a few weeks later about loitering at a park. Semiautomatic rifle parts were found in his car's trunk, but no charges were filed. About this same time—just weeks before the attack at Emanuel—Roof was arrested at the same shopping mall and convicted of misdemeanor trespassing; he received an extended three-year ban.

In late spring of 2015, Roof purchased a .45-caliber handgun from a West Columbia gun store with money his father had given him for his twenty-first birthday; it was the weapon he allegedly used to kill the Emanuel Nine. Following the Emanuel shooting, the FBI noted that a criminal background check should have prevented Roof from buying the weapon because he had admitted to drug possession in February.[36]

From a shy schoolboy, Dylann Roof grew to become a young man who purchased a weapon to kill human beings. In the hours after the shooting, his paternal grandparents, Joseph and Lucy Roof, expressed sincere grief and were visibly upset. According to one of their neighbors, "They said they were going to stay prayed up and ask the Lord to help them through this. A lot of people feel children . . . are taught intolerance and discrimination. I don't feel that is something Joe Roof would have taught or tolerated. Someone had to teach [Dylann Roof] that." Another family acquaintance said Dylann Roof's father and grandfather both live in neighborhoods with African American neighbors and that when Benn Roof held parties, he often invited his black and Hispanic employees.[37] Though none of this sheds light on where Dylann Roof learned to hate, his website told the story of a racist young man. "Integration has done nothing but bring Whites down to the level of brute animals," he wrote. It included pictures of him with patches from white-ruled African nations on his clothing and another of him with the Confederate flag. His clothing also was adorned with the number 88—a reference to the white supremacist code for "Heil Hitler." Police reported that on

Roof's website, he posted a nearly twenty-five-hundred-word essay on black crime, with reference to the white supremacist group Council of Conservative Citizens.[38]

The racial rhetoric that might have been absent from Roof's speech before he dropped out of the ninth grade began to appear when he was reunited with childhood friends via social media. In 2015, he joined Facebook and contacted Kimberly Konzny's sons, his friends in Lexington. Roof spent several nights a week sleeping on Konzny's sofa, watching movies. Because he had a car and pocket money, he chauffeured his friends and provided bottles of domestic vodka. Twenty-year-old Joseph C. Meek Jr., Konzny's older son, was quoted as saying that after he reconnected with Roof, he found Roof to be "a lot more quiet. He was, like, emotionless." Meek's fifteen-year-old brother, Jacob, said Roof "doesn't use the N-word. He says 'African-American.'"[39] But Joseph Meek revealed that he knew Roof talked about doing "something big" and that he was prone to have racist views—although Meek didn't attempt to inform police. He didn't know then that Roof wanted to start a race war. "He wanted it to be white with white, and black with black . . . He had it in his mind, and he didn't really let nobody know (what he was going to do)," Meek said.[40]

Although Roof did occasionally make racist statements, he was not linked with any particular racial groups, so Meek didn't take him seriously. But after Roof said on June 10 that in seven days he wanted to carry out a mass shooting at the College of Charleston, Meek and another friend, who is an African American, took Roof's gun from his car and hid it. They had been drinking vodka, and Meek hid the handgun until they all sobered up. Meek returned the weapon after another friend became concerned that Meek should not have it while he was on probation.[41]

After a search began for a suspect, Carson Cowles, Roof's maternal uncle, called police to identify his nephew. "The whole world is going to be looking at his family who raised this monster," Cowles said.[42] "He's guilty as hell. He'll get no sympathy from us, any of us."[43]

THREE

THE FLAG COMES DOWN

As information about Dylann Roof's racist ideology—complete with photographs of him waving the Confederate battle flag—permeated the Internet and news media, the response from Charleston church and civic leaders was immediate. Presiding Elder Joseph Darby, who was also the first vice president of the Charleston branch of the NAACP, pointed out that Roof's "manifesto is instructive to those who throw around reckless language for political gain . . . They have to first remove the blood from their hands."[1]

Charleston's Mayor Riley spoke openly about the ways in which the Confederate flag was co-opted by Roof and others as a symbol of racial hatred. Protesters demonstrated repeatedly in front of the South Carolina statehouse, demanding the flag's removal from the capitol grounds. Six days after the church shooting, almost every major South Carolina political figure, including Governor Nikki Haley, called for the removal of the flag. The prevailing sentiment was that if the flag didn't come down under these dire circumstances, then there was something deeply, deeply wrong with South Carolina. It was a redemptive gesture, but one with profound meaning for the people of the Palmetto State. There was an urgency around the issue because Senator Pinckney would be lying in state under the capitol dome on Wednesday, June 25, and the notion that his casket would have to pass by the Confederate flag still flying in front of the building was abhorrent to those demanding its removal.

But the battle over the Confederate flag has a long, contentious history in this state, and one's view of history (in particular the reasons for the Civil War) often determine one's attitude toward it. The Confederate flag was first raised in the state House chambers in the late 1930s; then it was raised in the Senate in 1956, but passion for the flag really heated up in the 1960s, during the civil rights era, when the flag was raised over the statehouse dome on April 11, 1961, to commemorate the centennial of the Civil War. This action came with no end date to take it down and was seen by many to be a clear political statement against desegregation and civil rights reforms. During the decades that followed, African American leaders and others called for the flag's removal, and in 1994 the chairman of the NAACP and many African American ministers threatened a boycott. The mayor of Columbia, along with business leaders, sued to force removal of the flag. The state legislature, however, did not vote to remove the flag. The next year, legislators passed a law while the statehouse was being renovated, giving lawmakers complete power over the flag's removal. In 1996, Republican governor David Beasley suggested moving the flag to a monument on the statehouse grounds. His suggestion was met with vociferous disapproval, and although he lost his bid for reelection, he never regretted the decision and was awarded the Profiles in Courage Award by Caroline Kennedy—the only South Carolinian to receive the honor.

In 2000, there were numerous marches and rallies at the statehouse. The NAACP boycott of South Carolina started on January 1, 2000, and was followed by a protest march of approximately forty-five thousand people that took place on the weekend of Martin Luther King Jr.'s birthday. (There was a subsequent pro-flag rally of six thousand.) In April,

Mayor Riley participated in the start of a five-day, 110-mile march to Columbia to call for the flag's removal. Thousands marched with the mayor, and a protest with thousands more convened at the capitol. That spring both the Senate and the House voted to remove the flag, and a compromise arrangement was reached and signed into law by Democratic governor Jim Hodges. On June 30, the Confederate flag was transferred from the dome, and a smaller version of the flag was raised on a flagpole at the monument to South Carolina's Confederate dead, directly in front of the statehouse building facing Gervais Street, which is a central thoroughfare in downtown Columbia.

But this compromise really didn't change or solve anything. The next year the National Collegiate Athletic Association (NCAA) banned the state from hosting postseason sporting events. Three years later, on MLK Day, a march to the statehouse called for the flag's removal. It became a hot-button issue in both the state and national political arenas—a kind of litmus test for a candidate's attitudes about race and social justice issues. As late as 2014, the Democratic candidate for governor, Vincent Sheheen, called for the removal of the flag in his failed attempt to unseat Governor Haley. Following the election, the state poet laureate's inaugural poem was banned from the inauguration ceremonies in January 2015, because the poem mentioned the flag and the civil rights issues it represents.

It took the massacre of nine innocent African Americans by a young white supremacist to finally get the Confederate flag off the statehouse grounds and placed under glass at the South Carolina State Museum. Even under these circumstances it almost didn't happen, although calls for the removal of the Confederate flag began almost immediately after the massacre.

On June 22, Mississippi House Speaker Philip Gunn, a Republican, called for the removal of the Confederate symbol from that state's flag. In his statement he described himself as a Christian and urged that a dialogue on the subject should commence. Less than a week after the church shootings, Governor Haley and US Representative James Clyburn, a Democrat from South Carolina, and US Senator Tim Scott, a South Carolina Republican—both African Americans—called for the removal of the flag. "One hundred fifty years after the end of the Civil War," the governor stated, "the time has come."[2] But there was still much opposition, and it would take a late-night battle in early July to gather the necessary votes. Business and community leaders throughout the state continued to call for the removal of the flag.

As the days passed, calls for changes involving a myriad of Confederate symbols went out across the country. Walmart pulled Confederate battle flag items from its stores. Amazon, eBay, Sears, and Kmart quickly followed. The flag was not the only target. Kentucky leaders called for the removal of a statue of Confederate president Jefferson Davis from the capitol rotunda. On June 23, Governor Terry McAuliffe of Virginia announced the state would begin to phase out specialty license plates for the Sons of Confederate Veterans organization, whose logo includes the Confederate battle flag. Nathan Deal, the governor of Georgia, made a similar announcement regarding specialty license plates in his state. It's worth noting that the day of the shooting in Charleston, the Texas Supreme Court ruled that Texas was within its rights to disallow license plates with the Sons of Confederate Veterans logo. In Tennessee, lawmakers demanded that a bust of Confederate general Nathan Bedford Forrest (also the first Grand Wizard of the Ku Klux Klan) be removed from their statehouse grounds. In early July the mayor of New Orleans asked the city council to remove the statues of generals P. G. T. Beauregard and Robert E. Lee and the president of the Confederacy, Jefferson Davis. And as far north as Baltimore, plans were announced by city officials to change the name of the city's Robert E. Lee Park.

Other reactions were more spontaneous. An American flag was burned by protesters in Denver at a rally outside the Colorado state capitol in support of removing the flag in South Carolina. Activists in Minnesota called for the renaming of a lake named after John C. Calhoun, and the Robert E. Lee Elementary School in San Diego considered changing its name. Political figures around the country began to weigh in. White House statements indicated the president believed the flag belonged in a museum.

Democratic presidential candidate Hillary Clinton called it a symbol of a racist past,[3] and former Republican presidential candidate Mitt Romney, who had made statements in favor of the flag's removal during the primaries in 2008, tweeted, "Remove it now to honor #Charleston victims."[4] The 2016 Republican candidates weighed in as well. Both Jeb Bush and Florida senator Marco Rubio issued statements suggesting the state would "do the right thing."[5] Even flag manufacturers decided to stop making it.

A seismic shift seemed to be happening within the very bedrock of the Christian South, when even the president of the Southern Baptist Convention's Ethics and Religious Liberty Commission, Russell Moore, wrote in a June 19 blog post, "The cross and the Confederate flag cannot co-exist [*sic*] without one setting the other on fire."[6]

In South Carolina, debate inside and outside the halls of government heated up. Randy Burbage, a Charleston leader of the Sons of Confederate Veterans, told the *Post and Courier*, "The flag didn't cause Dylann Roof to do what he did."[7] College of Charleston president and former state senator Glenn McConnell, well known for his local Civil War memorabilia store and his longtime support of the flag, made no comment. Many state lawmakers did the same.

There were numerous rallies and protests at the statehouse, and although they were overwhelmingly in favor of removing the flag, there were plenty of pro-flag demonstrators as well. At dawn on Saturday, June 27, the same day funerals were held in Charleston for Cynthia Graham Hurd, Susie Jackson, and Tywanza Sanders, thirty-year-old African

American activist Bree Newsome climbed up the flagpole in front of the statehouse and took down the Confederate flag. Newsome and her supporters felt that they couldn't wait any longer for the legislature to take action. She was arrested almost immediately and charged with defacing a monument. And within an hour a replacement flag was raised.

The battle over the flag came to a showdown on Wednesday, July 8, when the South Carolina House of Representatives was engaged for ten hours in a heated debate. The Senate had passed a measure the day before in favor of removing the flag, but events in the House were not so smooth. One representative in particular, Republican Mike Pitts from Laurens, South Carolina, repeatedly introduced amendments to derail the flag bill. More than sixty amendments were offered. Debate became emotional. Democrats and some Republicans accused an extreme faction of Republicans of delaying the vote, but the wind was largely blowing the other way—even the son of the late US senator Strom Thurmond, a segregationist, spoke about the need to remove the flag.

After hours of debate Jenny Horne, a Republican representative from Summerville—a city near Charleston—made a heartfelt plea to her colleagues, which seemed to turn the tide. She described being a descendent of Confederacy president Jefferson Davis, and with tears streaming down her face and anger in her voice, she pleaded: "I cannot believe that we do not have the heart in this body to do something meaningful, such as take a symbol of hate off these grounds. . . . If you cannot be moved by the suffering of the people of Charleston, then you don't have a heart."[8] And finally, during the early hours on Thursday, July 9, 2015, the first approval vote came in at 93–27, and a second came in at 94–20. People throughout the state stayed up all night to watch the televised debate unfold. Later that day Governor Haley signed the bill that called for the removal of the flag from statehouse grounds. She used thirteen pens, nine representing the families of those who lost their lives in Charleston. Some of their relatives attended, as well as former governors and dozens of lawmakers. That day, on the floor of the US House, Republicans tabled a bill that would allow Confederate flags at cemeteries managed by the United States Park Service. The hateful, racist associations with this flag suddenly seemed obvious to almost everyone.

Twenty-three days after the church shootings at Mother Emanuel, at 10:10 a.m. on Friday, July 10, the Confederate battle flag was ceremoniously removed from the flagpole in front of the statehouse as ten thousand citizens stood by and thousands more watched from their homes and offices on computers, cellular telephone screens, and televisions. It was taken to the South Carolina Confederate Relic Room and Military Museum, located about a mile away. Soon the flagpole and fence surrounding it were removed. It all happened so fast it was hard to believe how difficult and fraught with conflict the path to that day had been—a day many never thought they would see in their lifetimes. For African Americans and others who had fought so hard for so long to remove the symbol of hate, it was a moment for tears of joy.

Poet Nikky Finney, the daughter of the state's first African American jurist on the South Carolina Supreme Court since Reconstruction, spoke for multitudes in her prose poem "A New Day Dawns," which appeared beside a photograph of the empty flagpole on the front page of the *State*, a South Carolina newspaper, the next day: "In all our lifetimes, finally, this towering undulating moment is here."[9]

FOUR

THE SIN OF SLAVERY

On June 17, 2015, Dylann Roof pushed open the massive wooden door to a wide, ground-floor room at Emanuel AME Church that parishioners call the basement, an incongruent label in an Atlantic coast city that floods at high tide. Before the twenty-one-year-old Roof made it all the way inside, he knew what he would find—black church members seated with their pastor, most of them twice his age, for Bible study. Instead of choosing to mingle with young, mostly white college students his age who frequent night spots at a nearby commercial district, Roof drove to this house of worship with a history vastly different from his upbringing. A camera captured his image as he entered the vintage church, but modern technology couldn't detect the hatred Roof harbored or the weapon he toted that would trigger one of South Carolina's most heinous crimes.

Students of Charleston's history might find meaning in the date of Roof's visit to Emanuel on June 17, because 193 years earlier on approximately that date, one of the church's leaders, Denmark Vesey, had planned to start a slave rebellion. Although no such rebellion ever occurred and Vesey and others were executed by the state, Vesey's name has been reviled by some whites who have labeled him a murderer and a genocidal maniac.

On his way to Charleston, Roof drove past other historic AME churches and other black churches in cities such as Columbia, the state's capital, and Orangeburg, the seat of two black campuses of higher learning, one of which is South Carolina State University. In February 1968, the college became the site of major civil rights activism promoting the desegregation of a bowling alley near the campus. After three nights of demonstrations South Carolina highway patrolmen entered the campus. As tensions escalated, some of the patrolmen opened fire, killing three students and injuring twenty-seven others. Known as the Orangeburg Massacre, it was the first time anything like it had happened on an American campus and continues to influence many South Carolinians' ideas regarding race.

If Roof's intentions were to start a race war in Charleston, those details may have been significant for his diabolical plan and his distorted understanding of America's racial history. Roof imagined slavery as a benign institution and perhaps viewed Vesey as an evil by-product of it. In his website screed he bemoaned the failure of the Confederate "nation" and nurtured complaints against people of African descent as the tormentors of his own aggrieved race. On the night Roof arrived at Emanuel, he was blinded by such intense hate that he could not see the humanity his victims shared with him as God's creations.[1]

In his 1951 novel *Requiem for a Nun*, William Faulkner wrote, "The past is never dead. It's not even past." How true this is—especially in the South and in a city like Charleston, where its past as the cradle of slavery and its present as a tourist mecca meld as seamlessly as its historic and modern buildings. The hatred that motivated Roof's assault rose like heat from the *sin of slavery*, a crime against humanity that antedates the founding of the American nation. That sin has festered for centuries and coexisted with the most fundamental democratic traditions based on the presumed dignity and equality of men. The sin of slavery and its long-term implications have shaped and distorted attitudes toward people of

African descent in this country. That night in Emanuel's basement, it seduced Roof.

The African American experience in South Carolina, particularly in Charleston, is filled with contradictions. Surnames such as Drayton, Pinckney, and Middleton are the well-known Lowcountry names of slave-owning families. Today many well-educated and influential African Americans carry those names. Local people who know this history understand those linkages, but even the most astute observer may not know the real and sustained impact of the juxtaposition of slavery and freedom, liberty and human bondage, for our society today.

In Virginia as early as 1619, Captain John Smith described buying twenty "Negars" from the Dutch, after describing the first elections in the New World.[2] This contradictory interconnection of black bondage and American freedom is deeply embedded in American history. It has pushed this nation into war against itself. It is a source, albeit usually unspoken, of our contemporary racial malaise. We still cannot fathom it—a murderer who makes a church the scene of his crime—and yet this is just one of many examples of how history shapes the complex story of events, such as the shooting at Emanuel.

※

The New World brand of slavery was unique in that for the first time in human history, bondage was based on race. In the classical world of the Greeks and Romans, masters and slaves were often of the same race. Later, in the medieval years, European slavery was practiced widely in the societies between Scandinavia and the Black Sea. The modern word *slave* results from the fact that so many Slavic people were enslaved by other Europeans in this premodern period.[3] However, when Europeans settled the Western Hemisphere, they only enslaved people of color and Africans in particular. There were no European slaves in the New World.

For reasons beyond the scope of this book, the racial and social differences between the enslaved and their masters were greatest in the United States, where, generally, people with even the slightest African ancestry were classified as black. Such arbitrary definitions led to the identification of slaves not as persons but as property, deprived of all human rights, and the development of a voluminous literature rationalizing the enslavement of Africans based on race. Such a system readily promoted the perception of Africans as inferior to Europeans, and in the United States, once emancipation occurred, something had to replace slavery as the means of regulating race relations. The old system was replaced with racial segregation. There is no counterpart to it in any other earlier period of enslavement. These are the factors that make ours a unique system of oppression with a deeply embedded legacy.

The Atlantic slave trade that began in the mid-fifteenth century was the mechanism for transporting masses of Africans to the New World to work in silver mines or on sugar plantations. Today people have no idea of its magnitude or that this was the largest forced migration in human history. Furthermore, and contrary to popular belief, before 1820, of that swell of people who crossed the Atlantic to the Americas, fully three-quarters were Africans.[4] The Atlantic slave trade lasted for approximately four centuries and linked the human and commercial destinies of the New World to Europe and Africa, simultaneously enriching the former while devastating the latter.

The slave trade created the first global economy. Based on one model known as the triangular trade, consumer goods manufactured in Europe were transported to Africa and exchanged for people. The enslaved Africans were transported to the Caribbean, where they were exchanged for sugar, which was taken back to Europe. The process was repeated regularly, although with geographical variations.

Guns were among the most important commercial goods Europeans introduced to Africa in the course of the Atlantic slave trade. The new weapons ensured the trade would be fueled by warfare as African leaders and states competed with one another to gain access to guns. Warfare escalated, typically between traditional enemies, and prisoners were taken. Once captured, Africans were marched to the coast, where they were delivered to Europeans waiting at castles or forts that were sometimes referred to as "factories," and were stripped naked and inspected. In the final step of their dehumanization while still on the African continent, people were branded like cattle with their owners' marks and loaded onto oceangoing vessels.

Most Africans had never seen a ship, and now disoriented from their capture, they were sold into the hands of strange-sounding and harsh-looking Europeans. Imprisoned in the dark bowels of the vessel, captives faced an unknown future as they experienced a horrifying Atlantic crossing known as the Middle Passage. Enslaved people were chained and jammed together in confined spaces and forced to lie in excrement, blood, and other bodily fluids. Without adequate food, water, and fresh air, sickness was widespread, and the atmosphere quickly became putrid and stultifying. Sometimes women were separated and allowed time outside the darkness of the ship's hold, but this only made them vulnerable to their captors' sexual abuse. Crossing the Atlantic might be completed in as few as *three weeks*, but on average the Middle Passage took about *two months*.

Under these circumstances large numbers died before they ever reached their destination. Some captives found their confinement so intolerable that they jumped overboard while others lived to plot shipboard rebellions. Although these insurrections were occasionally successful, they generally only resulted in the further loss of African life. It is estimated that 12 to 13 percent of those who embarked did not survive, with most having succumbed to disease.[5] That said, during the period of transatlantic slavery, approximately eleven million Africans landed somewhere in the New World. For those who managed to live, their arrival to the New World simply started ·a new phase in their oppression as they were forced to adjust to lifetimes of harsh labor in new cultural and physical environments.

✳

The English did not invent slavery. They inherited the practice from the Portuguese and the Spanish, who had been at it for centuries. Labor was scarce in the New World because the European settlements developed plantation-based economies to supply the world with lucrative crops such as sugar. Sugar was probably the New World's most complex and labor-intensive crop because its production involved not only planting and harvesting but industrial processing. Later, other products, such as tobacco and cotton, cultivated on the North American mainland, while less taxing than sugar, further contributed to the labor demands of the New World. In South Carolina—and particularly in the coastal lowlands north and south of Charleston—rice was the crop that made plantation owners wealthy. That wealth was accumulated at a huge cost of African life, and ultimately demand for labor guided increasing numbers of ships to the African continent.

Initially, indigenous Native American populations were sources of labor, but aspects of their backgrounds made them unsuitable as plantation workers. Africans were less vulnerable to European diseases and had well-developed agricultural traditions. Once enslaved in the New World, Africans were especially easy to control because they were now in a strange landscape where their racial differences made them readily identifiable should they flee.

Virginia was founded in 1607, and as early as 1616, Jamestown settler John Rolfe had developed a mild form of tobacco that suited European tastes; tobacco production and export soon sustained the colony and later other colonies, such as Maryland. Tobacco was more labor-intensive than the crops that Europeans traditionally cultivated. Jamestown soon became a boomtown not unlike those that later developed during the 1848–1855 California gold rush. In the mad pursuit of tobacco, the demand for labor was intense. The first Africans arrived in the Chesapeake colony, where slavery became law in the late 1600s. Before then slavery was practiced as a social custom in Virginia and Maryland.[6]

The perception the English held of Africans was based on color, religion, sexuality, and gender. The complexion of Africans was called *black*; this term signified something dirty, foul, or polluted. Conversely, Europeans were *white* to convey purity, cleanliness, wholesomeness, and morality. That differences in skin color made a great impression on the English should not be surprising given their location in the North Atlantic, which placed them farther away from darker people than most other Europeans.[7] Secondly, in their encounters with Africans, the English and other Europeans did not find the practice of anything they considered a legitimate religion. Sub-Saharan Africans were generally preliterate, and most didn't possess books. They didn't have the equivalent of European churches; instead, they worshiped gods and spirits found in the natural world. Christians of that time considered Muslims heathens even though they shared much with Christianity: Muslims built mosques and had written sacred texts, which even included characters from the Bible. Many sub-Saharan Africans practiced Islam but most did not, so when the English encountered Africans, they concluded they lacked religion entirely, and this suggested a total absence of civilization.[8]

Gender and sexuality also influenced the European perception of African life. Since they lived in the tropics, Africans had different standards of clothing compared to the English; because their bodies were less than fully covered, Europeans concluded they lacked morals and were promiscuous and without shame. The practice of polygamy was another source of degradation, suggesting to observers that only men with animalistic sexual appetites needed to have multiple wives; women in such relationships were deemed similarly lecherous.[9] According to some observers, such as the early eighteenth-century traveler Pieter de Marees, African women could give birth relatively painlessly and recover very quickly just like animals in the field. The African women were not only different, but in the European mind they were inferior, savage, and thus so degraded they could legitimately be enslaved.[10] If these conclusions could be reached about women, it stood to reason they applied even more to the men.

These cultural judgments about Africans contributed mightily to the status they would occupy in the Chesapeake. This is readily observed in a 1640 Virginia judicial decision. In this case three indentured servants, two white and one black, ran away together and were apprehended and punished. The two whites had four years added to their indentures, but the black man was condemned to serve his owners for the rest of his life. To discourage servants (mainly white) from absconding with slaves, the Virginians enacted an additional law in 1661. It required runaway servants apprehended in the company of fugitive slaves to make up the time that the slaves were absent.[11]

The social and legal distance between blacks and whites increased and divided this society along racial lines. Over time these attitudes have persisted, shaping the perception of people of African descent in modern-day America—and may have been among the racial factors that distorted Dylann Roof's perception of black people in the United States and of the church members at Emanuel.

The decade of the 1660s also witnessed the increased sophistication of the Virginia colonists in the legal operation of the slave system. During this period, they eliminated legal loopholes and expanded the owners' authority over their chattel. For example, one of the justifications for the enslavement of Africans was that they were religious heathens. Debate eventually arose over whether the baptized children of slaves were entitled to their freedom. The matter was laid to rest with the

Virginia Act of 1667, which stated that conversion did not alter the status of slavery or freedom in such cases.[12]

Virginia's slave population grew significantly in the latter part of the seventeenth century, and masters wanted to ensure they had all the necessary power to control the expanding black labor force. To get a slave to obey the rules or to work hard, that slave had to be made to fear for his or her life. However, the slave owners had to be protected from legal liability, should—in the course of punishing "misbehavior"—they kill a slave. Legal statutes generally provided this protection to the master class, and in Virginia it was the Act of 1669 that served this purpose. The title of that law is particularly revealing: "An act about the casual killing of slaves."[13] *Casual* and *killing* would not usually be used together when discussing human beings, except if a certain class of beings was fundamentally considered to be property. Such language shows how little in the relative sense black lives mattered at this time.[14] The chances that taking a black life would lead to retribution were slim. The attitudes associated with the system of slavery didn't end with emancipation in 1863 but were passed on to subsequent generations. Was Dylann Roof influenced in this way and from these sources?

A series of statutes enacted during the years 1670–1705 further divided society along racial lines. The language used in the statutes is also revealing because frequently the term *Christian* was used synonymously with *white*; religious conversion was not sufficient to overcome the burden of blackness in this society. Slaves were prohibited from attempting to strike a white person. A 1691 Act prohibited miscegenation between singles or married people and imposed banishment on the white person who married a black, mulatto, or Indian. By this time the prevailing view was that freed slaves had no legitimate place in this society.

As the seventeenth century ended and the Chesapeake region was becoming a slave society, another settlement to the south was just beginning. This was the Carolina Colony, and its significance for black life would be immediate and profound. In contrast to the Chesapeake region, where African slavery was not part of the initial vision, in Carolina the institution was embedded in its very conception. In the earliest planning phase, even before the first settlers arrived, the decision was made to rely on slave labor. This was in part because several of Carolina's founders had plantations or investments in Barbados, the slave-reliant sugar-producing island in the English Caribbean, founded half a century earlier. Since Carolina was founded much later than other slave-based English colonies, it was able to anticipate and surmount some of the potential problems associated with slave labor. The initial organizing principles for the settlement were contained in its 1669 Fundamental Constitution, and the document anticipated the matter of slave conversion to Christianity, declaring that afterward the enslaved person remained in the "same State and Condition as he was in before." It was a rather peculiar document that points out another of those interesting and amazing contradictions in Carolina's racial history. The Fundamental Constitution granted religious liberty to slaves but simultaneously confirmed the masters' "absolute power and authority over Negro Slaves, of what opinion or Religion soever."[15] Once again liberty and slavery joined together.

Those first years of settlement were characterized by experimentation to place the colony on a firm economic footing. By the last two decades of the seventeenth century, Carolinians began making extensive efforts to produce rice. Rice cultivation proved successful because of the colonists' ability to harness African technological know-how. The English lacked any experience with a tropical crop like rice, but Africans from certain parts of the continent were thoroughly familiar with every aspect of its planting, harvesting, and consumption. Rice production became the major economic enterprise, accounting for more than half the value of South Carolina's total exports in 1720; it completely transformed every aspect of colonial life in the colony.[16] Rice was probably the most labor-intensive crop in the mainland colonies and required a large labor force, which came originally from other Caribbean sources but was increasingly obtained directly from Africa.

We know that black people were present in the very first year of Carolina's settlement. One of the earliest was a slave named Emanuel who was owned by a carpenter and may have helped construct the earliest buildings in Charleston. By 1740, Africans comprised 66 percent of the slave population in Carolina. Rice planters were more selective than most slave owners when constructing a labor force, and they preferred to purchase people already familiar with rice culture when possible. About 40 percent of all the Africans entering the British mainland colonies passed through the port of Charleston in the eighteenth century. Emanuel African Methodist Episcopal Church is situated only a few blocks away from Gadsden's Wharf, which was the most significant of the city's several historic wharfs where so many Rice Coast Africans and others disembarked.[17]

Based on the growth of labor demands, as early as 1708 Carolina developed its most distinctive demographic characteristic: it was the only one of the mainland English colonies with a majority black population. At first it was only a slight majority, but it rose to two-thirds by the eve of the American Revolution.[18] As South Carolina's black labor force grew and reduced whites to minority status, their fears rose accordingly, especially given their perception of African people. Carolina's first comprehensive slave code, passed in 1712, confirms this. After its preamble explains why slavery was an absolute necessity, it issued a stern warning about the dangerous presence of African people. The Negroes, it said, "are of barbarous, wild, savage natures," wholly unfit to be governed under the enlightened law of the province. Therefore special laws were required "for the good regulating and ordering of them, as may restrain the disorders, rapines and inhumanity, to which they are naturally prone and inclined; and may also tend to the safety and security of the people of this Province and their estates." Under these circumstances and to maintain order, it was necessary for all whites to cooperate and, if necessary, use violence to enforce the law. The 1712 Act required whites who apprehended slaves without passes to administer "moderate whipping" or face a fine. Furthermore, if a slave refused to show a pass or attempted to run away under questioning, the law empowered any white person to "beat, maim or assault" the slave; if the person could not readily be taken alive, a white citizen could kill the recalcitrant.[19]

Slavery was legal in all the original thirteen colonies. Most enslaved people lived in the South, but there was a small but significant black presence in the northern settlements also—particularly in Rhode Island, New York, and Pennsylvania. Some of the regions (such as the Hudson River Valley, Long Island, and northern New Jersey) that specialized in supplying foodstuffs and livestock to the Caribbean islands tended to have larger slave labor forces. There were also rural industries (such as tanning and ironworking) that relied heavily on slave labor. In some of the wealthiest agricultural counties of New Jersey in the mid-eighteenth century, male slaves outnumbered free workers.[20]

While most slaves lived and worked in the countryside, northern slavery was disproportionately urban. Large numbers of women and some men were used in domestic service while others, mainly men, were owned by artisans. Urban slaves were employed in maritime occupations, such as boatmen, sailmakers, dockhands, and fishermen. In most cases urban slave owners only kept one or two people because large numbers simply were not required and could have been a disadvantage given the scarcity and cost of urban housing.

Northern slave usage also influenced certain crucial aspects of black life. Just before the American Revolution, only about one-third of the black adults in Massachusetts were foreign-born, and evidence from New York shows that even the foreign-born black people there typically came from a southern colony, the Caribbean, or some other New

World location; there were few direct shipments of people from Africa.[21] Since northern masters owned small numbers of slaves and frequently worked along with them, they preferred people who were already at least somewhat acculturated. Even in the countryside it was not unusual for enslaved people to live in their owners' homes or in a nearby outbuilding. Unlike in the South, there was no separate slave street or quarters. The cultural impact of these factors was that northern slaves acculturated more quickly and extensively to Anglo-American values and behaviors than their southern counterparts.[22] By contrast, the black population in the Carolina Lowcountry had so many Africans, who retained and adapted their traditions to the new environment, it created a distinctive African American culture called *Gullah*. Among other things, it had its own food, language, and spiritual practices.

In the northern colonies the enslaved population maintained some traditional African behaviors and adapted them to the new environment to form a new African-based culture in America. One of the most significant and revealing examples is Negro Election Day. It was an annual celebration throughout New England in which slaves chose leaders, who were then given honorary titles such as governor, selectman, or sheriff. The elections were contested, and often the owners assisted their enslaved workers to get elected by financing parties or other events to build support. During the election period, there were many festivities, culminating in an inaugural ball. In Hartford, Connecticut, when the new black governor was installed, an observer noted he was accompanied by "a troop of blacks, sometimes a hundred in number, marching sometimes two and two, sometimes mounted in true military style and dress on horseback."[23]

Negro Election Day featured dances and songs rooted in African culture but also reflective of New World adaptations. Many of the kings or governors elected, however, had some connection to Africa; they might have been born in Africa or claimed descent from African royalty.[24] Only a slaveholding regime that was convinced of its hegemony would allow such celebrations. However, these occasions were not conceivable in the South, where the black population was proportionately much larger and potentially more dangerous.

Certain colonies in the North were also distinctive in the legal and customary rights they were willing to cede to the enslaved. The best example is Massachusetts Bay, where the 1641 Body of Liberties (ironically) set conditions under which people could be enslaved. It also conceded that slaves were required to "have all the liberties and Christian usages which the law of God established." This provision ensured that in Massachusetts court proceedings, slaves and white servants were frequently accorded the same legal rights and protections.[25] New York was more typical of the northern colonies—slaves had greater legal protections there than most places in the South. In a 1735 case in which a master was accused of maliciously beating his slave to death, a coroner's jury held that the death was the "work of God."[26] Decisions like this one in New York made it clear that as long as Africans were chattel, all their supposed rights were at the mercy of those with power.

It is a long and ugly history, and surely the reader wonders why it has taken so long for so many wrongs to be righted in this modern day and age, when *we know better*. But the reader wonders also what is it that has grown and festered in Dylann Roof's damaged imagination. What passed-down legacy of America's history of racism set him, the night of June 17, 2015, on the path to Mother Emanuel? With the church's past shaped by racial tensions in Charleston, its very existence symbolizes African American tenacity, talent, and triumph. Such a powerful black symbol stands open to attack.

FIVE

REVOLUTIONARY IDEAS AND THE RISE OF AFRICAN METHODISM

When news bulletins about the shooting at Mother Emanuel first flashed across the nation, many had never heard of the African Methodist Episcopal (AME) Church. Even now most Americans would be surprised to learn that this denomination was the first established by African Americans in the country, that it is almost as old as the nation itself, and that the two—the church and the nation—share much in common in their early histories. At the end of the eighteenth century, America was an improbable new nation that had won its independence against all odds from Great Britain, a far superior military power. The founder of the AME Church was Richard Allen, a man whose biography was similarly improbable. Born into slavery, Allen defied the odds to gain his freedom during the American Revolution and then to become bishop of a new branch of Methodism. In addition to biblical tenets, the foundation of the new church drew upon the ideas of the revolutionary era and demanded the nation apply its fundamental creed of liberty and justice to all people.

By the 1760s, the relationship between Great Britain and its thirteen North American colonies had begun to fray because of new taxes and tighter imperial administrative policies to ensure they were actually collected. In Boston, outraged colonists' ire boiled over in December 1773, when some of them dressed up like Native Americans and dumped tea worth almost two million dollars into the harbor. The depth of their anxiety could be seen in the rhetoric they used to oppose British policy; they charged over and over again that the British intended to reduce them to "slavery." This was the starkest metaphor they could use and reflected the most hopeless state of dependency they could imagine. Six months after the Boston Tea Party, George Washington suggested the British intended to reduce them "to the most abject state of Slavery that ever was designd [sic] for Mankind." British designs were also clear to fellow Virginian Patrick Henry. In the most famous speech made before the Virginia House of Burgesses, he asked, "Is life so dear, or peace so sweet, as to be purchased at the price of chains and slavery? . . . I know not what course others may take; but as for me, give me liberty, or give me death!" A month after the famous battles of Lexington and Concord, Washington now lamented that "the once happy and peaceful plains of America are either to be drenched with Blood, or Inhabited by Slaves."[1] Washington chose to lead the Continental Army, and the American Revolutionary War formally began with the Declaration of Independence in 1776.

In the run-up to the revolution, the atmosphere was rife with calls for liberty by American patriots, and when paired with the dreaded metaphor of slavery, the effects were especially striking among the slaves. Enslaved domestics overheard conversations about natural rights at the tables they served. Urban slaves sometimes found copies of pamphlets that justified overthrowing "oppressive" British rule. Not surprisingly, they applied the revolutionary rhetoric to their plight. They wondered how slave owners could decry schemes to "enslave" them, while holding human beings as property. The obvious contradiction inspired bold and remarkable actions by some slaves, who called on American political leaders to grant their freedom.

In keeping with the spirit of the era, some patriot leaders began working toward emancipation. Even while the war was still being fought, Pennsylvania passed a law in 1780 that gradually emancipated its slave population. Three years later Massachusetts courts effectively abolished slavery in a decision asserting "all men are born free and equal." Other states in the region embraced emancipation, and in 1804, well after the war had concluded, New Jersey was the last former colony in the North to institute gradual abolition.[2] The impact of the revolutionary philosophy was not universal—slavery remained entrenched in the South—but clearly freedom was on the march in the Northern states, where slavery soon disappeared entirely.

❋

Richard Allen's life began in Philadelphia in 1760, on the eve of these momentous times. His family was owned by Benjamin Chew, a prominent attorney, but by 1768, Chew sold them to Stokeley Sturgis, whose farm was near Dover, Delaware. Before long their lives were upended again when Sturgis's financial difficulties forced him to sell off individual members of Allen's family until only Richard, a brother, and a sister remained together there.[3] Richard and his brother were field hands; fortunately for them, Sturgis was not a harsh master. In fact, Allen described him as "what the world called a good master. He was more like a father to his slaves than anything else." However, their owner remained heavily in debt, and the two brothers worried that upon his death they would simply be auctioned off like any piece of property. Allen confessed that he was sometimes so deeply troubled at this prospect that he was "brought to weep;" this was a major reason why he described slavery as

51

"a bitter pill," even under a "good" master. Despite it all, Allen continued to hope and even expect that he would be free someday.[4]

Allen moved closer to achieving his goal once he was introduced to the circuit-riding Methodist preachers who held camp meetings near his farm. He and his brother began attending these meetings, and after recognizing their spiritual depravity, both converted in 1777. But Allen soon began to doubt that he was truly "saved;" he still felt so burdened with sin that he was convinced that hell would be his destiny. But after plaintive cries to God, Allen later wrote, "All of a sudden my dungeon shook, my chains flew off, and glory to God, I cried. My soul was filled." Finally convinced he was forgiven of his sins, he joined the Methodists and began to exhort his friends about the goodness of God.[5]

Richard Allen's affinity for Methodism was not unusual; many slaves preferred the denomination. Its evangelical style, emphasis on the conversion experience rather than formalism and theological complexity, and its message that all souls are spiritually equal and entitled to salvation, along with the use of lay preachers, all made it attractive. The fact that the Methodists were vehemently antislavery at this time didn't hurt either; the Quakers were the only sect that matched their antislavery zeal.[6] From this point on, Richard Allen always associated Methodism with both spiritual and physical freedom.[7]

Soon Richard Allen obtained his master's permission to invite Methodist preachers onto his plantation. After several preachers visited over a period of months, the famous minister Freeborn Garrettson, a former slaveholder, came to the Sturgis farm, perhaps in September 1779. After Garrettson delivered a sermon with clear antislavery themes, master Sturgis was convinced slavery was sinful and his soul was in jeopardy because of it. He arranged for Richard and his brother to hire out for wages in order to purchase their freedom, and they started 1780· with great expectations. Their joys must have been magnified when Pennsylvania enacted its gradual emancipation act that year. Even though Allen was unsure how he would make a living or secure the purchase price, he eventually found work chopping wood, working in a brickyard, and driving wagons for the Continental Army. His hard work was rewarded, and in August 1783, he paid two thousand dollars in exchange for freedom. It was an auspicious time: the formal end to the American Revolution followed within days of Richard Allen's manumission.[8] Now having achieved his personal independence, this newly freed man was ready to enter a new nation and make his mark.

The end of the Revolutionary War gave Allen the opportunity to travel, and he launched enthusiastically into preaching. Having already witnessed the power of Methodism to dramatically transform lives, Allen joined with other itinerant preachers and traveled widely, preaching the gospel. In the course of the next few years, he journeyed through New Jersey, Pennsylvania, and Maryland in the company of many well-known clerics. He did so on a volunteer basis, without even the meager compensation the church could provide. He explained, "My usual method was, when I would get bare of clothes, to stop travelling and go to work, so that no man could say I was chargeable to the connexion."[9] Race seems not to have been a serious barrier to Allen's efforts, as most of those he ministered to were white, and his talent as a preacher won him great success. Nevertheless, he longed to spread the Word more extensively among his own people. The city of Philadelphia provided just such an opportunity, and it was the perfect location for Allen.

Symbolically Philadelphia was a city that stood for freedom. In the conflict with Britain, leading to the revolution, it was host to the First and Second Continental Congresses, where American leaders criticized imperial rule and finally signed the Declaration of Independence. The city was home to large numbers of Quakers, whose abolitionist sentiments were widely known. They inspired creation of the Pennsylvania Abolition Society, the oldest antislavery organization in the English-speaking world, in 1775, just days before the famous battles at Lexington and Concord. The society continues to operate today. Slavery was in rapid decline in the city also. In 1765, Philadelphia only had about one hundred free blacks and fourteen hundred slaves. But by 1783, free blacks had soared to more than one thousand people, and the slave population was reduced to around four hundred. Philadelphia was a major center of Methodism, and the first meeting of its itinerant ministers was held there at St. George's Church.[10]

In February 1786, Richard Allen was called to Philadelphia by the elder in charge of St. George's Church and began preaching there. He relished the opportunity to minister to his "African brethren," whom he described as "a long forgotten people"—only a few of which ever attended regular church service. Allen gained the support of the leadership of black members and began preaching as early as five o'clock in the morning and frequently delivered four or five sermons a day. One of his supporters, Absalom Jones, worked with Allen as he established prayer meetings and a society of forty-two people. Allen soon proposed a separate building for the black members, but with the exception of Jones and two others, this plan was rejected by the most influential African Americans in the city, as well as by the white leadership at St. George's.[11] As Allen's ministry flourished, more blacks attended the services, and many were forced to stand along the walls; finally black members were confined to seats in the balcony. A dispute over seats in this area resulted in white officers attempting to physically remove Jones as he prayed. The date for this incident is not clear due to ambiguity in the record, but it seems to have been around 1792. Regardless of the date, black members' response was unequivocal. Allen reported, "We all went out of the church in a body, and they were no more plagued with us."[12]

When black members left St. George's Church, they gravitated to the Free African Society, which had been organized in 1787, under the leadership of Allen and Jones, who had become concerned about the "irreligious and uncivilized state" in which most African Americans found themselves. The goal of the Free African Society was to promote mutual aid, social uplift, and ecumenical spiritual growth; all who led lives of Christian virtue were eligible for membership. The first meetings were held at Allen's home until the membership grew too large. Dues were paid monthly; a committee visited members and monitored their spiritual and moral condition, and in the case of illness or death, the society provided financial support. The organization held religious services and served as a temporary "church home" for those who left St. George's.[13]

Sectarian differences within the group eventually produced two different black congregations. The majority of those who left St. George's opted for the Episcopal tradition and remained under the authority of the Episcopal Church. This group established St. Thomas's African Episcopal Church during the summer of 1794, under Jones's leadership; it was the first black Episcopal church in the United States.[14] Allen remained committed to the Methodist tradition because of what it had done for him and because he believed it was particularly suited to the genius and sensibilities of African Americans. He relocated a blacksmith shop to land he'd purchased in 1791, and this became the home of the original Bethel AME Church, also dedicated in the summer of 1794.[15] This was the first church in a new African American denomination.

When Richard Allen initially proposed an African church while at St. George's, the white minister was dismissive and, Allen recalled, "used very degrading and insulting language to us, to try and prevent us from going on." Once black members physically left the church, St. George's officials launched a sustained campaign of vilification and intimidation against them. They claimed that the Allen group had violated church law by establishing a separate body and that Bethel actually belonged to the conference rather than to its black members. The elder at St. George's claimed spiritual authority over the church; he claimed the right to preach there whenever he desired and to assign others to that pulpit at will. On more than one occasion when the elder attempted to take charge, he found his path to the pulpit physically blocked by Bethel members. Ultimately the elder at St. George's took the dispute to the Supreme Court of Pennsylvania, which handed down a decision in 1816 favoring the autonomy of Bethel AME Church.[16] It had been an arduous struggle, and success was far from certain. But according to one observer, men such as Richard Allen and Absalom Jones were "animated with some of the spirit of those days, resolved to introduce a new order of things among themselves."[17] They shared this penchant for liberty with the founders of the new nation, and it, along with their tenacity, carried them on to an improbable victory.

The successes won in Philadelphia encouraged African Americans in other places who yearned for spiritual liberation; Baltimore was such a place. While located in a slaveholding state, Methodism was influential in Baltimore, but it also had detractors. Obviously pro-slavery advocates opposed its antislavery policies. Others worried that Methodism's emphasis on spiritual equality would undermine the subordination required of slaves and embolden free blacks to seek new liberties—perhaps even social equality. This was one reason why in 1795, a year after Bethel was established in Philadelphia, Bishop Francis Asbury denied the request by black Methodists in Baltimore for their own church building. Undeterred, however, they created a Colored Methodist Society that hosted prayer meetings in members' homes.[18]

By 1802, the bishop had a change of heart and allowed the all-black Sharp Street congregation to form; however, like several mixed-race congregations in Baltimore, it remained under the control of the Methodist conference. Thus, even though this church allowed its members to control many of their affairs and gave opportunities to black lay preachers, they were still subordinate to white officials, who often treated them contemptuously.[19] Daniel Coker, an African American from Maryland, who had received ordination in the Methodist church before joining at

Sharp Street, was most frustrated with the situation there. He was highly respected among Baltimore's black Methodists and also corresponded with Richard Allen. By May 1815, when the situation was no longer tolerable, Coker led a small band out from Sharp Street Church and established the African Methodist Bethel Society in a rented building. It has been called the first independent black church in the slave states. By 1817, its membership had grown to more than six hundred, creating the largest black congregation in the city. Tension developed between the Bethel church and Baltimore's Methodist officials, who punished whites who cooperated with Coker's church, but it never escalated to the level experienced by Allen supporters in Philadelphia.[20]

Richard Allen was aware of several other African Methodist congregations with similar backgrounds and experiences. So he convened a meeting in Philadelphia, in 1816, to discuss their problems, consider collaboration, and to "promote union and harmony among themselves."[21] Those attending came from Philadelphia; Baltimore; Attleborough, Pennsylvania; Salem, New Jersey; and Wilmington, Delaware. They formed a single church body known as the African Methodist Episcopal Church; they elected Allen as their bishop and agreed to operate under a single discipline.[22] In keeping with the language of liberty, according to Allen, the decisions they made would protect them "from that spiritual despotism which . . . [they] have so recently experienced."[23]

From the beginning, Richard Allen conceived of dual roles for the AME church, one spiritual and the other secular, yet they were overlapping and not completely distinct from each other. He saw the church as a powerful instrument of social uplift that could inculcate its members with values that would make them successful. Allen believed in hard work, discipline, and sobriety—all of which had contributed to his extraordinary life—so he promoted them frequently in his sermons and writings.[24] He knew that an African American's enemies would use any opportunity to disparage the race, and as a prominent church leader, he felt obligated to refute such attacks. An important example of this occurred after the 1793 Philadelphia yellow fever epidemic. Assuming African Americans had immunity, prominent whites asked black Philadelphians to assist in relieving the city's suffering. Motivated by a sense of civic responsibility, Allen and Absalom Jones persuaded their church members and others to do this deadly work. Some, such as Allen and Jones, administered medical assistance, another group provided foodstuffs, while hundreds gathered and buried corpses, and others filed reports. It was a monumental effort. After the epidemic ended, the two ministers were shocked when some white writers criticized blacks in general for stealing, price gouging, and vile behavior. Allen and Jones immediately responded with a widely circulated pamphlet challenging the charges point by point, detailing acts of black heroism and also describing loathsome examples of whites' behavior.[25]

An even greater challenge occurred with the creation of the American Colonization Society by Robert Finley in 1816–17. Based on the twin assumptions that free blacks could never prosper in American society and would be victims of racial discrimination, Finley's group argued that they should immigrate "home" to Africa. If the assumptions were not troubling enough (that racial discrimination would be unrelenting and that Africa, not the United States, was their home), prominent slaveholding men, such as James Monroe, Henry Clay, and Andrew Jackson, were in leadership positions of the American Colonization Society, and it truly alarmed African Americans. In reaction, a mass meeting attended by approximately three thousand people was held at Bethel AME Church in 1817. Many present expressed fears that the activities of the Colonization Society would lead to blacks being forced from their homes, and they vowed never to abandon the slaves to their abject status. A committee of prominent black Philadelphians (including Richard Allen) was formed to organize a sustained opposition to colonization.[26]

Sometimes the threat to free blacks was more immediate and direct—particularly in Pennsylvania, which sat astride the Mason-Dixon Line dividing slave and free states. Even here the prospect of kidnapping was ever present. In fact, in 1806, a Southern slaveholder obtained a warrant for Bishop Richard Allen and attempted to seize him as a fugitive. Fortunately Allen was a man of such prominence that he was able to rebut the claim, and the would-be kidnapper was sent to jail for his efforts. However, before the man completed his sentence, Allen intervened in an extraordinary act of Christian charity and had him released.[27]

We don't know the precise impact of this event on Richard Allen's life because he didn't discuss it, but it must have shaped his activism, perhaps even increasing his commitment to antislavery work. This personal knowledge of how precarious liberty was for free blacks may explain his wife's, Sarah's, intense commitment to assist fugitive slaves. Observers noted that she aided "the poor, flying slave, trembling and panting in his flight . . . those eyes, kindled with peculiar brightness as she would bid them God speed to the land of liberty." The Allens continued this commitment for the rest of their lives; their "house was never shut against the friendless, homeless, penniless fugitives from the 'House of Bondage.'"[28] Aiding fugitives was illegal but was not unheard-of in the free states. In the South, and particularly the Deep South, it could have been deadly to both life and limb if discovered.

※

As a Deep South state and one with a majority black population, South Carolina had a harsh slave code with severe penalties for violations. White South Carolinians knew what would happen should they lose control of that population. The Stono Rebellion of 1739, which was the deadliest of the eighteenth century, occurred not far from Charleston. As a port city Charleston also received many refugees fleeing from the particularly bloody Haitian Revolution, which began in the 1790s. Their gruesome tales circulated for decades, kindling fears not easily forgotten.[29]

It is no wonder that when Methodism first arrived in Charleston in 1785, the reception was swift and hostile. The early Methodist ministers reported attacks against the church buildings and disruptions during their worship services. Many whites were put off by the evangelical style of Methodist preaching, but the greater threat was posed by the denomination's antislavery reputation, though that reputation was fairly quickly modified. Although the 1785 Methodist Discipline contained a bold condemnation of slavery, objections in the South led to an amendment of the section on slavery to allow local quarterly and regional conferences to regulate the matter. But periodically, efforts were made at general conferences to require the membership and ministry to free any slaves they owned. Finally, in 1804, in an effort to prevent future wrangling over slavery and build support in the South, two versions of the Methodist Discipline were published. The version applicable to Virginia and the region to its north contained directives on slavery, but the version applied to the lands south of Virginia had no such statements.[30]

As Methodism acquiesced to the demands of slaveholders, the denomination overcame the initial hostility—and even grew. That growth was overwhelmingly due to increasing slave members who rapidly comprised the majority of the mixed-race churches in Charleston. In 1811, for example, 81 white members were added, compared to 415 black members. Likewise, in 1815, the total number of white members in the city was 282 compared to 3,793 blacks.[31] The denomination provided opportunities for black members to exercise leadership positions in the church bureaucracy as class leaders and even as lay preachers. In Charleston they also had a tradition of managing their own Quarterly Conferences or business meetings, including collecting and dispersing monies. These matters became a point of contention when Reverend Anthony Senter was placed in charge of the churches in 1815. He found that the black leaders had misused church funds by apparently pur-chasing and then emancipating slaves. Obviously enslaved people had a different vision of the social gospel than Senter. Because of this, new, more restrictive policies were instituted, severely limiting the activities of the black church leaders and subordinating virtually all their deci-sions to white church officials.[32]

The new order of things created quite a stir among black members of the congregation, and they vowed to act. They knew about Richard Allen's church and sent two of their leaders, Morris Brown and Henry Drayton, to confer with him in Philadelphia and to be ordained as ministers of the AME Church. After their return, a dispute with church officials over the use of a burial ground became the precipitant for a break with white Methodists. In 1817 or 1818, Morris Brown led 4,367 black members from the white Methodist churches, and in the latter year they founded their own branch of the AME Church in Charleston. Over three-quarters of all black Methodists elected to join with the secession-ists, and one observer noted, "The galleries, heretofore crowded, were almost completely deserted, and it was a vacancy that could be *felt*."[33]

Morris Brown and his supporters next purchased land at Hanover and Reid Streets in Hampstead, an area beyond the city limits, and they petitioned the state legislature for permission to build a church there. This was necessary because in a slave society like South Carolina, it was illegal for too many free blacks to gather together without special permission. The state denied the request, but they built a church any-way, and eventually two missionary branches were established; one was located on Anson Street, very near Boundary Street, which is close to the present Emanuel AME Church.[34]

The revolutionary significance of what had already happened would be hard to exaggerate. Several thousand black Carolinians had asserted their religious independence from white authority and cast off white domination just as their brothers and sisters in Christ had done in

Baltimore, Philadelphia, and other cities to the north.[35] They refused to accept racist definitions of who they were and what they required. By doing so in Charleston, and then joining their destiny to a black, Northern abolitionist church, Morris Brown and his supporters launched a ministry of liberation unseen before in the Deep South. Those in authority immediately recognized what was at stake and vigorously fought the threat to white supremacy—and did so with deadly consequences.

SIX

THE SLAVE CONSPIRACY

June 7, 1818, was a Sunday, and by late morning the congregation was beginning to assemble on the grounds of the African church. Peninsular Charleston was small enough that many could easily walk here. Others came from farther away, from across the Ashley or Cooper Rivers west and east of the city, and they took ferries or other watercraft to complete their trips. Regardless of how early they started or where they came from, upon arrival they exchanged enthusiastic and heartfelt greetings. If Reverend Morris Brown had glanced across the crowd that morning as he prepared to call the service to order, he would have seen a diverse group of black people. Most were probably slaves, but many were free blacks emancipated by various means, including self-purchase or as a result of loyal service to their owners. Most were probably native Carolinians, but there was a substantial number of Africans in the church.

When services began, undoubtedly there were energetic songs of praise and Scripture readings to buoy the congregants' spirits. At some point the pastor, or perhaps a class leader, knelt before the congregation to offer prayers of thanksgiving to the Lord for another week in the land of the living and to ask for strength and deliverance in the days to come.

We do not know the precise sequence of events, but at some point during the afternoon, the Charleston city guard arrived in force and disrupted the service. Between 140 and 150 worshipers were arrested, taken to the guard house, and confined there overnight. The next day they were brought before city magistrates, who informed them they had broken laws in effect since 1800, and admonished them not to do so again. The charges were apparently dropped against most of the accused, except for those described as ministers. Five were sentenced to imprisonment for one month or "to give security to leave the state." Eight others were sentenced to "receive ten lashes, or [to] pay a fine each of five dollars." Despite such warnings, these church men and women held a subsequent "large and unlawful assemblage . . . as they had done before," as described by one local paper. They were detained again; however, the penalty, which could have included corporal punishment and imprisonment, was "inflicted only on a few of the ring-leaders."[1] Life in a slave society was routinely abusive for black people, but the attacks on the African church were so deeply disturbing that some of its members and supporters now contemplated violence as the only way to gain control over their lives. Denmark Vesey is a case in point.

※

Destined to become the most famous member of the African church, Denmark Vesey was born on St. Thomas in the Caribbean around 1767. At age fourteen he was purchased by Captain Joseph Vesey, who plied the slave trade mainly between St. Thomas and Saint-Domingue (today's Haiti). The French island of Saint-Domingue was known for the richness of its sugarcane harvests and for the brutality of its slavery. Denmark worked mainly for Captain Vesey on shipboard until 1783, at the end of the American Revolution, when the captain settled in Charleston and continued his trading operations. Denmark continued as Vesey's slave until the captain allowed him to purchase his freedom with the winnings from a lottery; so in 1800, Denmark Vesey started the new century as a free man. Over the next two decades he worked about the city as a carpenter, and developed close common-law relationships with two slave women and one free black woman, all of whom may have borne his children.[2]

While it seemed that Denmark Vesey was leading a successful life, he must have been discouraged if not exasperated by the difficulties that free blacks faced regularly. They were outside the political system; they could not vote and had no absolute right of petition. Nor could they testify in court in cases involving whites. Free blacks accused of committing crimes were tried in slave courts; certain acts were deemed criminal only when committed by those of African descent, and there were crimes for which slaves or free blacks were punished more harshly than whites guilty of the same acts. Free blacks were also required to pay a special "capitation tax;" failure to do so could lead to public sale and a term of servitude.[3] As if these everyday examples of racial subordination weren't sufficiently troubling, Vesey's manhood was assailed further by the fact that other men owned his family members; he was never able to purchase freedom for either of his "wives" or his children.[4]

Over the years the maddening frustrations of free black life embittered Vesey, and he found it difficult to contain his anger. Sometimes he was even purposely provocative in order to kindle the resentment of other black people. Someone once remarked of him that he looked for opportunities to engage in "conversation with white persons when they could be overheard by negroes nearby . . . during which conversation he would artfully introduce some bold remark on slavery." Even when strolling on the streets of the city, Vesey took every opportunity to enlighten other black Charlestonians and to upbraid those who degraded their manhood by cringing before whites. He was allegedly heard to proclaim that such people "deserve to remain slaves." Vesey vowed never to denigrate himself in this way because all men were equals.[5]

Denmark Vesey was a class leader in the African church and a devoted student of the Bible. Based on his understanding of the Scriptures, slavery—at least the kind under which African people in South Carolina languished—was inconsistent with the will of God. To promote his antislavery message, Vesey frequently held meetings at his home and read from the Bible. One slave who observed him said that "he studies the Bible a great deal and tries to prove from it that slavery and bondage is against the Bible."[6] Beyond this, Vesey developed a version of what would later become known as *black liberation theology*. It was not unusual for slaves to identify with the book of Exodus and the deliverance of the Israelites from the clutches of their Egyptian masters. Vesey embraced this view of a God who favored the oppressed and did all he could to convince Lowcountry slaves that as God's people, they also shared in the destiny of the Hebrew children. One of his favorite biblical passages was Zechariah 14, which showed the fiery trial through which Jerusalem passed before its ultimate salvation and elevation above its enemies through divine intervention. According to Vesey's theology of liberation, that same God would deliver black Carolinians and similarly vanquish their enemies who held them in such an unjust and inhumane slavery.[7]

The breaking point seems to have been reached when the Charleston authorities began harassing and persecuting members and leaders of the African church. Once this commenced, a slave reported that Vesey held a meeting at his home and said, "We were deprived of our rights and privileges by the white people, and . . . our Church was shut up, so that we could not use it." Rather than remain passive in the face of such an egregious insult, Vesey boldly asserted "it was high time for us to seek for our rights" and to "conquer the whites." Vesey was just as certain, though, that God would not do for enslaved people what they must do for themselves. Underscoring this argument, he pointed to enslaved people on Saint-Domingue, who had achieved something the world had never seen before. Beginning in the 1790s, they not only emancipated themselves by making war on their French owners, but they then went on to eject their former masters and rule the country they renamed Haiti as an independent black republic, the world's first. But first Vesey admonished black Carolinians to be courageous, to unite as the Haitians had done, and to gird themselves for the battle to come.[8]

That struggle would be violent; death on both sides would inevitably result because the master class would certainly oppose black freedom at every turn. The racial apocalypse Vesey envisioned was justified by the Holy Scriptures, which often showed common people used as the instruments of God's retributive justice. As in Haiti, Vesey believed that once the insurrection began, the forces of liberation could not afford to be squeamish in dealing with enemies who had proven to be most deadly in the past—for their own safety. Vesey and his chief lieutenants espoused these lessons as they persuaded or cajoled others to support an audacious bid for freedom, often under the cover of class meetings, prayer meetings, or other gatherings connected to the African church.[9]

On that tragic evening of June 17, 2015, another prayer meeting was held at Charleston's Emanuel AME Church—but its composition, tenor, and circumstances were wholly different from Vesey's meetings. Vesey's were illegal and usually clandestine gatherings that could have been dispersed by authorities wielding corporal punishment for the blatant threat they posed to white supremacy. Vesey's meetings were also exclusively male, which made their potential threat even greater. His teachings relied on the Old Testament and a God of judgment, justice, and physical deliverance, providing the means for black people to gain freedom and control over their own bodies.[10] How different was the scene in Emanuel's modern and spacious fellowship hall: only a small number were gathered, but their grandest wish was for the multitudes to come and hear the good news of the gospel proclaimed, to study and discuss it so their souls might be saved. Most of the attendees were women, which was not at all unusual, particularly for the modern church. Prayer meetings were public gatherings that broke no laws; the participants had every expectation of safety in God's house.

That night's lesson was drawn from the New Testament, based on the fourth chapter of Mark's gospel. The verses in that reading devoted to the parable of the sower are particularly relevant for understanding the events of that evening. Here the scriptures explain why God's Word had a differential effect on its hearers. Using the metaphor of the farmer who casts seeds to represent the person who preached God's Word, sometimes the words fell on fallow ground, germinated readily, and produced lives of deep devotion to Christ, manifested in good works toward others. Even the most cursory examination of the lives of the Emanuel Nine show their special receptivity to both the spiritual and secular missions of the church. But the same passage also warns that after the word had been preached, to some "Satan cometh immediately, and taketh away the word that was sown in their hearts" (Mark 4:15 KJV). Other times the hearts of men are like "stony ground" (v. 16 KJV). Other hearers prefer "riches" and "other things" of this world, and their "lusts" for them "choke the word, and it becometh unfruitful" (v. 19 KJV).

Dylann Roof was in the latter group. He came to the meeting under the guise of a fellow sinner seeking salvation through God's grace. Even though white and a stranger, he was welcomed into the fold. After an hour he stood up; for a split second Roof hesitated to attack people who, by his own admission, were "so nice to him."[11] But his ultimate goal to start a race war failed, just as Vesey's bloody apocalyptic vision remained unfulfilled.

Denmark Vesey's insurrectionary scheme was formulated with the assistance of several principal African and black Carolinian organizers and was originally scheduled to begin on the night of Sunday, July 14, 1822. Sunday was a logical choice because it was the day of the week that most slaves were free from their daily labor routine. Many came to the city to attend church services, to visit friends, or to recreate, so it

would not have been unusual to find rural slaves present in large numbers.[12] The plan was to organize several cadres of slaves, in Charleston
and the surrounding area, who would converge on the city under the
cover of darkness. Once the city guards were overpowered, they would
further arm themselves with weapons taken from local arsenals and set
fires at strategic locations around the city. When white citizens joined
with the local militias to quell the disorders, they all were to be engaged
in battle in the streets and alleyways of Charleston. The strategy was to
create enough chaos and to strike such a fearsome blow against white
Charleston to enable the insurrectionists and their supporters to reach
the docks, board ships, and achieve the ultimate goal of sailing off to
Haiti, the world's singular bastion of black liberation. Vesey seemed not
to have any expectation that this single episode would end slavery in the
state. He planned for as many people as possible to stage a grand "exodus" from the American "Egypt."[13]

Many of the details are still murky, but Vesey expected that the
Haitians would provide the rebels assistance in some form once the
insurrection began. After all, Vesey had been enslaved there, and Haiti's
reputation as a source of revolutionary ferment was well-known in
Atlantic port cities; Charleston had become home to many who fled the
country during the long and bloody rebellion. Vesey pledged to corre-
spond with the Haitian government—with help from black sailors on
Charleston ships that sailed between the two countries—to determine
what might be possible. As part of the plan, Vesey warned his followers to
make sure they did not kill the ships' captains because their skills would
be necessary to effect the escape plan.[14]

Every effort was made to maintain the secrecy of his plot so the
conspirators could preserve the advantage of a surprise attack. So, for
example, the principal organizers agreed not to inform Morris Brown
and some of the other mainstream leaders in the African Church of the
arrangements. Their assumption was that Brown and those like him

would never accept a radical plan of liberation that involved violence and, if informed, might even feel compelled to notify officials. In the end they could not prevent word from reaching officials. In late May, after a slave was informed of the plan but refused to join, the knowledge of what was about to happen proved too burdensome for him, so he told his master, who promptly notified officials. Once an investigation began, Vesey moved up the date for the rebellion by a full month, to Sunday evening, June 16. But it was too late—arrests, court proceedings, and convictions ensued. For a while it seemed that Vesey had escaped, but he was eventually captured. Altogether there were 131 arrests; Vesey was executed along with thirty-four others, and thirty-seven conspirators were sentenced to transportation outside the state under the pain of death upon return. Although it is likely that Morris Brown knew nothing of the conspiracy, as the pastor of the African Church, he fell under suspicion, and in this volatile atmosphere he fled the city to take refuge in Philadelphia.[15]

After the punishments were meted out, other actions were taken to make Charleston more secure against any similar future threats. The African Church was heavily involved in the conspiracy, and at least 60 percent of those executed were from among its ranks. As a clear source of subversive ideas, the church building was destroyed by order of city authorities, and the congregation scattered as a result.[16] In South Carolina free blacks had long been the objects of white misgivings; Denmark Vesey's actions confirmed the need for greater repression against this population. In the fall of 1822, a group of white Charlestonians petitioned the state legislature and stated that "although the immediate danger has passed," unless something was done quickly and decisively, "a series of the most appalling distresses" would soon follow.[17]

By December the state legislature responded to white fears with new laws. Now free blacks were required to pay new taxes annually, and males over fifteen years of age were required to have white guardians who could vouch for their respectability. One of the most effective ways to assert control over free blacks was to limit their ability to travel. Until this time free blacks had traveled to and from the state easily, but now the law prohibited those who left the state from reentering it. First violations were punished with imprisonment and second offenses with enslavement. Such stringent policies were necessary to ensure that free blacks did not abuse their rights by traveling to the North, where they might fraternize with abolitionists and bring dangerous ideas back to the state. Charleston also required free blacks to register with authorities twice annually and to account for any absences.[18] To minimize potentially dangerous outside influences on black Carolinians, the legislature passed the Negro Seaman Acts in 1822 and 1823. According to their provisions, black crew members from ships docking in the port were required to report to the municipal jail, where they were confined for the duration of the vessel's stay in the city. During the period of late July through September 1823, 154 black sailors disembarked at Charleston and were confined at the jail. Ship captains were responsible for paying the expense of their detention; if the fees were not paid, the free black seaman would be sold into slavery.[19]

Enforcement of slave law was the responsibility of Charleston's city guard, which was reorganized in 1823 to improve its communications and operational efficiency. To ensure adequate protection for the citizenry, white Charlestonians requested that the state establish a more modern arsenal in the upper part of the city. An old warehouse on Boundary Street was temporarily used for this purpose. By the mid-1820s, though, a more substantial building was under construction and included an arsenal, barracks, and mounted cannons surrounded by a high wall. After the events of 1822, white Carolinians certainly knew that survival in a slave society required that white men who were skilled in the art of war be present in the general population. To produce this group, the South Carolina Military Academy, also known as the Citadel, was established at this location in 1842. Citadel cadets were responsible for firing the artillery shots that eventually led Union troops to evacuate Fort Sumter in Charleston and brought on the Civil War. They were also responsible for training Confederate troops on the front lines of the war, particularly those involving the defense of Charleston.[20]

✳

Today the Citadel is South Carolina's public military college and counts African Americans and women among its distinguished graduates.[21] It is no longer located at its original site in the middle of Charleston's historic district but was relocated to the city's west side on the Ashley River in the early 1920s. Along the southern border of Marion Square, the site of the original Citadel building, stands a towering monument to John C. Calhoun, one of the South's major architects of the pro-slavery argument and the doctrine of nullification (the idea that states could declare laws that they deemed unconstitutional null and void). It is the tallest figurative monument in the city. The old Citadel building, which still resembles a fortress, is an Embassy Suites hotel. On the south side of the building is a small historical marker, erected many years ago, explaining the significance of the site. It says the building "was first constructed as a two-story armory and fortress as a result of the Denmark Vesey slave uprising." The marker is so small and in such an out-of-the-way location that the uninformed observer might never see it unless he looks very carefully. Similarly, the "Brief History" section on the Citadel's website has no discussion at all about the school's organic connection in its early days to the preservation of slavery and white supremacy; it's not there.[22] This omission, like so many others in South Carolina, represents the way the racial present is either still unreconciled with the past or just now coming to grips with it.

The best example involves Denmark Vesey. Among the black

community, Vesey has historically been the most well-known and revered member of the African Church—the congregation from which Mother Emanuel is descended. Before his brutal assault on its church members, Dylann Roof traveled to many Lowcountry sites of significance in African American history, and we know his view of that past was a distorted one. He contended that slavery was a benign institution, that black men routinely raped white women and violently victimized whites in general. *Where did he get these ideas?* Did he know anything about the Vesey trial record, in which witnesses predicted widespread violence against whites? As previously noted, the timing of Roof's assault against Emanuel is certainly food for thought; regardless, it is a tragic example of how the racist perversion of the African American past clouds our present.[23]

Charleston is a city where the past is on prominent display in the public square. Along the streets or in the parks of the historic district, the past takes on an immediacy through historic buildings, markers, and monuments. Only a relative few of these are reflective of the African American past, but the number is growing. As might be expected, the attempt to memorialize Denmark Vesey has been contentious and protracted. In 1976, when the Gaillard Municipal Auditorium was being outfitted, Charleston's young—and still relatively new and progressive—mayor, Joe Riley, commissioned local artist Dorothy Wright to paint a portrait of Denmark Vesey to be placed on display in the auditorium, which is proximate to the original location of the African Church and oblique from the current site of Mother Emanuel. In the months before installation of the painting, in private conversations or through letters written to the local paper, whites ridiculed or denounced the idea of displaying the image of such an infamous character on public property. Shortly after Vesey's portrait was installed, it was stolen—only to be returned after Mayor Riley vowed to have a replacement painted. It was then more securely mounted on the wall to prevent theft.[24]

In 1996, Henry Darby, then a high school history teacher and now one of Charleston County's elected officials, organized the Denmark Vesey and the Spirit of Freedom Monument Committee to memorialize Vesey in Marion Square. The committee envisioned a figurative monument as an important step toward making black Charlestonians' experiences more visible in the city's streetscape. Marion Square was the most logical location because it is down the street from Mother Emanuel and directly across the park from the old Citadel building. The park is owned, however, by Washington Light Infantry and Sumter Guard—two private militia units that originated in the early nineteenth century—and they lease the grounds to the city.[25]

Not surprisingly, even with the mayor's support, the Vesey committee could not win approval for the monument on the square. In the years the committee worked on the project, the usual detractors and arguments were brought against the wisdom of such a choice. The *Post and Courier* published letters (presumably from white writers) calling Vesey's plan "a Holocaust" and accusing Vesey of advocating "ethnic cleansing." The opposition of some was deeply personal. When Robert Rosen, a prominent white lawyer, supported the monument, he received a phone call from a colleague who told him, "If Denmark Vesey had succeeded in his plot, I would not be here." Despite such characterizations (and with the city's unflagging support), a site was eventually selected for the Vesey monument in the upper part of the city in Hampton Park. During the Civil War, this area was used by the Confederacy as a prison camp for Union troops; more than two hundred died there and were buried in a mass grave. After the war, black Charlestonians created a proper cemetery for these men and staged a mass march to the site; many believe it was the first example of a Memorial Day celebration.[26] The park was later named for the Confederate general Wade Hampton III.

On Saturday morning, February 15, 2014, after eighteen years of frustration and hard work, the Denmark Vesey and the Spirit of Freedom Monument was unveiled in a ceremony witnessed by hundreds of bystanders. The African Church's most famous member had finally found a place in one of Charleston's most scenic parks. The text on the base of the statue speaks to the universality of the quest for freedom and situates Vesey's bold, liberating plans in the context of the rise and demise of the African Church. Reverend Joseph Darby, a presiding elder in the AME Church, was one of the speakers that day and said, "Some people see Denmark Vesey as a dangerous terrorist, [but many more] see him as a freedom fighter. My hope is that this monument will add to the full story of our southern heritage."[27] And it will probably accomplish that purpose, although not in the way the Marion Square location would have, with the visual juxtaposition of the buildings where the struggle between slavery and freedom was fought.[28]

In Charleston—where the connection of racial histories to buildings and other sites has not always been clear—the most striking ironies arise. Such was the case on the evening of June 17, 2015. After relatives of the victims (and others) began to converge on the church, clamoring for information, the authorities began directing them down the street to the Embassy Suites Hotel, less than two blocks away. Soon more than 250 people were gathered on the hotel's second floor, where they encountered church officials and chaplains who tried to comfort family members as they waited for information on survivors—and they were waiting inside the old Citadel building. Imagine the irony: descendants from the African Church, whose church building was destroyed by city authorities, now being comforted within the walls of the structure that once housed and trained men who were responsible for suppressing their antebellum ancestors.[29]

※

Even after new, more racially repressive policies were instituted in 1822–23, the fears of white Charlestonians were never completely allayed.

This was in part because white Carolinians continued to live in the midst of an enslaved black majority population. Then, in 1831, Virginia's famous Nat Turner insurrection took sixty to seventy white lives and sent a shock wave of fear across the South, reconfirming the high cost of life in a slaveholding society. The threat of insurrection continued unabated, due to the rise of the Northern abolitionist movement, which denounced the slaveholding South in ever more strident terms. Northern white men, such as William Lloyd Garrison and Wendell Phillips, were among slavery's most vociferous critics. So were the Grimké sisters— Sarah and Angelina—of Charleston, who renounced their slaveholding birthright and left the city for the North, from which they denounced slavery as insiders.

While the AME Church was suppressed in Charleston, the denomination continued uninterrupted in the North, where it made substantial contributions to the abolitionist movement. In 1830, Bishop Richard Allen organized the first meeting of what would be known as the Negro National Convention Movement at Bethel AME Church. This was the first of twelve such meetings to occur before 1865. They were designed to convene African American leaders from the North to systematically examine the plight of slaves and free blacks and to formulate abolitionist and antiracist strategies for achieving racial justice in America.[30]

These national conventions were also the model for smaller state and regional conventions of black leaders. These were the forums in which black men, such as Frederick Douglass and William Wells Brown, both fugitive slaves, and others like them rose and denounced slavery while demanding they be accorded the rights of men. In 1843, in one of the most militant speeches given at one of these abolitionist conventions, Reverend Henry Highland Garnet rose and appealed to the slaves directly. He commended the memory of Denmark Vesey to them, calling him a "martyr to freedom" worthy of emulation. Going further he reminded them of the stark choice to be made: "However much you and all of us may desire it, there is not much hope of redemption without the shedding of blood. . . . rather *die freemen, than live to be the slaves.*"[31]

Under the relentless attack of such abolitionist rhetoric, white Carolinians feared that it would not be long before words translated into acts that threatened their lives. One article in the *Charleston Courier* observed the abolitionists were trying to destroy the slaves' natural affinity for their owners through lies and distortions—and when successful they might as well "have armed him as with a dagger, and placed about a master and his family an enemy capable of conceiving their destruction."[32] Under these circumstances, Carolinians calculated the value of remaining in the Union, and after John Brown led a racially integrated assault on the federal arsenal at Harper's Ferry, Virginia, the future seemed clear. The election of Abraham Lincoln in November 1860, as the candidate of the antislavery Republican Party, was the last straw. White Carolinians were a racial minority in their state, and with almost half of its white families owning slaves, South Carolina had the highest rate of slave ownership in the South. They would take no chance on finding out what life would be like in a country now governed by a man they considered an abolitionist—because slavery was the bedrock of their society. As John S. Preston, one of its most ardent defenders, declared: "Slavery is our King—slavery is our truth—slavery is our Divine Right." Men have always sacrificed their lives for the glory and defense of their kings, and this time would be no different. On December 20, 1860, South Carolina became the first state to secede from the Union; the broken nation plunged into fratricidal war within months.[33]

SEVEN

RESURRECTION

Within weeks of South Carolina's secession, several other like-minded Southern states left the Union, and in February 1861, they formed the nucleus of the Confederate States of America. According to its vice president, Alexander H. Stephens, this was a unique government in that "its cornerstone rests, upon the great truth that the negro is not equal to the white man; that slavery, subordination to the superior race, is his natural and moral condition."[1] Such a position notwithstanding, it was this government's policies that set the stage for the almost inevitable conflict with the United States. After the Union army refused demands to abandon Fort Sumter in Charleston Harbor, the Confederates fired on it on April 12, 1861, which led to its surrender and evacuation two days later. The struggle over slavery and its implications that had smoldered in American life and politics for decades now burst into a raging conflagration. The trial through which the nation would pass brought the potential not only to destroy it but also to consume the South's slaveholding order and to create a "new birth of freedom."[2]

Early in November 1861, at the Battle of Port Royal, Union forces invaded the southern coast of South Carolina and successfully occupied the area. One slave reported what many must have experienced there when he said, "We saw the lightning—that was the guns! [A]nd then we heard the thunder—that was the big guns."[3] These scenes of unprecedented combat were remembered for generations up and down the coast as the "Days of the Big Gun Shoot." These events were also interpreted in a religious framework and according to W. E. B. DuBois, an astute observer of Southern black life, "This was the coming of the Lord."[4] It was the famous Day of Jubilee that so many had waited for, and despite every method their masters used, including threats and coercion whenever Union troops came near, the slaves were encouraged to escape into their lines. This was because as one man observed, "Yankee fight fo' free we!"[5]

Slavery's demise proceeded unevenly and only reached Charleston late in the war, when the city finally fell to Union occupation on February 18, 1865. Black Charlestonians received freedom with the same ecstasy witnessed across the South. One month after the city's evacuation, African Americans organized a huge parade to celebrate their new freedom. Stretching over two miles, the procession was led by black Union soldiers; it included a mock slave auction and culminated with a hearse bearing the "body of slavery." Boldly written on the hearse for all to see were the words: *Slavery Is Dead* and *Sumter Dug His Grave on the 13th of April, 1861.*[6]

Charleston was fittingly the location for a national celebration commemorating the end of the war and slavery. On April 14, 1865, national politicians, military leaders, and abolitionists, as well as black and white soldiers, sailors, and marines, converged on Fort Sumter. William Lloyd Garrison, the famous white abolitionist, was there along with the acclaimed antislavery minister (and brother of novelist Harriet Beecher Stowe) Reverend Henry Ward Beecher. An estimated three thousand people were inside the fort, and thousands more were on boats of all kinds around its perimeter. Among those boats was the *Planter*, commanded by the fugitive slave and now famous war hero Capt. Robert

Smalls. Smalls was accompanied by abolitionist Maj. Martin R. Delany, the highest-ranked black officer in the army; and by the son of Denmark Vesey. Along with throngs of others, these men witnessed the reraising of the American flag over Fort Sumter by Gen. Robert Anderson, who had been forced to surrender the fort to Confederate occupation four years earlier. Joyous tears streamed down the faces of the many who immediately understood the meaning of this hour.[7]

A new racial landscape unfolded across the South and the nation, but it was purchased at a tremendous price. More soldiers died in the Civil War than in all of the country's wars from the Revolution to the Korean conflict combined. One-fifth of the South's men of military age died in the war, and in South Carolina the figure may have been as high as 35 percent.[8]

The specter of death even claimed the life of the first American president to die from politically and racially inspired violence: shortly after Confederate Gen. Robert E. Lee's surrender, Abraham Lincoln discussed plans for reconstruction in a speech to the nation. In doing so, he became the first president to publicly support extending the right to vote to "very intelligent" African Americans and to black Union soldiers. Hearing these words, the actor and rabid Confederate supporter John Wilkes Booth, a man who already considered the president a tyrant, had his rage further kindled at the prospect of "nigger citizenship." Booth vowed this would be Lincoln's last speech, and only days later, on the evening of April 14, he assassinated the president in Washington's Ford's Theater.[9]

Dylann Roof and John Wilkes Booth share much in common. Both were deeply committed to the ideals of the Confederacy. At one point Booth contemplated riding through the streets of Washington waving the rebel flag; photographs of Roof show him actually waving a Confederate flag and burning the American flag.[10] Although separated by 150 years, both were men without a country; neither could accept the social, political, or racial order he felt was unfairly thrust upon him, and each lashed out at the forces and the people that threatened white supremacy. In 1865, the triumphal president of the United States was the enemy, and in 2015 the enemy was the black church, an institution that could only flourish after that same president vanquished the Confederacy and ended slavery. And it did flourish, by aiding the freedmen in reorganizing their postwar lives and serving as the foundation for much of the racial progress that occurred during the next 150 years. The black church was deeply rooted in Charleston, the "Holy City," and African Methodism was destined to play a particularly important role within that larger story.

The restoration of the AME Church in South Carolina actually began during the Civil War when, in May 1863, Bishop Daniel Payne dispatched Northern missionaries to the state to begin working among the freedmen in the Port Royal area.[11] As the Union army extended its control over the area, these men were also able to expand the range of their preaching and teaching. Now, for the first time since 1822, there were official representatives of African Methodism in the state, although the formal organization of the denomination had to wait until after the Union occupation of Charleston in February 1865. Three months later Bishop Payne, himself a Charlestonian who had been forced from the city in the 1830s because of its oppressive laws against free blacks, now returned triumphantly to establish a new Zion. On Monday, May 15, he convened the first session of the South Carolina Conference of the AME Church. One participant emotionally noted, "The new era has dawned, the sun has lit up the horizon, and humanity is rising to a just appreciation of the crisis."[12] According to Reverend Richard H. Cain, the events of that day could not be understood without remembering the life of Denmark Vesey and his compatriots, who died "as martyrs to human liberty." The church was subsequently "demolished," and Cain asserted further that "from that day to this, our people have had to wear the accursed yoke of religious bondage."[13] But now it was a new day, a resurrection day, and God's glory showed forth as never before.

In this first meeting AME leaders challenged certain misconceptions and misrepresentations of the denomination that had been circulated, especially by Northern Methodists who saw the African Methodists as unwelcome competition. In a series of resolutions, for example, the conference denied that the term *African* meant that their church excluded mulattoes or whites from full participation in the denomination. Occurring in the wake of President Lincoln's assassination, this body also passed resolutions expressing both grief and revulsion over this malicious act, the intent of which was to undermine free government and "perpetuate the horrid crime of negro slavery."[14]

At this first conference the administrative structures of the church had to be established, and the various missionary stations were created for an episcopal district that originally included not only South Carolina but also Georgia, North Carolina, Florida, and Alabama. Those men who attended were from various locations North and South; some had been free while others were newly emancipated slaves. Some had been sent to South Carolina from other districts of the church, but others simply showed up to be of service. Some were fully ordained, and others were candidates for the ministry. In services described as dignified, solemn, and deeply impressive, candidates who qualified were ordained into the holy orders, and others were placed in the ministerial course of study. The district was divided into seven areas, and each was assigned a field superintendent to coordinate the work. Richard H. Cain was placed in charge of southern South Carolina and was based in Charleston.[15]

Richard Cain was born free in Virginia but spent his youth in Ohio, where he joined the AME church in Cincinnati. Bishop Payne discovered him in the 1850s and had him trained in the Indiana Conference and at Wilberforce University in Ohio. During the Civil War, Cain relocated to Bridge Street Church in Brooklyn, and he later founded Fleet Street

Church there. Cain was not only an able minister, but he was a deeply committed abolitionist who was personally acquainted with some of the leading antislavery men of the day, such as Frederick Douglass and Henry Garnet.[16] Bishop Payne recognized Cain's talents, brought him to South Carolina, and placed him in charge of the church's efforts in this vital state.

With Cain on the scene as representative of the new social and religious order, black Carolinians had to make a choice. They could remain under the old dispensation in the congregations of their former masters, or they could leave the houses of bondage and fully achieve their freedom. Given the eloquence and the charisma of Cain and the compelling story of African Methodism, the choice was an easy one for many. That's why in less than two weeks of its organization, the black members of three of Charleston's Methodist Episcopal churches—Bethel, Trinity, and Cumberland—joined the South Carolina Conference of the AME church.[17]

Cain threw himself into the work and took steps to secure a building in Charleston for regular services. Although he was granted use of Trinity Methodist Episcopal Church South, he opted not to use it in favor of meeting at Zion Presbyterian Church on Calhoun, near Meeting Street. This was a church originally constructed for Presbyterian slaves and was not far from one of the branches of the original African Church.[18] These were difficult economic times. Much of the lower part of Charleston lay in ruins, but Cain proved his ability to organize people and to raise monies. Astoundingly, on September 25, 1865, an estimated crowd of three thousand people gathered to witness the ceremonial laying of the cornerstone for Emanuel, the city's first postwar AME church building. Cain—who became the church's first pastor—proudly announced that the edifice was designed by Robert Vesey, the son of Denmark Vesey. The two-story wooden frame building was estimated to cost about $10,000 and to have a seating capacity of about twenty-five hundred people.[19] The rise of Emanuel Church as a building was both symbol and substance of the boldness that had characterized the antebellum African Church. For a people who dared to dream of emancipation, this site must have exceeded their fondest expectations; as the building went upwards, their spirits soared in reply.

Although simply constructed, the church represented the converging vision of African Methodism as a denomination with Richard Cain's philosophy of black nationalism. The AME Church stood for a gospel of freedom, which rejected the values and limitations imposed by slavery and replaced them with a vision of the race defining its own goals and achieving its potential for full development, in accordance with Northern values. Cain's black nationalist philosophy amplified church goals. His fundamental idea was that African Americans had a unique identity and should "rely primarily on themselves in vital areas of life—economic, political, religious and intellectual—to effect their liberation."[20] This is what makes the connection between Robert Vesey and Emanuel so vitally significant: when Cain described the construction of the building, he stressed the fact that every worker "is a colored man." This is also why every minister who participated in the cornerstone-laying ceremony was a black man.[21] Cain was not anti-white but understood the value of race patronage.

Undoubtedly some of Emanuel's success was grounded in the knowledge that African Methodism was a racial enterprise that also offered unique forms of spiritual fulfillment. For many this was exactly what they sought in a church, and the congregation grew rapidly. In 1875, one church official thought its membership was the largest in the entire denomination; observers sometimes said it had a "mammoth congregation." By the mid-1870s, it had 2,764 members; 372 probationers were served by one main (itinerant) pastor, 14 local preachers, 7 exhorters, and 70 class leaders. By 1882 as the membership crept closer to 4,000, many in the congregation began clamoring for the church body to be divided because the responsibilities were too much for one pastor. Emanuel had already given rise that year to Mount Zion AME Church, and Morris Brown AME Church was also established from its congregation in 1866.[22]

✳

Starting with Richard Cain, the ministers of Mother Emanuel have had an expansive view of their role in the community. The secular needs of its congregation have often required the church to address material and spiritual concerns simultaneously. The church had an immediate role in strengthening black family life, and its ministers encouraged Victorian values in marriage and family relationships. Most freedmen never had a real marriage ceremony; many were eager to have their marriages solemnized, and most ministers were willing to accommodate. In addition, the church was national in scope and published the *Christian Recorder.* Its columns were frequently used to identify and locate family members who had been separated from one another during slavery or wartime. Sometimes family life was threatened by individual moral failings. This is why ministers frequently discussed how best to promote temperance and warned their congregations about the great ills that proceeded from intemperance. One group of ministers considered intemperance not only a threat to family life but "the great enemy of the human race."[23]

Churchmen regarded education most highly as they considered both sacred and secular aspects of their work. The AME missionary James Lynch observed that in South Carolina, schools "have demonstrated the natural capacity of the colored race, and [have] done much to make the white people of the North believe" in racial equality and the "natural capacity of colored persons." He also stressed that education was the surest safeguard against those "designing men" who posed an ongoing threat against black freedom in the South.[24] These were reasons why ministers argued that every church ought to have a Sabbath school to secure the needs of future generations. At the time Emanuel was constructing its first building, it already maintained two Sunday schools that served 340 students. The major problem it faced was a serious shortage of books, paper, and teachers.[25] Higher-level education was also required to increase the ranks of professionally trained and qualified ministers. South Carolina ministers and church members, including those at Emanuel, financially supported Wilberforce University, the denomination's college in Ohio. There were also those Carolinians who saw the need to offer advanced educational opportunities closer to home. To that end, in 1871, the Payne Institute was established in Cokesbury in Greenwood County. In 1880–1881, the college was transferred to the more central location of Columbia and renamed Allen University, after the founder of the denomination. At this time the school added a law department, which graduated its first class in 1884. Allen University was the first college in the state established and maintained by African Americans.[26]

The post–Civil War years, and the unprecedented educational opportunities they afforded, produced significant numbers of ministers in South Carolina who could claim professional training for the first time, and these men assumed important leadership roles in their communities. In all of the nineteenth century, none was more significant than Richard H. Cain because of the myriad roles he played and the energy he brought to each. While pastor at Emanuel he also purchased additional property in Charleston and organized Morris Brown Church there. Although approximately half the size of Emanuel in the 1880s, it was also considered a "first class" congregation. In supervising the work of the church, Cain was personally responsible for establishing numerous other congregations along the coast north and south of Charleston as well as in the interior.[27]

Cain's commitment to African Methodism and his black nationalism were mutually reinforcing, and he used a variety of means to promote the interests of black Carolinians. For example, at an early date he understood that the people he served needed to have a black-controlled newspaper that valued them and fairly represented their interests. In 1866, he purchased the *South Carolina Leader,* which he renamed the *Missionary Record;* Cain served as its editor and published it until the early 1870s. The newspaper's masthead described it as the "organ of the Colored People and exponent of their views and desires." Within its pages the reader could find the latest information in the areas of literature and the arts, politics, and science, and it routinely contained the latest information on AME activities. This was the first such publishing venture controlled by African Americans in South Carolina.[28]

Not surprisingly in this time when African American men were beginning to receive their full rights as citizens, a number went into politics. With a 60 percent black majority, South Carolina was potentially a fruitful field for men with political ambitions, and between 1868 and 1877 black men dominated the lower house of the state legislature.[29] From an early date Cain was involved in state and local politics as another means of promoting the interests of black Carolinians. In 1867, he participated in a series of meetings that organized the Republican Party in the state. He was later elected to the January 1868 South Carolina Constitutional Convention, where he played an important role protecting the freedmen's voting rights, promoting public education, and the acquisition of land by small farmers. In 1868, Cain was elected to the state senate, where he vigorously and successfully promoted the creation of a state land commission to help freedmen and other small farmers purchase their own land and avoid the exploitative sharecropping system.[30] He also purchased more than five hundred acres of land about twenty-five miles north of Charleston and sold lots to African Americans. These initial sales were the basis for the settlement of Lincolnville, which Cain planned to become an all-black town in which the residents could show their capacity for discipline, order, and prosperity. Finally Richard Cain was elected to the United States House of Representatives in 1873–75 and 1877–79; while there he worked with other Republicans to pass the country's first federal public accommodations law.[31] Without question Cain established a high bar for achievement, and to this day his record of accomplishment is unsurpassed among African Methodist clerics. More importantly, it served as an inspiration for many of those pastors who followed him at Emanuel.

Anyone who knew Clementa Pinckney knew of his love for history— particularly for the history of Mother Emanuel. He could go on for hours talking about events from days gone by that had occurred at his beloved church or in the surrounding community. He was a pastor who drew strength and inspiration from that history. In this way he resembled Richard Cain. On one occasion in 2013, he welcomed a group of doctoral students to the church with a prayer. In part he said, "God, we welcome and invite you into this place, your house. We thank you for the spirit that dwells here, the spirit of Denmark Vesey. The spirit of R. H. Cain. The spirit of Dr. King. The spirit of many of the unsung heroes of our people." He called the ground upon which they sat, sacred, and he went on to discuss the vital roles Richard Allen, Morris Brown, and Denmark Vesey had played in the history of the denomination and in the history of Emanuel.[32]

Despite being pastor of such a storied church—and he reveled in it—Pinckney was quick to tell people that Emanuel was not a museum but was still a place "where we can hopefully work on the hearts and minds and spirits of all people."[33] As a pastor he nurtured and taught his members but understood that the church's mission only began with the congregation. He believed, like Cain before him, that all Christians were responsible for transforming the communities in which they lived according to godly precepts. These ideas were rooted in biblical prin- ciples and the traditions of his church, and they were the reasons public service was such a crucial extension of Pinckney's ministry. He entered politics to become the senator for the southern region of the state around Jasper County, an area that lagged behind the state in development and overall measures of well-being. He promoted bills that sought to empower people. Thus he vigorously opposed restrictive voter ID laws, championed wage increases for hospitality workers, supported Medicaid extension, and he fought hard for a port development project to bring jobs so sorely needed in Jasper County. More recently he played a pivotal role in passing the law that now requires the police in South Carolina to wear body cameras. This reform measure resulted from the April 2015 killing of Walter Scott, an unarmed African American, by a white police officer in North Charleston. Standing up for such a policy in the senate, in the cordial yet firm way he did it, demonstrates why Clementa Pinckney was long known as the "moral conscience" of the general assembly.[34]

Taking stands on the issues that he felt deeply about was what it meant to be African Methodist. According to Pinckney, this church stands for a "universal vision of all people being treated fairly under the law as God sees us in his sight."[35] But doing so had its costs, and Pinckney was aware of this also. On one occasion he informed a group of visitors to Emanuel's sanctuary that to promote God's vision for humanity, "sometimes you got to make noise to do that. Sometimes you may even have to die, like Denmark Vesey, to do that. Sometimes you have to march, struggle, and be unpopular to do that."[36] Little did we know how soon he would pay such a price, and the kind of challenge his death and that of the others would pose for the church, its community, and the nation.

But Emanuel had seen challenges before. Like the denomination of which it is a part, its entire history was punctuated with challenges met and surmounted. In Emanuel's case an important historical example began on August 31, 1886. At approximately 9:50 p.m., Charleston and the surrounding areas were struck by the most severe earthquake ever recorded along America's Eastern Seaboard. Those who have studied it claim it was more powerful than the 1989 earthquake that destroyed the Oakland freeway or the 2010 Haitian quake in which hundreds of thousands of people perished.[37] In the Charleston area the effects were horrifying. One observer in the nearby town of Summerville reported that "without a moment's notice a sudden trembling shook the earth." It seemed as though "a thousand tons of powder had been buried beneath and was forcing its way out from its concealed cavern. Then a noise followed as though a subterranean cannonading had taken place. Houses were falling, chimneys were tumbling down, water spouting out of the earth, [and] streets becoming flooded," as shrieking people witnessed "terra firma . . . passing us down to terra incognita."[38] The situation must have been even more frightening in Charleston, with its denser population and built environment; the damage was so extensive the city was crippled for weeks. The religious community was particularly hard hit; one resident reported that "nearly every church in the city is damaged more or less." Of the three major AME churches in the city, Emanuel seemed to have sustained the most physical damage. A newspaper reporter who visited the church concluded it was "seriously damaged," with fallen plaster and a listing western wall, and that the organ had been knocked out of place and was "heavily damaged." According to L. R. Nichols, Emanuel's pastor, an inspection of the church revealed about $2,800 in necessary repairs.[39] Over the next several weeks some of Charleston's AME ministers used the columns of their national newspaper, the *Christian Recorder,* or traveled to locations as far away as New York to appeal for funds to repair their buildings.[40]

The plight of the city quickly became a national news story as detailed coverage of the mammoth earthquake made the pages of newspapers from coast to coast. The American people also showed their generosity then, just as they did in the days, weeks, and months following the mass shooting at Emanuel Church in the summer of 2015. Contributions to the relief efforts poured into the city as people from around the nation extended credit, pledged relief-related services, and made monetary contributions ranging from under one hundred dollars to thousands of dollars. The *Charleston News and Courier* acknowledged this sense of unity with Charleston in a series of news stories with titles such as: "The Whole World Kin," "Universal Sympathy with Charleston in Her Great Calamity," and "All Hearts Beat as One."[41]

The support from near and far was still insufficient to address Charleston's immediate, enormous needs. With their homes and businesses destroyed, and the extensive aftershocks that followed the initial quake, fearful residents were thrown out into the elements to seek shelter: a series of tent camps sprang up in the city's numerous parks, squares, and vacant lots. Some of the tents, such as those located on White Point Garden in the city's most affluent neighborhood, were made of heavy-duty materials and even had covered floors. Far from typical, these tents were occupied solely or overwhelmingly by whites. More often than not, black Charlestonians gathered whatever scrap materials they could find—such as tin, old rugs, and bedsheets—in the wreckage on the streets, to assemble makeshift tents that provided varying degrees of shelter; when it rained the inhabitants had little real protection. Eventually regular tents were made available, and the city constructed some wooden sheds for residents, but the process was slow and uneven, which meant that many—particularly black Charlestonians—were left to fend for themselves.[42]

The set of circumstances the earthquake created had significant implications for the city's race relations, particularly when competition over scarce resources led to physical and cultural collisions between Charleston's black and white populations. Of the tent cities that arose after the earthquake, some housed either black or white residents while others included the two groups in the same general area. In the heart of downtown, Washington Square was a racial transition zone. During a September stroll around the city, an observer noted that the previous week whites had sought refuge there but that now "the colored people have taken entire possession of this square" after having "driven" the whites away. White Charlestonians were not physically driven off, but they found African Americans' exuberant religious services—which lasted well into the evening—intolerable and, therefore, abandoned the square. This criticism of African American religiosity was common in the city: A. Toomer Porter, a well-known white Episcopal minister, sternly directed blacks to refrain from "the loud howling, singing and praying . . . in the streets" by which they disturbed the city's peace.[43] These cultural differences contributed to rising tensions between blacks and whites as they were forced into the same public spaces.

The way the relief effort was managed was also a source of racial tension. When Mayor William Courtenay created an executive relief committee to decide how the city could best alleviate the suffering and disorder following the earthquake, all his appointees were white business-men, and many were former Confederate veterans. This, coupled with the fact that certain African American tent settlements, such as those in Washington Square, never received the city services available to whites elsewhere, led black Charlestonians to question the fairness of the administration. That's why a letter to the *New York Freeman*, critical of Charleston's relief efforts, charged that "colored people are the greatest sufferers. All money is in the hands of white men."[44]

Black ministers took a leading role in trying to correct this situation. William Heard of Mt. Zion AME Church, L. R. Nichols of Emanuel, and others organized a committee to publicize the plight of their people to the country and to solicit funds nationally for their relief. This initiative won only scorn and criticism from whites who accused them of what is in today's vernacular called "playing the race card." A. Toomer Porter publicly entreated these black clerics against voicing any questions about race. Francis Dawson, editor of the *Charleston News and Courier*, responded to these ministers by denying that any discrimination existed in the provision of relief. He also went on to say that the charges they leveled were damaging because they suggested that blacks were neglected by city authorities, when according to Dawson, they had actually received more and better housing than whites.[45] The weight of black criticism would eventually bear fruit when the city finally decided to employ black canvassers for each of the city wards who were responsible for identifying those in need and referring them to the city's relief committee for action. Even so, complete authority for decision making on matters of relief remained solely in the hands of white men, and for the duration of the crisis, black men were never appointed to the city's relief committee.[46]

The committee's composition was a testament to the ironclad rule of white supremacy, which (although penetrated briefly after the Civil War) remained firmly intact at the end of the century. In fact, the years following the earthquake witnessed a steady deterioration in race relations across the nation and in South Carolina as disenfranchisement, racially inspired violence, and the rise of Jim Crow, or the system of legally established racial separation, further marginalized African Americans. Emanuel Church, however, would be a strong refuge against these outrages. Like the proverbial phoenix, it had risen from its antebellum ashes, and now, most recently, it had even withstood some of the earth's most violent forces. The memories and inherited knowledge of this history and the values embedded within it represented a powerful bequest, preparing those who availed themselves of it for their own challenges.

EIGHT

JIM CROW

Within days of the murders at Emanuel, two historic monuments were defaced in Charleston. One, located more than a mile away on the Battery across the harbor from Fort Sumter, was a tribute to the "Confederate Defenders of Charleston." The other—the tallest figurative statue in the city at eighty feet—is one-half block west of the church and directly across Marion Square from the Old Citadel; it immortalizes John C. Calhoun. The statue symbolizes virtually everything that is antithetical to Mother Emanuel, but it would be a touchstone for anyone driven by racial hatred.

According to one of Charleston's late-nineteenth-century newspaper editors, Calhoun was considered "a great statesman" and "the most eminent man South Carolina has ever produced."[1] Over the course of his career, Calhoun served as secretaries of war and state, vice president, and as a US senator. He was also known as one of the most ardent defenders of states' rights and of the institution of slavery. The original inscription on the monument to Calhoun reads, "Truth Justice and the Constitution," to which someone added in bold red spray paint *And Slavery*; also the painted base read "Calhoun, Racist."[2] The identity of the vandals remains unknown, and in today's atmosphere of social awareness, there is little reason to assume that the vandals were black rather than white. Historically, though, it was much different because black Charlestonians showed a general contempt for Calhoun, who, in their experience and memories, represented the state's most virulently oppressive forces. That animosity continued long after Calhoun was dead since his rise to greater visibility in the cityscape also corresponded with increasing difficulty in the lives of blacks.

John Calhoun died in 1850; an elaborate funeral procession through the streets of the city marked the occasion. After his death, Boundary Street, the most important thoroughfare in the northern part of the city, was renamed Calhoun. In the decade before the Civil War, intersectional tension between North and South reached a fever pitch and Southern whites felt the need to surveil the slave population more carefully to guard against abolitionist influence and the possibility of rebellion. Times also became more difficult for free blacks because they were increasingly viewed as misfits in a society that proclaimed slavery the best of all possible statuses for people of African descent. In the final years of the decade, there were debates in South Carolina and throughout the South over whether the free black population ought to be expelled or enslaved. Rather than wait to see the outcome, many free black Carolinians fled the state for the North.[3]

After the end of Reconstruction, white supremacy took a quantum leap ahead in the 1880s and 1890s, and these decades each witnessed the erection of a Calhoun statue. The first was erected in 1887, but displeasure with its design led to its replacement by the much taller present version emplaced in 1896. That year was the occasion for the Supreme Court's infamous *Plessey v. Ferguson* decision, which provided the legal basis for and therefore encouraged the creation of two American societies, one black and one white, separate and supposedly equal, except by design the latter never happened.[4]

The way the Calhoun statue was defaced after the shooting at Emanuel contained an implicit question: Why don't we tell the whole story about men who are lionized in Charleston's landscape? The hand-written descriptors added to the Calhoun statue are only the most recent display of a deep-seated and widespread animosity toward the fact of white supremacy, its symbols, and the long roots in Charleston's history.

The former slave Elijah Green was one of the five men who dug Calhoun's grave, and he cleared off the land where the monument is located today. He was unusually honest in sharing his contempt for Calhoun with a white interviewer in the 1930s. He said, "I never did like Calhoun 'cause he hated the Negro." Green wanted to make it clear that many other black Carolinians shared his feelings, and he asserted "no man was ever hated as much as him by a group of people."[5] One youthful observer from the early twentieth century recalled that "blacks took that statue personally" because he embodied the whites' sentiments toward blacks. Walking nearby, she recalled, there was Calhoun staring down at you with the message: "Nigger, you may not be a slave, but I am back to see you stay in your place." That's why she said that children and some adults sometimes threw objects at the statue to show their disdain.[6] There were many new policies that were instituted in the late nineteenth century and early decades of the twentieth that signaled a harsher era of race relations—and Calhoun was the symbol of their plight.

One of the most troublesome developments in the new racial order was the rise of disenfranchisement. Even after Reconstruction ended, African American men continued to vote and hold office in South Carolina, albeit in much-reduced numbers. There was at least one black Republican state legislator until 1900, but the last African American congressman from the state left office in 1897. Almost a century passed before another was elected.[7] The black electorate was being under-mined across the South through methods that can only be described as legal sleight of hand and political manipulation. In South Carolina the process began in the 1880s, with the introduction of more complicated voting procedures that only intensified in the next decade. In 1895, with leadership from the rabidly racist senator Ben Tillman, South Carolina convened a state constitutional convention expressly designed to disenfranchise black Carolinians. The 1895 constitution included a variety of provisions including residency, literacy, and property qualifications, all of which made it more difficult to vote.[8]

Some of the new requirements also allowed election officials sufficient latitude to administer the laws unfairly. Blacks who attempted to register to vote frequently faced more difficult questions than their white counterparts, and when this was not sufficient to discourage them, fraud could always be used. In the opening years of the twentieth century, a black Charlestonian complained to a visitor about the way such political chicanery had nullified his community's vote. "To his certain knowledge" the Charlestonian said, he and other black men "cast Republican ballots; but the result, as announced, showed not a single Republican vote." The foregoing methods were effective and ultimately destroyed the black electorate. This is how—despite South Carolina's black majority in 1900—Senator Benjamin Tillman could still announce that of its 114,000 registered voters, only 14,000 were black.[9] Simultaneously with their elimination from the voter lists, black men also had less influence over the criminal justice system. In the 1880s, Charleston black men (and some from other places around the state) continued serving on juries, but by the turn of the century, they had been completely removed from this civic responsibility.[10]

The deterioration of race relations could be further seen in the proliferation of legally enforced racial segregation that physically separated the races in public spaces. The South's duo-chromatic order followed the Civil War as blacks and whites gravitated to different social spheres—but these early racial divisions were established by custom, and they were not rigid. In the two decades following the Civil War, it was possible for the races to interact on the basis of equality on public conveyances and in recreational areas, such as parks and theaters. The rise of white supremacy in the late nineteenth century, however, dictated a more complete and thoroughgoing separation of the races embedded in law.

This new system was informally known as *Jim Crow*; the origin of the name is central to understanding the purpose of the system. Jim Crow was originally the name given to an antebellum character found in a type of popular musical known as the *minstrel show*. He was portrayed by whites who darkened their faces and then performed caricatured and demeaning representations of "the Negro" that demonstrated his inferiority and unfitness for freedom. The widespread use of this term to describe the system of racial segregation reveals a twofold purpose. First, Jim Crow was devised to separate and insulate whites from the contamination of a group of people who were deemed their inferiors in every way.[11] The second function of Jim Crow was educational: the segregated facilities were never equal in quality, and thus the differences provided a constant and pervasive stream of visual cues that established and seemingly reaffirmed the evidence of white superiority and black inferiority.

In 1889, South Carolina repealed its civil rights law passed two decades earlier.[12] Over the next two decades, Jim Crow facilities, with "Colored" and "White" signs, spread across South Carolina like an invasive kudzu vine, choking off any resistance and trapping the state in a racial mire from which it has yet to become fully disentangled. The process began with the railroads: the first law establishing racial segregation on first-class railroad cars was passed in 1898, and two years later new legislation required trains with multiple cars to maintain separate coaches for each race. In 1917, railroads were prohibited from even unloading and loading black and white passengers at the same locations. During this time, steamboats and ferries were segregated. At the turn of the twentieth century, black Charlestonians still had access to most seats on the city streetcars where the old, informal customs still applied.[13] The old practice was that blacks would take seats in the back and fill forward, while whites would take seats in the front and move further into the car; the two groups would meet somewhere in the floating middle. One black Charlestonian saw the absurdity in this arrangement and noted, "If you could be looking from above—if you could see it as God saw it—you would see black and white 'stripes' getting wider and thinner as black people and white people got off and on the car . . . [with a] blank stripe in between." The unwritten rule was that the two races could not sit next to each other on the same seat. A new law passed in 1912 destroyed the system's earlier flexibility and relegated black riders to the back seats.[14]

The segregation laws extended to most other areas of life, including major institutions, such as theaters, hospitals, jails, and schools—and even included the more mundane but apparently crucial water fountain. In the early twentieth century, public parks may not have been officially segregated, but the police and other white officials warned African Americans away, unless they had official business in these places. White Point Gardens (also known as the Battery) at the tip of the peninsula and Hampton Park to the north were examples of such interdicted zones. The one exception at the Battery was the Fourth of July, which many white Charlestonians still regarded as a "Yankee" holiday. On this day the park was turned over to black Charlestonians, who frequently had picnics and formal programs that included reciting excerpts from Abraham Lincoln and Frederick Douglass speeches, as well as singing the Negro National Anthem.[15] The general lack of access to public parks ensured that church grounds like those of Emanuel would be important locations for African Americans' outdoor activities.

Public and private schools were segregated by law, and this had a devastating effect on African American education. In keeping with the real goals of Jim Crow, black children attended schools that were physically inferior to those of their white counterparts: they were usually more crowded, and their educational materials were often items that had already been discarded by white students. The lack of attention to black students is evident in racial disparities in school funding; in 1926, for example, Charleston County spent five times more on white schools compared to its black schools.[16]

Although white students had access to a public high school for decades, Charleston failed to provide a public high school for African Americans until the eve of World War I. Even then, it was established as the Charleston Colored Industrial School and specialized in teaching manual skills, such as carpentry, bricklaying, and needlecraft, while lacking college preparatory courses. The prevailing belief among whites was that black Charlestonians had no need for an advanced or classically oriented education to fill the limited jobs that would be available to them. A private high school operated by the American Missionary Society, Avery Institute was available for black students. It had a fine reputation and prepared many of its students for college. In certain respects, Avery was the antithesis of what a Jim Crow education was supposed to produce. Eugene Hunt graduated from Avery in the 1930s and became a well-known South Carolina musician and educator. Reflecting back on his high school years, he believes many whites had little fondness for Avery, which they saw as teaching "negras" to become "smart alecs" who didn't know their place. One of the school's greatest achievements, according to Hunt, was "teaching blacks that they were the equal of anybody and need not apologize to anybody."[17] Those attitudes shared by the teachers, administrators, and students explain why Avery Institute became an important site for civil rights activism.

There was a peculiar exception to strict segregation in Charleston city schools, though—in the early years of the twentieth century, black teachers were generally excluded from employment in the city schools, even the ones for black students.[18] These urban jobs were reserved for whites because the school buildings were more substantial with more inviting work environments compared to their rural counterparts. City employment also allowed teachers to avoid having to travel long distances into the countryside, which often required taking ferries or being rowed across rivers to reach schools in the country.

Teachers often used public institutions to supplement their teaching—fields trips to theaters, libraries, and museums. As an educational institution, the Charleston Museum had only been patronized by whites, but in 1915, for the first time, its new charter *explicitly* designated the institution for the benefit of white citizens. The museum soon deviated from strict enforcement: in 1920 a progressive-thinking director arranged special hours on Saturday for African Americans to attend.[19]

While education was designed to improve people and fit them for participation in society as responsible citizens, racial segregation—particularly in education—undermined those goals and ultimately produced a corrosive effect on human relations. Mamie Fields, who grew up in late-nineteenth and early-twentieth-century Charleston, watched Jim Crow expand and become more comprehensive. Observing its effects, she concluded that segregation "made friends into enemies overnight." For years, she recalled, her brother had played with a German child across the street, but the tightening grip of segregation choked their former relationship; the two boys began to use racial epithets and to sometimes fight. Fields observed the same behavior among black and white children on the street as groups of kids walked home from school. Previously they might speak, but under Jim Crow as they approached one another, their bodies stiffened and threats were exchanged, which sometimes resulted in violence.[20]

※

Violence—which had a long and well-established place in Southern history—was the implicit force lurking behind racial segregation. If one stepped out of line or transgressed the accepted racial etiquette, one's life could be in danger; there was not a year between 1882 and 1900 that South Carolina did not have at least one lynching.[21] The threat was increased with the rebirth of the Ku Klux Klan in 1915—almost simultaneously with the release of the ultra-racist film *Birth of a Nation*, which depicted black men as corrupt Reconstruction-era politicians and rapists. The mass migration of Southern blacks to Northern cities during World War I, combined with the recession following the demobilization, brought these tensions to a boiling point in 1919, when the country experienced twenty-six race riots.[22] The very first flared up on the streets of Charleston.

Outside a pool hall in the city, a group of black men clashed with sailors stationed at the naval base in North Charleston on May 10, 1919. The conflict began inside the hall, probably over a minor matter, but then escalated outside into a violent confrontation using cue sticks and fists. As the fight intensified, two white sailors shot and killed an unarmed black man. It didn't take long for the brawl to boil over into a race riot when white Charlestonians joined the sailors to chase black men through the streets, shooting at any black face they saw. One black man was pulled from a streetcar and killed while diners in a nearby restaurant looked on in horror. The mob at one point grew to several thousand, taking control of the downtown area as the black men shot at the sailors on their return to the navy base.[23]

The riot lasted about four hours before three black men were killed and scores of blacks were beaten and shot. City officials pledged to investigate the riots, but many black Charlestonians doubted it would be fair or thorough. Edwin G. Harleston, president of the NAACP local branch and owner of the funeral home across the street from Emanuel, conducted a probe into the riot and characterized it as an outright lynching. Harleston and the NAACP joined with the Interdenominational Union of Ministers, which included Emanuel's Reverend T. R. Nelson, to demand the city prosecute the mob and take action to prevent more violence. The ministers also called for an expansion of the police force to include black officers, upgraded housing in the city, and better sanitation and education for black residents.[24]

The navy eventually convicted six of the sailors involved in the riot, but the black community in Charleston considered it a small gesture and not a full remedy to a much larger problem. Because he didn't relent in his calls for improvements for blacks in Charleston, Harleston's life was threatened, but he refused to walk away from the challenges. "We are continuing this work," he told an NAACP convention that summer. "We have the right to live in Charleston in pursuit of happiness. We keep it up [but] if we go down we want you, The National Association to know we go down fighting."[25]

A number of the ministers that eventually came to Emanuel had been active in the fight against the racial strictures imposed in a Jim Crow society and were prepared to continue the struggle to expand the opportunities available to African Americans. The effect of Jim Crow on public school funding and operations was one of the top concerns among black educators, including R. E. Brogdon. In 1910, Brogdon was on the faculty of Allen University, an AME-supported campus in Columbia, and joined a group of nearly twenty black grade-school and college educators who brought their concerns to the state's secretary of education. Representing "the best sentiment and hopes of our people, assembled here," they sought the creation of supervisors of rural schools to bring order to the curriculum and inspect the work of teachers and students. The supervisors would also advise schools on sanitation. They also contended colleges should require courses in practical economics and industrial training.[26] This educational work showed Brogdon's interest in the social gospel and helped prepare him for the pastoral work he would assume twenty years later in the pulpit at Emanuel. With each succeeding Emanuel pastor, social activism was lifted to another level, either as a result of the pastor's personal mission, or experiences with Jim

Crow–related racism. For Benjamin James ("B. J.") Glover, who arrived at Emanuel in 1953, it was likely the latter.

Twenty-one years before Glover moved to Charleston, he had boarded a train for Cincinnati—to attend high school in preparation for theological studies at Wilberforce University, an AME-supported campus in Ohio. He intended to follow his father, Reverend C. G. Glover, into the ministry. Sending B. J. north for school was part of the elder Glover's plan to ensure his children would acquire the education they needed to live outside of Promised Land, a small community in Greenwood County, South Carolina. Situated midway between Charleston and Atlanta, Georgia, the approximately one thousand residents of Promised Land were descendants of freedmen who made a living as small farmers or sharecroppers.[27]

B. J. Glover returned to Promised Land an educated man who could read not only English but Latin and Greek. He was bursting with the idealism of a typical black youth of the 1930s—eager to engage in social reform. He was assigned the pastorate of an AME church in Due West, South Carolina, fewer than twenty miles from Promised Land. The causes he espoused to his congregation were inconsistent with those of a Jim Crow society. Glover spoke about advancing the "Southern Negro" through educational parity and voter registration. He established a "no drop-out program" for the children in his church and encouraged local teachers to work with him to ensure that youth returned to the classroom after the annual harvest. When like-minded black teachers ran into trouble with white supervisors and lost salary as a result, Glover devised a successful plan to help them obtain their back wages. He quickly built a reputation as a problem solver.[28]

In 1936, Glover put his words into action. He walked up the steps of the courthouse in Abbeville, South Carolina, and attempted to register to vote, a move that extended his social activism into a direct challenge of disenfranchisement. Although Glover easily passed the literacy test, after conferring with a supervisor, the clerk dismissed his application with the definitive declaration, "I just can't register you." An emotionally charged Glover left quietly, but that Sunday he preached from his pulpit in Due West about the unfairness of the voting laws and the need for black people to vote.[29]

Glover was not only getting attention from blacks, but whites, too, were now taking notice of his activities, especially after his courthouse confrontation. In September 1939, the Klan found out that Glover was leaving Due West for Greenwood; he was kidnapped, blindfolded, stripped down to his underwear, sexually taunted, and beaten for hours. His tormentors asked, "What you doing, nigger? Why don't you leave things like they are?" They said the KKK made examples of "uppity smart nigger[s] from the North" who came back with wild ideas.[30]

Left alone to die, Glover was discovered unconscious by a prostitute who happened along, and who knew him from the community. She ran the considerable distance to Glover's father's home, yelling, "They killed B. J.! They killed B. J.!" His relatives brought him home, where a black doctor stayed with Glover through the night until he regained consciousness the following day. The young men in the community took turns standing watch around the Glover home until they were certain the Klan didn't plan to bother him again. No one was charged, although the attackers were known to the black men in Promised Land. Glover recovered fully, and was never deterred from his mission of social activism.[31] He brought that zeal with him to Emanuel Church, where he was well prepared to join the emerging civil rights movement in Charleston.

People were attracted to Emanuel because of its unique position as the founding congregation for African Methodism in the state, for its pastoral leadership, and also because it was an important hub of community and denominational activity. Emanuel was routinely the site for the meeting of the South Carolina Annual Conference of the AME Church, but sometimes there were special meetings held there too. When the

Council of Bishops met at Emanuel in February 1937, church members
and ministers came from all around the country and various parts of the
world to witness the deliberations of one of the highest councils of the
church. In addition to strictly religious matters, ministers and lay leaders
also gathered to discuss race relations, Christian missions, education,
crime prevention, and many other issues to strengthen the church and
uplift the race.[32]

A variety of lectures and programs were held at Emanuel. On one
occasion a lecturer provided the latest information on Liberia and Sierra
Leone. During the interwar years of the twentieth century, Thomas
Miller, the former president of the Colored State Agricultural and
Mechanical College, spoke on the needs of the race and how important it was to remain on the land. Emanuel also planned a week-long
Chautauqua program devoted to remembering Bishop Daniel A. Payne,
who was a famous AME bishop from Charleston.[33] There was also a
variety of musicals performed at the church. One of the most popular
was titled "Heaven Bound" and depicted aspects of African American's
religious beliefs. The notice placed in the newspaper noted that whites
would receive special accommodations. The Allen University College
Choir also appeared at the church.[34]

Emanuel supported other organizations such as the Workingman's
Cosmopolitan Club, allowing it to use the church for meetings. It sponsored a musical performance to raise funds for the American Red Cross.
Emanuel also assisted the Federal Council of the Churches of Christ
with its Race Relations Sunday. Its purpose was to bring people together
across racial lines to further understanding.[35]

Emanuel AME Church fulfilled its mission within an all-pervasive
system of racial segregation. It was an oppressive system that demeaned
people and denied the common personhood shared by all humanity.
This meant that in addition to serving the traditional role as a source of
spiritual instruction and enlightenment, black churches like Emanuel

had to heal souls in another way. Much of what occurred at Emanuel was designed to directly or indirectly blunt the destructive force of Jim Crow. This was done formally from the pulpit, by supporting organizations with progressive goals. This was also achieved by serving as the thriving center of an alternative world, where black people interacted freely with one another and reinforced their humanity, while obtaining the services required to navigate the larger, harsher, white world outside.

NINE

LIFE IN THE BOROUGH

During the 1950s and 1960s, three blocks down from Emanuel Church on Calhoun Street, the lights were switched on for the next Little League baseball game. Other boys too small for the Little League diamond improvised a game by swinging a broomstick at a fast-pitched half of a rubber ball; it curved sharply. Pipe-puffing women laid rags on smoky fires to repel the "skittas." Children chased lightning bugs. Palmetto leaves rustled in the sea breeze.

Businesses around Emanuel lured people in search of new shoes, polished shoes, pressed clothes, haircuts, groceries, sweet treats, and liquor. From pushcarts, street vendors hawked fresh vegetables and sea-food on ice. Big trucks carried cut firewood before mothers cooked with gas. Through the Arch—an opening in a wide, even *stout* building—loomed a congested three-tiered tenement, where drunken gamblers engaged in knife fights, laundry was dried on banisters, and courtyard privies were the only toilets. It made for real-life theater, of the kind portrayed in *Porgy and Bess* decades before the Broadway folk opera reached a Charleston stage.

The distant hoot of a tugboat whistle echoed on the busy Cooper

River, signaling arrivals and departures of oceangoing vessels. White men in hard hats and bulky overalls filed in the shipyard to bend, bang, and weld metal. Some black men worked there, too, but it was a white domain. Outside the shipyard's chain-link fence, the livelihood of black dockworkers was set long before—in contentious labor struggles after the Civil War. By day the waterfront's prosperity glistened in the shiny cars driving down Calhoun Street near the baseball field where the big boys played at night.

These sights and sounds blended into a neighborhood mosaic of the Borough, a name derived from the Ansonborough Homes, a federally funded project built on low-lying land at the east end of Calhoun Street in the late 1930s when the city launched its first effort to eradicate "Negro slums." Within the projects, bounded by Washington, Concord, Calhoun, and Laurens streets, and in the wider Borough neighborhood just beyond it, nearly all needs could be met within walking distance of the white world. Sometimes white police patrolled, but more frequently it was a white insurance salesman at the front door to collect the weekly premium. "Mama! Dah 'surance man," a child called out in the Gullah accent.

The Borough was like other black neighborhoods, but its position against the Cooper River and at the end of a major street conjured a feeling of insulation within a space of friendly faces. The Borough's children knew immediately it was a sheltered place to mature, where adults assumed responsibility for all the neighborhood children. To use an oft-quoted cliché, it was the proverbial village that raised the child. Children later learned, however, it was not a place to live as an adult, and many left for the military, college, or work; some left because they were sent to prison. They had not been taught, and they could not have imagined, that their neighborhood had been shaped by Charleston's history. Much of what they saw, heard, and feared was set in motion centuries before their birth. Black children wouldn't have learned those harsh lessons until the Borough was some distance behind them, or if they had been one of the unfortunate ones to taste the sting of racism at an early age. In one sense Emanuel was an extension of this safe space, tending to the spiritual and community needs just as Buist Elementary School across the street was a place to play and learn. The Borough, like many other communities in the city, was tight-knit and not always welcoming to people from other neighborhoods, regardless of race.

※

The city owed its seventeenth-century beginnings to Englishman Ashley Cooper, who was memorialized with rivers that bear his name flanking the peninsula that comprises the city's historic core. Charleston is so old, at least by American standards, that some residents boastfully claim the two rivers combine to create the Atlantic Ocean. Nevertheless, Calhoun Street extended east and west across the peninsula between the two bodies of water. The west end overlooked the Ashley River. Calhoun Street stopped at the Borough three miles away. On the peninsula's eastern edge, East Bay Street carried traffic north from the historic Battery against a panoramic harbor view of a distant Fort Sumter, where the Civil War's first shot exploded. King Street, the city's central shopping district, was Charleston's commercial spine, where mothers trolled with youngsters in tow to buy new clothes at Easter, Christmas, and at the start of a new school term.

When the school bell rang to signal a new year in 1958, recent college graduate Walter Brown reported to work at Buist School across the street from Emanuel Church. He was a new sixth-grade math teacher and a recent graduate of South Carolina State College in Orangeburg, a predominantly black campus seventy-five miles inland from Charleston. The tall, lanky Brown moved with long strides down Buist's polished hallways as he explored the school that first day. The school and the church were the two most imposing buildings on the street. Built like a fortress, Buist was a sturdy, three-story, brown-brick structure that doubled as a fallout shelter in the event of a Soviet nuclear attack. The church was an equally imposing cathedral—with a gleaming white stucco facade topped with a copper-clad steeple that seemed to balance the blue sky on its peak. Nearby buildings were shabby in appearance but historic in style. Some of the homes were typical Charleston single houses: long, narrow structures, typically one room wide with a porch, an architectural style inherited from Barbados.

Brown was not new to the bustling Borough although he lived several blocks north of the community and Emanuel, on Columbus Street on the fringe of the old Hampstead neighborhood. He was reared in an AME family that worshiped at Ebenezer Church, and as a very young boy, he had deduced that Emanuel held significance in the AME realm because it was the "mother church." Emanuel was South Carolina's largest black church in 1950, with twenty-four hundred members when Frank Veal was its pastor. Veal helped return Emanuel to its former physical glory, restoring, redecorating, and stuccoing the church's magnificent brick structure. The city's chamber of commerce cited Veal and the church for contributing to improvements to the city's downtown.[1] During Veal's tenure at Emanuel, one of his members was ninety-seven-year-old Annie Ward Smith, who joined the church in 1865, when Richard Cain was its pastor. She was an important link to the past. She recalled the stories told about Denmark Vesey, and as a young girl, she helped carry wood to rebuild the quake-ravaged church. She lived long enough to assist in Veal's efforts to renovate the current church.[2]

Walter Brown was more than just a classroom teacher who stood in front of a blackboard. He shepherded his young students to sites beyond the neighborhood and the city limits. They saw an Egyptian mummy and whale bones dangling from the ceiling of a dark and spooky Charleston Museum. A massive newspaper press in the basement of the

News and Courier was a sight to see and hear too. From nearby Johns Island, a sea island, civil rights leader Esau Jenkins brought his bus to take Brown, sixth-grade teacher Juanita Jordan, and their students to Brookgreen Gardens, a former rice plantation north of the city. On the return they stopped at McKenzie Beach to sample Frank McKenzie's famous hot dogs. McKenzie, a black man, had a thriving Pawley's Island business when black people were barred from white-only beaches along the Atlantic coast.[3]

The excursions were the teachers' way to show students that classroom lessons could be applied to real life. Some of their students were Emanuel members who would be touched by the tragedy at the church in 2015. Myra Thompson, murdered that night during Bible study, was a student in Brown's class. Brown remembers her as quiet, serious, and smart. She lived over a corner store across the street from the baseball field and basketball court at the Calhoun Street playground that is today's parking garage at the end of Calhoun Street.[4]

Susie Jackson, the oldest person killed on June 17, was a regular at the school's Parent Teacher Association meetings, where she asked probing questions about her son, Walter, and his progress and behavior in school. Brown told Jackson that her son, like Myra Thompson, didn't give him any problems. He didn't tell her that sometimes he did have issues with her son because Brown could talk sense into young Walter and other boys. It was easier to do then, when teachers enjoyed respect from students and parents who didn't object to tough love in the classroom.

May Day was a big day at Buist and other black public schools in Charleston. Myra Thompson and Walter Jackson attended Buist at different times, but they shared similar experiences, such as wrapping the maypole on May 1, traditionally a fund-raiser for the school and a festive after-school event for children who went home to bathe before returning in crisp, clean clothing. Brown could tell which ones were the children of dockworkers who loaded and unloaded cargo from oceangoing ships.

They typically were better dressed because their fathers had some of the best-paying work in the city as union members on the waterfront. Longshoremen spent money liberally with businesses on King Street and along a three-block stretch of Calhoun Street between Emanuel and the Cooper River.[5] Their higher-than-average pay didn't come without a struggle.

※

The roots of the longshoremen's comparatively high wages were developed shortly after the Civil War, when newly freed slaves began to transform the character of work along the docks and in other sectors of the economy. Before the war, slaves played critical roles as dockhands, and later as freedmen they continued such pivotal roles by capitalizing on their numbers and organizing to improve their wages (and sometimes working conditions). Two years after the war, black dockworkers joined together in successful strike actions. In 1869, the men incorporated as the Longshoremen's Protective Union Association to promote greater unity. By the middle of the next decade, union membership was reported to be eight hundred to one thousand men, overwhelmingly black but with a few whites. On more than one occasion in the 1870s, the union went out on strike and completely shut down shipping at the port. By doing so its members were able to win regular working hours, higher hourly pay with overtime wages, and the exclusive use of union men on the waterfront.[6] This may have been the period of its greatest strength, but this union remained a force to be reckoned with into the twentieth century and eventually joined with the International Longshoremen's Association. In later decades among other sectors of Charleston's economy, two notable union disputes erupted, involving hospital employees and workers in the cigar factory.

At the turn of the twentieth century, Charleston's business leaders sought to boost the city's role in manufacturing, leading to a campaign to lure industry, including textile mills. At that time, Charleston led the state in industrial activity, but those gains could not keep pace with other Southern cities. With limited access to investors and national markets, Charleston never became an industrial hub, nor did it become a haven for textile plants, like cities in upstate South Carolina. But Charleston got a Christmas gift in 1882, when the machinery began to spin in the Charleston Manufacturing Company's "handsome" five-story cotton mill. It occupied a city block on the edge of the old Hampstead neighborhood, site of the old African Church and several blocks north of Emanuel Church and the Borough. Sunlight beamed through ceiling-to-floor windows. One side of the building overlooked the Cooper River. At night, gas-fueled lanterns lit the interior. Raw fibers flowed uninterrupted from the basement picker house through machines that produced cloth from cotton or wool.[7]

When the plant opened, black people were hired but only for custodial jobs. Skilled white workers from Northern cotton textile plants supervised local whites.[8] Blacks had been barred from textile jobs and other skilled positions based on white people's perception that black workers were best suited for low-level positions. As the mill began a slow decline using white workers, an attempt was made in 1897 to boost production with black employees. It was a historic decision, but the company only experienced mixed results and the plant closed.[9]

Two years later a final effort was made to revitalize the textile mill using a black labor force that included black women from nearby Sea Islands, but to no avail. Some whites seeking easy answers blamed the failures on the ineptitude of black labor, a claim that outraged black Charlestonians.[10] An infuriated Reverend M. W. Gilbert, pastor of Central Baptist Church in Charleston, penned a lengthy rebuttal that was published in the *News and Courier:* "It does look to us sometimes as though a gigantic conspiracy has been formed by the newspapers, especially the reporters, to magnify the negro's [*sic*] faults and minimize his virtues." Furthermore, "the poor negro [*sic*] is expected to do better in a given situation than a white man under more favorable conditions, to avoid the vigorous and merciless assaults of his enemies. He is expected to work a miracle in order to win a little praise."[11]

The textile plant switched from spinning fiber to rolling cigars in 1903 under the ownership of the American Tobacco Company. At the peak of the Great Depression, the factory employed about fourteen hundred people.[12] The precedent had been set to hire workers of both races when the plant made textiles; they were, of course, segregated. In 1931, the *News and Courier* reported that on the fifth floor "Negro workers are employed exclusively" to produce thirty thousand cigar boxes daily. Down in the basement "Negro men are kept busy" processing tobacco leaves.[13]

A decade later Marguerite Michel, Emanuel's oldest member at the time of the slayings at the church in 2015, went to work at the cigar factory in 1942. Michel was pregnant at the time, and her job was to position the outer layer of the cigar on a machine that rolled it into shape. Her pay was based on the number of cigars she made. "Don't ask me how many I made and how many it took to fill a box," Michel sharply warned her interviewer. "My memory is not what it used to be. At 104 years old, I thank God for what I can remember." She worked at the cigar factory for about a year but didn't return following the birth of her daughter and eventually took a maid's job at lower wages in the Francis Marion Hotel, located down the street from her church.[14]

When the United States entered World War II, some men—black and white—left the cigar factory for the military. Ninety-year-old Emanuel member William Black was hired there in 1942. Eleven months later the Army drafted him for the war in France. At age seventeen, Black had been on the fourth floor as a "fuller" boy, as he calls it in his Gullah dialect. He earned seventeen dollars a week placing the filler for the cigar's core in a machine that carried it to the next station.[15]

The war opened many jobs for women. Sumter County resident Lillie Mae Marsh Doster, who had just moved to Charleston, was lucky enough to be hired in 1943, on the first day she started looking. Some mornings, before the start of Doster's shift, she dashed up to the fifth floor to view a brilliant sunrise over the Cooper River.[16] It was a rejuvenating pause before the start of another day of mundane repetitive work. On the top floor of the factory, Doster and other black women and men placed labels on cardboard boxes before the conveyor carried them along. For black Charlestonians it remained the best-paying job available—at fifty cents an hour in the mid-1940s. But working conditions in the stiflingly hot plant, combined with the disrespect of black employees by white bosses, produced an intolerable situation. Black workers started a series of sit-down work stoppages, followed by talks with management. Workers had honored a no-strike pledge during the war, but when it ended, they demanded a twenty-five-cent raise and an end to racially discriminatory practices on the job. When their demands were not met, about a thousand workers, mostly young women who had formed a union, left the plant on October 22, 1945. Soon white workers followed them to the picket line to share leadership positions in the new union. The walkout was not limited to Charleston; it was part of the Food, Tobacco, Agricultural, and Allied Workers protest at other American Tobacco Company factories.[17]

Segregationists and police harassed Doster and her coworkers—young female workers—many of whom were so naive they weren't afraid of the potential ramifications of their actions. They should have been leery of challenging the company at a time when the Southern order was overtly crafted to keep workers—particularly black people—poor and uneducated so they would be ill equipped to stand up against authority.

Walter Brown also experienced this dispute when his mother, union leader Delphine Brown, and other women of both races didn't passively allow themselves to be exploited. Delphine walked the picket line from eight o'clock to noon. She and others watched as support from fellow workers dwindled when "scabs" of both races crossed the picket line.[18] Doster watched, too, as trouble was brewing. There already had been clashes on the picket line between striking women and others brought in from outside the city and smuggled in through a side door to work at the plant. Striking women boasted that they had already beaten some of the scabs and were planning to inflict even more pain. They had prepared sticks and ax handles spiked with nails. When the striking workers left the plant momentarily, Doster recruited a male striker to help her hide the arsenal. When the women returned and couldn't find their weapons, they erupted in anger and put a good cursing on Doster before battling with more scabs.[19]

That winter's extremely low temperatures, freezing rain, and a rare snowfall had tested the strikers' will. During the walkout, plant worker Lucille Simmons joined the picketers at the end of the day to sing a traditional gospel song, "We Will Overcome." It signaled the end of another day of protest and lifted strikers' spirits. From Charleston, the song became an anthem for labor and civil rights struggles across America and the world. Decades after the strike, Simmons's nephew, retired Circuit Court judge Richard Fields, discovered that it was his aunt who sang this early version of the iconic song. Simmons was a few years older than Fields, and they were raised like siblings. The song never again played a part in her life after the strike. She didn't sing it in their home, and she didn't mention it again.[20]

Lillie Mae Doster recalled that strikers joined in with "Down in our hearts I do believe we'll overcome someday. You think about that it's almost like a prayer of relief. We didn't make up the song. We just started singing it as a struggle song."[21] Several years later some of the strikers were invited to the labor movement's training grounds in New Market, Tennessee: the Highlander Folk School, founded by Myles Horton. Horton's wife, Zilphia, was stirred by the old gospel song and taught it to singer Pete Seeger and musician Guy Carawan. They sped it up, added new chords, and changed the lyrics for a growing protest movement.[22]

On April 1, 1946, strikers returned to work with a fifteen-cent raise and promises of better working conditions. When they won the contract, everyone benefited. The American Tobacco Company strike was far ahead of its time. It led to a biracial labor alliance that never happened again on the same scale in Charleston. The divisions between working-class Southerners of both races increased under the pressures of anticommunist and anti-integration rhetoric that was soon to come.

Following the strike, World War II vet William Black returned to the cigar factory, hoping to get his job back as a "fuller" boy. He was rehired—but not in his old job. Black was no longer a 120-pound boy. After three years in the military, he had become a strapping, 180-pound man and was assigned to a "floating gang" in the basement, where men muscled heavy bundles of tobacco into position. Black eventually moved up to an assistant supervisor under a white boss. After twenty years at the plant, the pay scale had been outpaced by other jobs in the Charleston area, particularly at the navy shipyard. Black regrets that he stayed at the factory so long before leaving to work on the housekeeping staff at Charleston's Veterans Administration hospital.[23]

At age thirty Black was ready to surrender a lifestyle that included trips through the Arch, where moonshine flowed freely. His step-uncle, John Polite, was a class leader at Emanuel and encouraged Black, who was more like a brother, to attend church. When Black joined Emanuel in the mid-1950s, Emanuel could boast the choice of two Sunday morning services for its sixteen hundred members. At that time Benjamin Glover was a newly arrived pastor who was preparing Emanuel for social activism in the streets.[24]

In later years Black became Emanuel's custodian. When his tenure ended, he handed the church's keys over to Ethel Lance, who lived around the corner on Alexander Street. Lance, the second woman in the church's history to serve as custodian, also worked as a custodian at the Gaillard Municipal Auditorium, named for Charleston mayor J. Palmer Gaillard.

Lance went to work at the auditorium when it opened in 1968, just as the labor dispute at the state's teaching hospital was brewing on the west end of Calhoun Street. The dispute would thrust the mayor, the city, and local churches, including Emanuel, into an international spotlight.

In the meantime, the auditorium's construction altered the Borough. With a federal urban renewal grant in the mid-1960s, the city began buying property for the start of the auditorium's construction. To make room for it, three square blocks of homes, businesses, and the slums behind the Arch were demolished, displacing seven hundred residents, most of whom were black.[25] Such a large exodus of Borough residents left a hole in the neighborhood and drained Emanuel of some of its membership as the displaced residents moved further up the Charleston peninsula or to North Charleston. Some of those who were pushed out found it difficult to make it back into the city on Sundays for service at Emanuel; many sought church memberships elsewhere.

The building that residents called the Arch—known by the city as the Arch Building—was saved and later restored because of its historical significance. Local lore has it that the two-and-one-half-story stucco building was built around 1800 and renovated fifty years later. It was originally built for the horse-drawn wagon business, wagons passing through its distinctive arch to the yard behind it.[26] The presence of the Arch Building at the east end of Calhoun Street, not far from Emanuel, might explain why two African American blacksmiths, Peter Simmons and Philip Simmons (no relation), operated shops in the Borough from the mid-1920s to the late 1960s. Philip probably received his most important education in the ironworks trade from Peter, the local blacksmith at the time, "who ran a busy shop at the foot of Calhoun Street."[27] Peter Simmons, who had been enslaved, probably learned the craft from his enslaved father, also a blacksmith. If so, the three men practiced a craft with roots in slavery and participated in the transfer of blacksmithing skills over a span of three generations and well into the twentieth century. Today Philip Simmons is remembered for his ability to adapt his skills as market demands changed—from making iron tools to decorative ironwork, such as the gates and window grilles that adorn many Charleston homes.

For many longtime black Charlestonians, the Arch's survival is a bitter reminder of how a black neighborhood was crushed in the name of preserving another neighborhood. That's because the demolition for the Gaillard Municipal Auditorium was done in tandem with saving the mostly white Ansonborough neighborhood, just south of the Borough, where residents were feeling encroached upon by "renters" in decaying houses of historical significance. This could not be tolerated in a city with an influx of tourists who were drawn by Charleston's high concentration of historic homes. To resolve the problem, the Historic Charleston Foundation launched a revitalization effort in the peninsula's historic core to preserve Ansonborough's architectural inventory.[28]

As the foundation saved some homes, the city began to destroy "the slum," called the Borough. Ansonborough was a concentration of historic brick and wooden structures, but the Borough was crammed with frame dwellings that had evolved into black tenements, many of them structurally unsound. This type of area had a new name—urban blight—and city governments across the United States were eager to put a stop to it. Removing the slum was important to create a buffer zone between the Ansonborough rehabilitation project and the predominantly black neighborhoods and the slums of the upper east side, north of Emanuel, that residents called Little Mexico. Ben Scott Whaley, the foundation's president, said at the time that the "eradication of urban blight in the heart of our community . . . would greatly improve the setting of the six blocks of significant period architecture in which we are working, and help us toward our goal of giving Charleston in-city residential areas which are also tourist attractions of great value."[29] The foundation was successful in its goal, but it began a process of gentrification that is still advancing through the city and deepening mistrust of city government among some black Charlestonians. That suspicion of government, however, first flared in the early 1960s, when a much larger relocation of black homes and businesses preceded the 1969 completion of the Septima P. Clark Expressway, which locals call the Crosstown, a six-lane extension of Interstate 26.

The Charleston Municipal Auditorium (later dedicated to Mayor J. Palmer Gaillard) opened on July 1, 1968. For the first two years, the auditorium was open to white audiences only. When *Porgy and Bess* came to the auditorium's stage for the city's tricentennial celebration in 1970, the nearly all-black cast performed before the auditorium's first integrated audience. It was not the first time, however, the city tried to stage a production of the 1935 Broadway show, which depicts black life in Charleston much as the daily life children in the Borough would have witnessed through the Arch.

As the color of springtime azaleas exploded across the city, plans were being made in April 1954 to stage a production of *Porgy and Bess* by the Stagecrafters, an all-black dramatic group, with sponsorship from the Dock Street Theater. But there was a problem. Jim Crow was in the wings at County Hall. To overcome South Carolina's prohibition of race mixing at amusement events, the Stagecrafters suggested a compromise, one that the local NAACP rejected. The civil rights organization's rejection of the proposed plan, to segregate the audience with whites on one side of the venue and blacks on the other, coupled with the state's ban on integrated audiences, resulted in the production's demise.[30]

Advancements to end segregation were not going to occur with the showing of *Porgy and Bess*, but the following month Jim Crow was shaken by the United States Supreme Court's decision to outlaw segregated schools in *Brown v. Board of Education*. It would take nine more years, however, before the curtain rose on integrated classrooms in Charleston.

TEN

CIVIL RIGHTS

Charleston's white community had no intentions of discussing racial inequities even a century after Abraham Lincoln's Emancipation Proclamation ended slavery in the old Confederacy. In early 1963, Charleston had settled into a comfortable social rhythm of racially divided schools, and lunch counters and retail jobs on King Street reserved just for whites, along with other bedrock Jim Crow restrictions. But this status quo was increasingly frustrating for Charleston's black population. In the spring of that year, the civil rights movement's "children's hour" in Birmingham, Alabama, gave nonviolent protesters there the upper hand against the police force.[1] A transfixed nation watched televised images of police dogs attacking children and high-pressure water hoses knocking them down. The NAACP in South Carolina used a similar strategy of engaging children on the front line for social justice.

An elaborate organization was designed in Charleston to stage meetings, prayer marches, restaurant and lunch counter sit-ins, theater stand-ins, parades, and picketing; this plan was backed by nearly twenty churches, a steering committee, and a woman's group of thirty-four people, all directed by James G. Blake, the NAACP's national youth chairman. Emanuel was selected as one of the sites for rallies, and B. J. Glover was assigned to recruit high-profile speakers for events.[2] Glover and Blake, a student at Morehouse College in Atlanta, Georgia, the alma mater of Martin Luther King Jr., may have both asked King to speak at Emanuel and lead a march down King Street.

Before the Charleston movement's launch on June 7, 1963, at Calvary Baptist Church, black South Carolinians had already secured federal court victories before District Court judge J. Waties Waring of Charleston, who was hailed by some as "the Moses for black people."[3] The corps of black lawyers who would take civil rights cases to state and federal courts in the 1960s resulted from a Waring decision. World War II veteran John H. Wrighten of Edisto Island near Charleston, a member of Mother Emanuel, was denied admission to the University of South Carolina Law School in Columbia in 1946, and his five attorneys, one of whom was NAACP lawyer Thurgood Marshall, filed a lawsuit in federal court.[4] The following year Waring ruled that Wrighten was entitled to the same opportunity and facilities available to whites who pursued legal training in South Carolina. Waring gave South Carolina three choices: (1) admit Wrighten to USC; (2) establish a law school at the Colored Normal, Industrial, Agricultural and Mechanical College of South Carolina in Orangeburg, South Carolina; or (3) close the USC law school.

South Carolina chose to open a law school at the Orangeburg campus. By the 1960s, Wrighten's lawsuit had produced a windfall for black activists. The law school not only trained Wrighten, who is considered the "granddaddy" of black lawyers in the state, but it also produced others who became the friendly faces in state and federal courts to argue civil rights cases. Among them were Emanuel member and South Carolina Circuit Court judge Daniel E. Martin Sr.; South Carolina Supreme Court chief justice Ernest A. Finney Jr., the first black man elected to South Carolina's Supreme Court since Reconstruction; and Columbia attorney

Matthew J. Perry, the first black lawyer from the Deep South appointed to the federal bench. Before the law school closed in 1966, fifty men and one woman obtained legal training there.

In the summer of 1947, when Waring decided the Wrighten case, he also ruled on a voting rights lawsuit that concerned the exclusion of black voters from Democratic Party primaries. Denying black people the right to vote helped South Carolina maintain "separate but equal" schools and public services, and Democrats had controlled party politics in South Carolina from the end of Reconstruction. Through the 1930s and 1940s, blacks had defected from the Republican Party as a result of Democratic president Franklin D. Roosevelt's New Deal policies to free the country from the grips of the Great Depression. In 1944, the United States Supreme Court ruled that white primaries were illegal. To counter that, South Carolina's Democrats reorganized their party as a private club to prevent black participation. Two years later South Carolina's all-white Democratic Party primary was challenged in federal court, and the following year Waring's ruling opened the primary to all voters.

William Watts Ball, editor of the *News and Courier* in Charleston, explained in an editorial that the state's primary operated like a private club. But Waring wrote that private clubs don't vote or elect the president and other elected officeholders. "It is time," the judge said, "for South Carolina to rejoin the Union" and accept the American way of holding elections.[5] A federal appeals court upheld Waring's ruling, and in early 1948, the United States Supreme Court refused to review it. In 1949, thirty-five thousand black South Carolinians voted in the Democratic Party primary, the highest number of black voters since the 1890s. In Charleston County and elsewhere, voting became an imperative. Charleston's social activism was well suited for Emanuel's pastor; Glover had defied the Klan in Greenwood County and almost paid for it with his life.

In the late 1940s, B. J. Glover pastored a congregation in Columbia near Allen University, where he taught Bible literature and psychology. After a few years he was assigned to Morris Brown AME Church in Charleston and, in 1953, to Emanuel Church, which had been restored to its present grandeur during the leadership of Frank Veal. Glover left Greenwood County far more educated and confident than when he had returned home from college. Years later in 1959, Glover spoke during the Palmetto Voters Association annual program: "I am not afraid of anyone. I speak my mind whenever I have the opportunity, and I tell [whites] I am going to stay right here [in South Carolina]." He explained that unless black people vote, "we are not going to make any further progress. Although we have made strides in education to a certain degree, and in some areas of human relations and some areas of economics," in politics black people had lost ground, and voting was the best means to uplift the race.[6]

Glover drew laughter when he reminded the audience that black people once could get much of what they wanted if they were subservient. "There was a time that we could go to the back door and whites would give us whatever we wanted, if we bowed," he said, repeating "if we bowed" several times for emphasis. "But that day is gone now. You can bow all you want, and all they will do is give you a kick out of the back door."[7]

Nearly a decade before voter registration efforts began to take hold across the state, in 1950, black parents in Clarendon County, South Carolina, filed a federal lawsuit challenging inequalities in public education. In South Carolina black children walked to classes in inclement weather as buses with white pupils rolled by. That inequity motivated James Miles Hinton, chairman of the South Carolina NAACP, to challenge an Allen University audience in December 1947 to recruit teachers or ministers to contest the discriminatory practices of the state's school bus system.[8] AME pastor Joseph Armstrong DeLaine was in the audience at his alma mater, and he heeded Hinton's words.

In addition to serving several small AME congregations, DeLaine was the principal of a small school near Summerton, South Carolina, a town that today is situated in the "Corridor of Shame," one of the state's most impoverished regions. Four years after that unexpected meeting and with help from the NAACP, DeLaine and a few Clarendon County residents, including Harry and Eliza Briggs, filed the lawsuit *Briggs v. Elliott* in federal court after the county schools refused to provide school buses for black children. In 1951, the lawsuit was expanded to go beyond a request for school buses to attack segregation. Two of the three judges ruled that the county schools must be equalized but not integrated. Judge Waring, who dissented, wrote that segregation in education can never produce equality. The decision was appealed to the United States Supreme Court, where it was combined with four other cases from around the nation to form the landmark case *Brown v. Board of Education of Topeka*.

While the country waited for the court's decision, South Carolina got busy demonstrating that racially divided schools could be equal. From the early to mid-1950s the state went on a massive construction program to build new schools and provide modern buses. Only a third of the money went to white students, who comprised about 60 percent of the school enrollment statewide. The sudden shift in spending for black children still was not enough to eliminate three hundred years of neglect.[9] South Carolina took other measures to buttress its "separate but equal" doctrine, believing that segregated schools were within the state's "police powers" to promote education to prevent disorder.[10] In May 1954 in *Brown v. Board of Education*, the Supreme Court outlawed segregated schools. South Carolina took a blow, but the fight was not over.

White voters passed a referendum to undo the constitutional requirement that the state provide education. White citizen councils sprouted up across the state to resist desegregation. Retaliation in the form of economic pressure that took away jobs, credit, and homes rained on those who opposed segregation. In 1956, the South Carolina legislature was so obsessed with fighting integration that *News and Courier* reporter William D. Workman Jr. called that legislative season the "Segregation Session."[11] One of that session's laws made it illegal for any public employee to join the NAACP, and it cost acclaimed Charleston educator and civil rights activist Septima P. Clark her job as a teacher—and her retirement benefits. Years later, seventeen members of Emanuel Church signed a petition in support of Clark receiving her retirement following an "illegal suspension" from her teaching position.[12]

The anti-integration effort was not limited to white lawmakers; whites from all walks of life embraced segregation. Although 20 percent of the state's white population could not read, a significant number of whites said segregation was more important than education.[13] Whites also cheered in 1952, when Judge Waring decided to retire.[14] Waring was a seventh-generation Charlestonian, but his lineage didn't insulate him from the backlash over his controversial court decisions. Starting with his ruling to end the white primaries to his dissenting vote in *Briggs v. Elliott,* whites in Charleston considered Waring a race traitor. He was vilified and ostracized to the point that he had become the "loneliest man in Charleston."[15] To make matters worse, Waring had divorced his Charleston-born wife and married a woman from Connecticut. He and his new wife entertained prominent members of Charleston's black community at their home. Eventually the Warings decided to leave Charleston in 1952, but not before black Charlestonians gave them a farewell dinner at Buist Elementary School across the street from Emanuel Church.[16]

Schools in the United States were segregated when Glover had to explain to his six-year-old daughter, Oveta, why she couldn't play in the playground at Julian Mitchell Elementary School across the street from Emanuel's parsonage, where he and his wife and their two daughters lived. The school and its park was for white children only, Glover told Oveta, but he promised her that one day she would be able to play in that park and attend that school. Meetings on how best to integrate the schools were held at Emanuel Church. When Glover left home to attend those strategy sessions with ministers, the local NAACP, and community leaders, Oveta tagged along.

While South Carolina obstructed the Supreme Court's ruling in *Brown v. Board of Education*, the NAACP in South Carolina would test the force of the court's decision. With few options for black students in Charleston to integrate schools, Oveta Glover and Minerva Brown, daughter of J. Arthur Brown, president of the Charleston NAACP, were selected to enroll in two schools in the fall of 1960. As a high school student, J. Arthur Brown was reminded most nights that just a few blocks away was a college he could not attend because of his race.[17] Through his bedroom window he heard the buglers' reveille in the morning and taps at night played at the Citadel, South Carolina's military college, "yet my parents who were taxpayers in this community had to bag me up and send me off to school," he said. "There were five Japanese boys attending the Citadel. They all rode together in a little blue Chevrolet car. You saw one, you saw five, and they were able to come from Japan to the Citadel when I couldn't go four blocks to the Citadel. And I think I took the position then that if I ever got a chance to hit [segregation], I'm going to hit it hard."[18]

Glover took Oveta to Mitchell Elementary School, the school across the street from their home, and Brown's twelfth grader, Minerva, and another student, ninth grader Ralph Dawson, attempted to integrate Rivers High School. The Glovers dressed Oveta in her best Sunday dress and shoes, along with lacy socks, and on the morning of October 10, 1960, she held her father's hand as they crossed the street to Mitchell Elementary School.[19] The hallway was lined with students, parents, and teachers, and a blond-haired boy stabbed her in the thigh with a pencil as someone yelled, "Nigger, go home!" As she turned to the boy, her father tightened his grip on Oveta's hand. In the principal's office they received another surprise. The Glovers were told Oveta couldn't enroll because the letter from her previous school, A. B. Rhett Elementary, didn't name the school she would transfer to.[20] Minerva and Ralph had similar setbacks at Rivers High School.

Following those failed attempts to integrate the schools, the Glover household experienced white hate. When the phone rang, Oveta rushed to answer it. The voice on the other end uttered words no child should hear. Callers made death threats against her father if he didn't leave the city. Lydia Glover was fired from her teaching job, which forced her to leave Charleston in 1962. For one year she taught home economics at Kentucky State University before rejoining her family. The Glovers' oldest daughter, Madrain, was enrolled in Boylan-Haven-Mather Academy, a black boarding school in Camden, South Carolina. Lydia and Oveta later went to live with Lydia's mother in Sumter, while Glover remained in Charleston to continue his civil rights work and lead Emanuel Church.

The next attempt to integrate Charleston's schools came on the first day of school in September 3, 1963.[21] Thirteen children had been selected, but that morning only eleven of them reported to the white campuses.[22] Oveta and her father arrived early at James Simons Elementary School and were greeted by the principal. White students and their parents had not yet arrived when they were escorted to Oveta's class. "Your seat is back there," the teacher said as she pointed to a chair at the rear of the classroom. As the white students arrived, one of the students, Kathy, sat next to Oveta. After a few days Oveta got the impression the teacher had paired them together. For the remainder of the school term, Oveta helped Kathy with her schoolwork, but at recess they didn't play together. Oveta had very little contact with the other children; it was as if she could hear them saying to themselves, "Don't sit next to the nigger girl." Her only enjoyment in school came during violin lessons. It was her time alone with her music teacher.[23]

Millicent Brown was enrolled in Rivers High School, located just a block north of the James Simons campus, but a bomb threat delayed part of her first day at school. For Millicent and Minerva Brown, being the daughters of the president of the Charleston NAACP had a profound effect because they experienced Charleston's civil rights movement as it intersected with prominent national and international activists who often met at their home. "Mike King was Mike King before he was Martin Luther King, and I think that that was such a very, very rich background to have had that made a big difference on me when I did go into Rivers that first day," Millicent said in retrospect years later.[24] At Burke High School, Brown was a rising tenth-grade student who looked forward to socializing with her friends and being a popular student on campus. But those youthful hopes were dashed when she walked into Rivers High School. She didn't experience physical violence there, but psychological trauma was cutting as white students seemingly on cue gave her wide berth in the hallways to strongly communicate they did not want to touch her. After graduating from high school, she saw enough of the world and America and education in this country to recognize that physical integration was superficial. "Black bodies being under the same roof as white bodies is not integration. And the harm, I think, that has been done to our feelings of self-worth, because we somehow thought if we could just be with white children that that was going to somehow alleviate our ills."[25] Sending black children to the white schools was not about going to school with whites, Oveta Glover explained years later. "If we had the same kind of books and educational material, there might not be any integration because it was all about equalization."[26] Millicent Brown and Oveta Glover and the other students were placed on the threshold of history at a time when black Charleston stepped up and confronted the city's segregated schools. Families willing to take those bold steps to integrate the school required courage, but "somebody had to do it."[27]

Before black students were enrolled in predominantly white schools, a protest of another kind against Jim Crow was brewing in Charleston. In 1958, Burke High School students decided to protest at the all-white lunch counters at Woolworth and Kress, variety stores on King Street. James Blake prepared the students for what they would encounter. "We went through a whole regimentation as to how you would act when you would go to a lunch counter. How you would act if you were arrested. What you would do if the police placed his hands on you. We took our folks through a course for about five to six weeks before we actually pulled the whole demonstration on them."[28] The protest in Charleston went mostly unnoticed outside of Charleston compared to a similar protest in Greensboro, North Carolina. The first salvo in the lunch-counter battle in Charleston may have come in early 1960, when forty students stood outside a Woolworth. They didn't enter the store, and they left soon after they arrived.[29] A year later nine teenagers and five juveniles were arrested at the Kress lunch counter. The teens were released on bond, and the younger protesters went home with their parents.[30] Four months later twenty-four high school students staged a five-and-a-half hour sit-in at the Kress store on King Street. The South Carolina Supreme Court later upheld the students' trespassing conviction, ruling that a private restaurant can select its customers on the basis of race.[31] By the spring of 1962, the protesting was beginning to yield some results in Charleston: at least two stores hired three black salesclerks.[32] Those small gains were not nearly enough to prevent stepped-up demonstrations, and by the summer of 1963, lunch counters weren't the only integration targets.

That night in 1959, when Glover spoke during the Emancipation Day observance on Johns Island, he speculated that black people could exert pressure on King Street merchants with a one-day boycott. In the summer of 1963, the NAACP initiated a selective buying effort as part of the Charleston civil rights movement. Many of the foot soldiers were high school students like seventeen-year-old Harvey Jones, who lived several blocks north of Emanuel Church. Jones decided that he was going to participate in the student protest because he'd had just about enough of Jim Crow laws. "I realized I would rather die than not be able to go into a restaurant and eat like regular people. I didn't want to be forced to go upstairs in a theater to watch a movie. I rather be dead than be treated as less than a human."[33]

Jones joined the picket line, and during one march, he had an opportunity to protest alongside Dr. King. During that march, activists were stopping at each of the businesses that had refused to integrate, when a white man came out of a bar and threw a beer on Jones. King saw what happened, and he told the teenager, "Son, don't do anything. If you feel that you have to do something, go back to the church." Jones assured King, "I am fine, Dr. King. I am fine."[34]

After numerous marches that led to many arrests and brief stays in jail, Jones was given a new protest target in July 1963. He and other students were asked to walk a short distance from Emanuel Church to the YWCA—to try to get in the pool. Glover also instructed them that if anyone attempted to block their entrance, they should throw their money on the counter and jump in the pool with their clothes on. That's what they did. The students weren't in the pool too long before they felt the burning sensation of chlorine the janitor had poured in the water as he yelled, "Niggers in the pool! Niggers in the pool!" The following month the local YWCA told the group's national board that it "cannot and must not" integrate, although the national organization had voted to launch a nationwide effort to speed up desegregation of local YWCAs.[35] The week of the YWCA pool demonstration, twenty-eight youths were arrested after they rushed into the city-owned pool on George Street and swam for about an hour before the pool was drained and the police took them away. While that protest was going on, eighty black people had left Emanuel and marched to the city's police station on St. Philip Street.[36] The protesters defied a judge's order in early July against mass demonstrations.

The following day a much larger group left Emanuel Church and returned to the police station, while inside the station, AME bishop Decatur Ward Nichols and four others were being booked on charges of trespassing at the Fort Sumter Hotel overlooking Charleston's historic Battery. One of them was former Avery Normal Institute teacher Ruby Cornwell, who was friends with Judge Waring and his wife.[37] As the protest dragged on, a flyer was circulated asking black people not to shop on King Street "because King Street merchants want our money, but we cannot work on King Street unless we are maids, janitors, or stock clerks." Black Charlestonians also were reminded they were the great-grandchildren of slaves, and the Charleston movement was "asking [that they] be treated as any other American because this is our home."[38]

Charleston's two daily newspapers—the *News and Courier* and its sister paper the *Charleston Evening Post*—gave the protest limited or no coverage, and often what was reported was one-sided. The newspaper's "blackout" was designed to prevent local blacks from being informed of what was happening in their city, but also to prevent outside supporters from joining the movement. James Blake observed, "So the people across the country never received the story of really what happened here."[39] Out of frustration, on July 16, 1963, about five hundred people took their songs and chants to the newspapers' doorsteps on Columbus Street for a late-night protest that became a "near riot."[40]

Harvey Jones wasn't supposed to participate in the nighttime march because he and the other youth protested during the day while adults were at work, letting the adults take over in the evenings. But Glover wanted the young people who had participated in previous marches to help manage the group; the older people had to be continually reminded to keep moving to reduce their chances of being arrested. Blocking traffic or a driveway could result in a trip to jail. The trouble that night started, Jones recalled, when someone in a nearby alley threw a brick that hit a policeman in the mouth. According to news stories, that triggered a rock-and-bottle-throwing melee that injured six police officers and a firefighter.[41] Police had their guns drawn, but no shots were fired; the dogs weren't released, and high-pressure fire hoses remained dry. Harvey Jones said, in retrospect, that police used restraint to avoid charges of brutality recently lodged against the police in Birmingham, Alabama. Besides, in the Holy City it would have been a national embarrassment if police dogs were released on the preachers. More than one hundred demonstrators were arrested, and later some of them were charged with rioting, including Harvey Jones. But if there were rocks and bottles thrown, he said, they didn't come from the organized protesters.

Glover was not jailed that night, but he promised that more marches would follow. "If those people think we will drop the demonstrations because others have been arrested, they've got another think coming." He urged his followers to engage in "peaceful street demonstrations." Mayor J. Palmer Gaillard responded that "the city would meet lawless force with overwhelming lawful force."[42] At the mayor's request, South Carolina's governor dispatched the National Guard to Charleston. The mayor said the protest had halted "adjustments" planned by King Street merchants who didn't want to be seen as yielding to mob intimidation.[43]

When Jones was released following eleven days in the county jail and the county's prison camp, Glover told him to go home, put on a suit, and go to Morris Street Baptist Church. The church was filled to capacity, and people stood outside waiting to get in. When they arrived, Jones and other youths who had been arrested outside the newspaper were asked to speak at a mass meeting. This was a big event, and Harvey Jones was just a teenager. He had experience participating in protests, but he knew nothing about public speaking. He was shaking with fear— and didn't have any idea what he would say. But he stepped up to the podium, opened his mouth, and as if it were divinely inspired, out came: "I just spent eleven days in jail for freedom and, if necessary, I would go back again."[44] The church erupted in applause and cheers.

After thirteen weeks of picketing, ninety King Street merchants met the NAACP's demands and were willing to allow black customers to try on hats, dresses, and other clothing; serve customers as they arrived without consideration of their race; hire black people for sales jobs; provide equal pay and rank to black clerks; use courtesy titles to black customers; and desegregate the lunch counters, fitting rooms, restrooms, and other services available to customers. The NAACP called the victory the most significant and productive breakthrough achieved as a result of a desegregation demonstration in the South.[45]

In 1965, Glover took a new job, leaving Charleston for the presidency of Allen University. At this point in his activist career, he had earned a reputation—the local newspaper recently called him the dean of the civil rights–era ministers in South Carolina.[46] Some parishioners at Mother Emanuel were sad he was moving to Allen, while others were happy he was leaving. Glover's tough talk and his practice of not backing down to police when ordered to return to the church might have inspired and impressed young demonstrators like Harvey Jones, but it made more conservative members of the congregation extremely nervous. In not-so-subtle attempts to force him out, some members of Emanuel held separate services at Harleston Funeral Home across the street from the church, and Glover's monthly salary was sometimes cut to six dollars. Some of the older people in the church believed that a pastor of Glover's status should not lead teenagers in street protests. The writing was on the wall for Glover.[47]

✳

The year 1965 was significant for another reason. The Voting Rights Act passed that summer, suggesting the ongoing strength of the civil rights movement; however, within days of its passage, the Watts section of Los Angeles erupted into one of the worst race riots to occur in American history. Soon other cities exploded in violence, and these episodes revealed that the civil rights movement was closer to its beginning than its end, particularly in the realm of economic justice.

Street protests marked with some violence also arrived in Charleston in the late 1960s, when the teaching hospital at Charleston's Medical College of South Carolina—located directly down Calhoun Street several blocks west from Emanuel—became the center of a major struggle for economic justice and human dignity. Black employees' grievances against this institution were long-standing. As late as 1965, the college had no black students, nor were there African American professional staff members or faculty.[48] In 1969, the firings of black licensed practical nurses (LPNs) and nursing assistants led Mary Moultrie (another African American hospital employee) to begin organizing a labor union.[49] This seemingly small step, in combination with other events, set the stage for a strike that grew into a class and racial struggle.

On March 20, 1969, black hospital employees—mostly women—walked out to protest the firing of twelve nurses' aides. They demanded recognition of their union, higher wages, and respect. In many cases black employees earned less than minimum wage and often less than white employees who did the same job. Additionally, some white supervisors referred to black nurses in derogatory terms, such as "monkey grunts," using such racial epithets openly.[50]

The walkout evolved into a strike, and for ninety-nine days several hundred employees and local residents took to the picket lines. The strike spread to the nearby Charleston County Hospital, and as it dragged on, services were reduced, forcing Medical College of South Carolina president William McCord to consider closing the state's teaching hospital. During the most violent period of the strike, a King Street business was burned, and the National Guard was deployed to enforce curfews. Medical College employees joined a New York–based hospital union—1199 Drug and Hospital Workers' Union—on its first organizing push to the Deep South.

The striking nurses were in the middle of one of the city's bloodiest and most bitter labor protests. Described by a *New York Times* editorial as "the country's tensest civil rights struggle," the protest represented a larger set of issues. It was a struggle between the "haves" and the "have-nots."[51] It was similar to the struggles that had already played out on Charleston's docks and in the hot cigar factory.

Lillie Mae Marsh Doster was still toiling away in the cigar factory when the hospital strike spilled into the streets. The union formed at the cigar factory during that strike continued to operate from an office inside the factory, where she served as the union secretary. The union office became a place where medical college worker Mary Moultrie and her fellow striking nurses and their community supporters could go to think and plan.

The striking workers also gained support from the Southern Christian Leadership Conference, one year after a sniper's bullet had killed its president, Dr. Martin Luther King Jr. It was the SCLC's first attempt in Charleston in the Poor People's Movement. During a massive protest on Mother's Day 1969, King's widow, Coretta Scott King, made an address at Emanuel Church. Doster and union organizer Isaiah Bennett had recommended that the hospital workers contact the hospital union in New York, and with the help of activist Septima P. Clark, the hospital employees got the SCLC's attention.[52] Moultrie and her followers were buoyed by the marriage of civil rights and labor that had come to support their cause in Charleston.

After the strike was settled in June 1969, the fired workers were rehired, but they didn't return to a welcoming work environment. They didn't get a contract or win union recognition.[53] The strike left painful memories among those who were disgruntled that its outcome didn't go the way they had expected.

The hospital strike transformed the city's race relations, and when it was finally over, it led to the creation of an agency to investigate workplace grievances within state agencies. In Charleston, the strike unified black residents across class lines to dispel myths that had sustained the racial status quo. Black voter registration also rose in the 1970s, giving voice to a black electorate that had been shut out of the political process. William Saunders, a community organizer who advised the strikers, points proudly at the accomplishments: "The strike solidified the black community and all people of good will. It also proved that there is power when the masses of people are organized properly and that power has to be reckoned with by the people who control the economy and police."[54]

ELEVEN

PEOPLE IN SERVICE TO THE CHURCH

Bishop Richard Allen was at his Philadelphia home in 1809, when twenty-six-year-old domestic worker Jerena Lee came unannounced to share her story of being called to preach and the troubling night she had fretting whether it was truly God's calling or the devil's trick. After listening to her passionate plea, Allen authorized her to lead meetings, prayer services, and unorganized gatherings in the AME Church, but he did not give her permission to preach from the pulpit. The AME Church Discipline, he told her, did not call for women preachers.

Lee's acceptance of the bishop's decision did not last long. For eight years she served as a Methodist minister without official recognition from the church. Based on the belief that her calling came from a much higher power, she gave an estimated 178 sermons, traveling widely. In her journal she posed this probing question: "Why should it be thought impossible, heterodox, or improper for a woman to preach, seeing the Savior died for the woman as well as the man?"[1]

Lee's travels eventually led her back to Bishop Allen during a Sunday morning service at his church on the day that a guest minister lost his voice and his place in the text during the sermon. As the distraught minister returned to his seat, Lee rose confidently from the audience to take the minister's place at the lectern, where she proceeded to repeat the text he had delivered and complete his unfinished sermon before an astonished audience. Because the platform was reserved for ordained ministers, Lee returned to her pew knowing she had violated church rules in the presence of the bishop who had earlier forbidden her from preaching from the pulpit. Although Allen informed the congregation he had refused to ordain Lee, he praised her evangelizing and the sermon she had just given. He then ordained her because he believed her calling was equal to that of any man. Allen assigned her to his church.[2] Lee opened a trail for other women ministers in the AME Church—such as Emanuel's first female minister, Hilda Blanche Scott, who in turn set an example for other women at Mother Emanuel.

The weight of the June 17 tragedy at Emanuel was heaviest on women, as six of the Emanuel Nine victims were women, and three of them—Myra Thompson, Sharonda Coleman-Singleton, and DePayne Middleton-Doctor—were ministers in the church. Nevertheless, the loss was sweeping, taking its toll on people—women and men—who gave their lives in service to the church and the Charleston community.

Service to the church defines many "strong women" of Emanuel, but Reverend Hilda Scott perhaps stands out because she challenged a male-dominated church to become not just a minister but also a role model for generations of Emanuel's children. The nattily dressed and feisty Scott moved quickly through the Emanuel sanctuary with a feverous devotion not only to the church but especially to the young people who lovingly called her "Mama Hilda." From the mid-1940s through the early 1990s, she served as Sunday school superintendent, presiding over teachers and students who assembled in the ground floor area where the Emanuel Nine lost their lives.[3] A thin line separated Scott's warmth from her stern discipline. Her hallmark punishment for misbehaving inattentive juveniles was a pinch to the upper arm or an earlobe yank.

Despite Scott's stern disposition, Emanuel trustee pro tempore Leon Alston remembered Scott as a warm, loving person in the church—and especially in the neighborhood where her husband, Oscar Scott, often stopped by the Alston home on Saturday mornings with a package of whiting (a local fish) for his mother from "your girlfriend Hilda." Alston tells the story of a day he and his friends spent the Sunday school hour throwing rocks at the John C. Calhoun statue not far from the church. "We had read in our book that he was one of the slave owners in South Carolina," Alston says. "Mama Hilda wanted to get us back in Sunday school, so she made us join the Sunbeam Choir. But after a couple of years of that, she realized I couldn't sing, so she said, 'I think you are best suited for the junior usher board.'"[4]

At Emanuel, Scott blazed a trail for women ministers, such as Thompson, Coleman-Singleton, and Middleton-Doctor. Emanuel steward emeritus Ruby Martin had mentored Thompson and Coleman-Singleton. She bought textbooks and a book on women in the Bible and supported them financially in other ways. "Sharonda was being ordained, and I took communion with her and her family, and Myra was about to rise to another level in her ministerial studies before she died," Martin says. "I knew Myra as a young woman. I made the motion for her to get a license to preach and wrote a letter to the board of examiners for her to preach, and I knew where she was in her Christian movement."[5]

✳

Anthony Thompson also knew Myra but when they were much younger. She used to come over to his house to play with his little sister, but to him she was a little kid, four years younger than him, and he didn't pay much attention to her. They never could have foreseen when they were children how often their lives would continue to intersect over the years.

The story of the Thompsons is the kind of love story that movies are made of. No matter what they were doing or where they were, they simply kept bumping into each other. Little by little their friendship deepened into the kind of relationship that everyone wishes for: a marriage based on mutual respect and admiration and a deep, deep abiding love.

Both Myra and Anthony Thompson grew up in Charleston, and as fate would have it, they both ended up at Benedict College in Columbia at the same time, despite their age differences. Anthony was finishing up his last year of college after a stint in the navy, and Myra transferred from Livingston College in North Carolina. Anthony was driving in his car one day when he saw Myra walking down the road. She was visibly upset because she had missed the bus to Charleston, where she traveled every weekend to see her baby son, Kevin, and to work at McDonald's. Anthony had a wife and son at home in Charleston, and he would also go home on weekends, so he offered her a ride. She told him that she knew he was going where she was going, but she didn't trust him. Thompson can smile about it now in retrospect: "She was no-nonsense. She was always focused and so serious."[6] Anthony was impressed. Soon, he gave her a ride home every weekend, dropping her off on Fishburne Street at "Miz" Mabel's house. Mabel took care of Kevin during the week when Myra was away at college. Myra graduated from Benedict with a degree in English education.

The years passed by, and Anthony and Myra both ended up back in Charleston. He was living on Line and Coming Streets downtown, and she was living on Coming Street near the fire station, so they would bump into each other occasionally. Then Myra got married and moved. Anthony and his family also moved away from the Coming Street area, but he and Myra, of course, relocated to the same neighborhood. They continued to cross paths, and her son, Kevin, got to know Anthony. Myra

The Library Company of Philadelphia

Rev. Richard Allen, first bishop of the African Methodist Episcopal Church, 1823

REUTERS/Brian Snyder

A crowd gathered outside the Mother Emanuel Church, following a nearby prayer service, June 19, 2015

REUTERS/Randall Hill

A family member at the burial of Rev. Clementa Pinckney, St James AME Church, Marion, SC, June 26, 2015

REUTERS/Jason Miczek

Jay Bender held an anti-Confederate flag sign
during a rally at the SC State House, June 20, 2015

Joel Woodhall

Local leaders and community members united in a prayer
circle during the early morning hours of June 18, 2015

Rev. Sharonda
Coleman-Singleton

Cynthia Graham Hurd

Susie Jackson

Courtesy of the National Afro-American Museum and Cultural Center

Bishop Daniel A. Payne, founder of the South Carolina Conference of the AME Church, circa 1870–90

Herb Frazier

A bronze statue of Denmark Vesey stands a short distance from the entrance to the Citade

REUTERS/Brian Snyder

A group held hands and prayed outside Mother Emanuel, June 19, 2015

Charleston Chronicle/Courtesy of the Lance family

Ethel Lance

Charleston Chronicle/Courtesy of the Doctor family

Rev. DePayne
Middleton-Doctor

Charleston Chronicle/Courtesy of
Rev. Clementa Pinckney

Rev. Clementa Carlos Pinckney

Rev. Richard Harkness (L) and Rev. Jack Lewin (R) sang with the congregation, "We Shall Overcome," during a prayer vigil at Morris Brown AME Church, Charleston, SC, June 18, 2015

Bethel African Methodist Episcopal Church, Philadelphia, 1829

A makeshift memorial outside Mother Emanuel grew as people remembered the Emanuel Nine

Charleston Chronicle/Courtesy of the Sanders family

Charleston Chronicle/Courtesy of the Simmons family

Tywanza Sanders

Rev. Daniel L. Simmons Sr.

Courtesy of the Thompson family

Myra Thompson

Malana Pinckney, daughter of Rev. Clementa Pinckney, gazed at President Barack Obama at the start of her father's eulogistic service, Charleston, SC, June 26, 2015

President Barack Obama spoke at Rev. Clementa Pinckney's funeral service, Charleston, SC, June 26, 2015

also gave birth to a baby girl named Denise. She eventually began working at the Cathedral School, where Kevin was a student, and Anthony would often run into her there. At the time, both of their marriages were troubled, and they began to talk to each other about what they were going through, which brought them even closer. A few years later they were married. According to Anthony, after decades of friendship, once they were married, "everything came together."[7]

Myra Thompson was always driven and focused. She worked as an English teacher, and she taught at both Cathedral School and Brentwood Middle School. She earned two master's degrees at the Citadel—one in counseling and one as a reading specialist. According to her husband, she did it for her students who needed help with reading, not for the paycheck: "When she did something, there was always a purpose behind it, and it was always to help someone else."[8]

Myra had a difficult childhood, and it's possible that her sense of purpose can be traced back to those earlier years and a need to create stability and independence. Her father was absent from her life, and her mother was a struggling alcoholic. When Myra was a student at Burke High School, her mother made arrangements with her next-door neighbor and friend, Kathy Coakley, to take her in, so Myra went to live with the Coakley family. They were members of Mother Emanuel Church, and Myra soon joined the church as well. She became a lay leader too; it's clear her church home was a solid, stable force in her life.

Myra's father was married three times, and he had multiple children from each marriage. But Myra was his firstborn child, and this is a role she took very seriously. Once she became an adult, she made enormous efforts to create family out of these disparate parts. "Her goal was to bring her family together, and she did everything she could to make sure her life with her children would not be like her life with her mom," Anthony Thompson comments, adding, "She was very strong; I admired that about her."[9] Myra and Anthony Thompson were married for thirteen years, and during that time they reunited with all of Myra's siblings, making many weekend trips to visit them. There were eleven in all—a few were her full siblings, but most of them were half sisters or half brothers. The family is so huge, in fact, they had to hire a bus for them for the funeral, because they all came. Myra had more than fifty nieces and nephews; a son, Kevin Singleton; a daughter, Denise Quarles; and a stepson, Anthony Thompson. She also had two grandchildren.

Myra even had the opportunity to see her father's mother before her grandmother died; they had met only one other time. Myra kept a photograph of her wearing a fur coat, and that was all she could remember about her. When the two finally met again, Myra was astounded at the similarities between them, their characters and mannerisms. Myra was thrilled to bring her children and grandchildren to meet her grandmother.

At Anthony's urging, Myra also reconnected with her father, and that's really when they began a relationship. Myra was in her forties at the time. She also maintained a relationship with her mother, who passed away some time ago. Myra's father lived in Hampton, South Carolina, and he helped start Clementa Pinckney's political career—driving him around town, talking about politics and how to run a campaign. According to Anthony, Clementa Pinckney got a kick out of that connection.

Myra Thompson and Rev. Pinckney worked closely together when she was the head of Emanuel's property committee, working to restore and maintain the historic church. She also served as the children's church instructor and trustee pro tempore and on numerous panels, including one to put in an elevator so everyone could have access to the sanctuary. It's not surprising, given her devotion to her church, that Myra would choose to become an AME minister. She pursued her seminary studies at night, and she had delivered a number of sermons as part of the process—all of this leading up to conducting Bible study on the night of June 17, a task usually undertaken by Daniel Simmons. According to her husband, she had thoroughly prepared for the evening and had practiced the discussion many times. She had received her license renewal earlier at the Quarterly Conference. It was a proud night for her.

Both Myra and Anthony Thompson had worked for decades in their chosen careers before making the profound decision to pastor, and the fact that they attended different churches and were of different denominations is a testament to their mutual respect and admiration. Anthony Thompson worked for twenty-seven years as a probation officer, and he started attending the Reformed Episcopal Seminary in Summerville, South Carolina, in 1985. He was also going for his MA in clinical counseling, and he and Myra agreed it was too much—the seminary degree was the one to pursue. He graduated in 1995 with a master's degree in divinity. He is now the pastor of Holy Trinity Reformed Episcopal Church, a small church in downtown Charleston, with a simple yet beautiful sanctuary.

Behind the building is a garden that Thompson's friends planted in the days following the church shooting. It's called Myra's Garden, and it is filled with a variety of flowering plants, benches, and a plain white crucifix against the back wall. Anthony's friends from high school spearheaded the effort. Tom McQueeny, who graduated from Bishop England High School with Anthony in 1970, was the ringleader, e-mailing photos of the garden to Anthony while he was still in Atlanta with his family during the days that followed his wife's murder. Neighbors contributed as well, and it is a lovely tribute to his beloved wife, whom he says had four spiritual gifts: helping, giving, teaching, and counseling.[10] This is what she spent her life doing. We hope he finds peace in that sacred space.

※

Sharonda Ann Coleman-Singleton wore many hats: mom to her three children, Chris, Caleb, and Camryn; track-and-field coach to the female runners at Goose Creek High School, where she also worked as a speech pathologist; and pastor at Mother Emanuel Church, where she worked with the youth and young adult ministries. She did it all with a big smile that radiated energy and love. Coleman-Singleton was a track star in college. Originally from Newark, New Jersey, she attended South Carolina State, where she competed as a champion hurdler; the team won the conference championship. She joined Alpha Kappa Alpha sorority, and her sorority sisters nicknamed her "Tookie." In 1991 Coleman-Singleton received her degree in speech pathology and audiology. She later received her MA degree from Montclair State University in New Jersey.

When she and her family moved to Charleston from Atlanta, Georgia, in 2007, they joined Emanuel Church. Her husband's grandparents were longstanding members of the church. She served as itinerant deacon there and helped the acting pastor in his work. In the pastor's absence she could perform baptisms, marriages, and funerals. According to her friend, Emanuel member Evelyn Sinkler, "When she preached, everyone seemed to listen; she always had a way to pull you in."[11] Ms. Sinkler expresses amazement at Singleton's stamina. No matter how long her days were at work, Coleman-Singleton always came to Bible study, and she often brought her children. "She embodied the spirit of love," Sinkler says.[12]

Coleman-Singleton's son Chris, a sophomore at Charleston Southern University, is on the baseball team. He often accompanied his mother to Bible study on Wednesday nights, but he had a game on June 17, 2015, and his life was spared. He arrived home from the game around 9:30 p.m. and received a call from his mother's telephone. A stranger asked if any other adults were around and told him to get down to the church as soon as possible. Once he heard from the coroner that eight people were dead, he says he cried so much he couldn't cry anymore.[13] Poised and talented, Chris Singleton made the following statement at a June vigil: "Love is stronger than hate, so if we just love the way my mom would, then the hate won't be anywhere close to where the love is."[14] He is a living testament to his mother, who was only forty-five when she was killed. Chris also led his summer baseball team, the North Charleston Dixie Pre-Majors, to a World Series win, after which the New York Yankees made a $150,000 donation to the Singleton Memorial Fund at Charleston Southern University.

❋

A six-foot DePayne Middleton-Doctor stood out in the crowd on June 5, 2015, the last day of school at Ashley River Creative Arts Elementary. She was among teachers and other parents with their children who mingled in the corridor outside the auditorium to exchange hugs, good-byes, the thrills of advancing to middle school, and well wishes for a happy summer. Because of Middleton-Doctor's stature, Linda Meggett Brown and her daughter Faith quickly spotted Middleton-Doctor and her youngest daughter, Czana, Faith's friend and classmate.[15] Twelve days after that brief exchange, Middleton-Doctor was among the nine murdered at Emanuel.

Brown and Middleton-Doctor shared more than just having daughters in the same class. They also were schoolmates at Baptist Hill High School in Hollywood, South Carolina, where Middleton-Doctor played for the girls' basketball team. As students, Brown didn't know Middleton-Doctor that well because she was a few grades ahead of her, but in the small community south of Charleston, she knew of her and her family. Years later Brown and the rest of the Hollywood community became even more acquainted with Middleton-Doctor's family life when she delivered a Sunday sermon that revealed how her faith sustained her through a divorce from the father of her four girls, Czana, Gracyn, Hali, and Kaylin.[16] In 2012, Wesley United Methodist Church, across the road from the Baptist Hill campus, invited Middleton-Doctor to be the speaker during a women's day program. Brown remains in awe of the sermon Middleton-Doctor delivered with a voice of authority, demonstrating she was a Bible scholar adept at relating Scripture to everyday life.[17]

Reared by parents who worked in service professions, Middleton-Doctor was the middle child of three girls born to retired AME pastor Leroy Middleton and retired social worker and Head Start administrator Frances Middleton. She followed a path of service to her community and church and was the third female minister among the Emanuel Nine. Middleton-Doctor did her trial sermon in the early 2000s at Mount Moriah Baptist Church in North Charleston, South Carolina, where she also sang in the choir. She and Dr. Brenda Nelson were the first two women ordained to preach at Mount Moriah before they moved their memberships to Emanuel.[18] Both received their local licenses to preach in the AME Church on the fatal night of June 17. Middleton-Doctor returned to the AME Church to rejoin her roots and find a church family that she could call home, and she found it at Emanuel.

In the pursuit of becoming an AME minister, Middleton-Doctor was a regular at the Wednesday night Bible study. She was a woman of God who not only was strong in her faith but also had a desire to help those in need. Middleton-Doctor administered grants for Charleston County that enabled residents to make repairs to their homes that they couldn't otherwise afford. In 2005, she retired as director of the county's Community Development Block Grant Program. The year before she died, Middleton-Doctor had joined the staff at Southern Wesleyan University as the admission coordinator in the school's Charleston learning center.[19]

Middleton-Doctor, who along with her daughters joined Emanuel on May 31, 2015, was a strong single parent who "functioned for the girls," Ashland Magwood Temoney, Middleton-Doctor's niece, says. She attended school and sporting events; "she was their rock." When Middleton-Doctor's marriage began to fail, she advised Temoney in making her decision to marry. She told her to make God first and be certain she was making the right decision. "She wasn't a party pooper, and she didn't let her situation," her divorce dampen her niece's excitement about being married, Temoney says. Years later on March 12, 2015, when Temoney gave birth to her son Archie Temoney II, Middleton-Doctor could not come to the hospital. But she came the next day. "She was excited for him coming, and I have a phone message she left me on my due date. 'Hey I am just calling to see if Try has made his arrival and see how you are doing.' I have saved it so I can hear her voice."[20]

❊

Three of the Emanuel Nine were tied not by pulpit affiliation but by blood. At the time of the shootings, Charleston city councilman William Dudley Gregorie was on the phone with his mother, longtime Emanuel member Marguerite Gregorie, who was in Cleveland, Ohio, visiting her daughter Ellenora and Ellenora's husband, Walter Jackson, Susie Jackson's son. In one night the Gregorie family lost not only Susie Jackson but also her nephew, Tywanza Sanders, and their cousin, Ethel Lance. Text messages from Dudley Gregorie's city council colleagues flashed on his cell phone that something had happened at his church. He went to the command center and was told the devastating news.[21]

Earlier that night Dudley Gregorie was concerned that he hadn't had an opportunity to give Susie Jackson a hug after the property committee meeting, chaired by Myra Thompson. When the meeting ended, he turned, but Susie Jackson's seat was empty. After the meeting he found Jackson in the basement, seated with Ethel Lance, cutting out coupons from the newspaper. So he did hug Jackson then, and they talked about her recent trip to Cleveland to see his mother. And he hugged Lance as they were joined by Nelson and Middleton-Doctor. That night Thompson had her license to preach renewed, and her chairmanship was coming to an end, but she assured Gregorie that she would continue to be active with the committee. Then they went into the Quarterly Conference around seven o'clock. Had the shooter arrived at the church an hour earlier, more than fifty people would have been gathered together.[22]

Susie Jackson, at eighty-seven, was a true matriarch at Mother Emanuel Church. Most of her family attends the church, and she lived right around the corner on Alexander Street. She had two children, but was known for opening her home to many others. "She was a mother to so, so many," Emanuel member Carlotta Dennis said on the day of "Ms. Susie's" funeral.[23]

Jackson grew up in Charleston and attended Buist Elementary School, located across the street from Mother Emanuel Church. Later she attended Burke High School. Over the years, she worked as a beautician and home health care provider, but her heart was with her church, where she was a trustee. She was also in the Willing Workers Club. According to her lifelong friend Evelyn Sinkler, "Ms. Susie was always willing to do her part in the edification of the children in our church. The Willing Workers Club sponsored a baby contest, a fashion show, and an Easter egg hunt."[24] Jackson also sang in the Jubilaires Choir and the senior choir, regularly attended Bible study, and was a member of the Women's Ministerial Society, the Missionary Society, and the senior citizens group.

If anyone was sick or shut in, she would pay that person a visit. Known for being soft-spoken, Susie Jackson was always thinking of others. She also loved to travel and was a member of the Traveling Partners—a group of women from the church who went on annual trips together. Her niece, Felicia Sanders, was in the group, as well as some of Jackson's sisters and her friend Evelyn Sinkler. Every year they chose a different destination to visit, and they often invited other friends to come with them. They had planned to go to Chicago on June 21, 2015. One of Ms. Susie's nieces told Evelyn Sinkler that her aunt had already started packing for the trip before she was killed on June 17.

Susie Jackson's cousin, Ethel Lance, often joined the Traveling Partners too. Lance, a lifelong member of Mother Emanuel, was a mother of five and a grandmother. Lance was known for singing the gospel song "One Day at a Time" to her friends at Emanuel Church. It gave her strength. Everyone who knew her described how much she loved to sing and dance. But most of all, she loved her church. At her funeral Norvel Goff described her dedication: "She was at the church seven days of the week. I believe if God gave her eight she would have been there eight days a week. . . . Mother Emanuel was deep down in her spirit, her soul."[25] Lance's funeral was held in the large Royal Missionary Baptist Church in North Charleston. At the service her oldest grandchild, Brandon Risher, said, "She was a victim of hate, but she can be a symbol of love."[26]

Ethel Lance was a longtime member of the usher board at Mother Emanuel, and she was also active in the senior citizen's group there. Most notably, she'd been the church custodian since her retirement, and lovingly cared for the old building. She was so devoted to Mother Emanuel that she once returned to the church from her home west of the Ashley River when Pinckney called her because he'd forgotten some food that someone had given him. She drove back downtown to the church to put the food in the refrigerator—she just couldn't let it spoil. This is a wonderful example of her love for her pastor and her church.[27]

The youngest victim on June 17 was twenty-six-year-old Tywanza Kibwe Diop Sanders. His nickname was "Wanza," and his big, sweet smile was infectious. His final words were, "Where is my Aunt Susie[?] I've got to get to my Aunt Susie."[28] At his funeral at Mother Emanuel Church on Saturday, June 27, 2015, Tywanza's brown casket was placed beside Susie Jackson's silver casket, having arrived at the church in two caissons led by white horses. So many members of this large family were in attendance that unrelated mourners were asked to give up their seats for family. The pews were filled with his young friends from both his Charleston childhood and his years at Allen University in Columbia.

Tywanza Sanders was an entrepreneur full of hopes and dreams— and he was serious about poetry. He was a spoken-word poet with a social conscience. His poem "Tragedy" was recited at his funeral. It ended with the lines: "Divided by color / So we are all trying to be equal."[29] His English teacher at Allen University was poet and assistant professor Charlene Spearen. Tywanza had shown her his poems when he was a student, and they continued to work together after graduation. Spearen says he was writing all the time, and he was very self-possessed and compassionate. "He took responsibility for any choice he made. For example," Spearen explains, "if he was having problems with a course, he took ownership of it. He was a bit older than your average college student; therefore, he was more mature."[30] According to Spearen, both Tywanza's writing and his life were based on a set of ethics taught in communities of faith. He respected his parents and loved his fellow man. He believed that we are our brother's keeper, and that there was a moral behavior that determined how we should treat one another. "When he saw something violate these principles," Spearen adds, "that's what he wrote about."[31] He also wrote about the realities of being a young black man in today's America. Tywanza worked with Spearen on the NEA Big Read Project featuring the work of writer Zora Neale Hurston, and he helped teach poetry workshops in Lowcountry schools. He would recite his poems and engage students wherever they went, and "the kids loved him."[32]

The Friday before Tywanza was killed, he called his English professor and told her he had about two hundred pages of his poems that he wanted to publish in book form. "'It's time,' he said. 'It's time.'"[33]

✳

The oldest man killed on June 17 was Rev. Daniel L. Simmons Sr. Known as Dan to his friends and family, Simmons was born in the summer of 1940 in the small town of Mullins in Marion County, South Carolina. Like Tywanza Sanders and Clementa Pinckney, Simmons attended Allen University in Columbia, South Carolina, where he received his

BS in education administration. But Simmons was drafted right out of high school. He started his college studies, then served in the United States Army in Vietnam, and returned to graduate. While in the military, Simmons was wounded and received a Purple Heart. Later he earned a master's degree in social work from the University of South Carolina. He married Ann Graham, who was also from Mullins. They settled in Columbia and had two children—Daniel Lee and Rose Ann. Simmons worked as a counselor for the Veterans Administration in Columbia. Before that, he worked as a teacher and counselor with the South Carolina Department of Corrections. Previously he worked as a coach operator for Greyhound Bus Corporation and an insurance broker for Metropolitan Life Insurance Company. Somehow he made the time to attend seminary, and in 1988 he received his master of divinity from the Lutheran Seminary in Columbia. For the next ten years, Simmons pastored at a number of churches in the Columbia area.

After twenty-four years of marriage, Ann and Dan Simmons were divorced; Dan remarried and divorced again. He moved in 1999 to Charleston, where he served as pastor at several AME churches. Simmons retired in 2013, whereupon he joined the ministerial staff at Mother Emanuel AME, where he generally led the Bible study on Wednesday nights. He had coached Myra Thompson on the Bible passage she used in the study June 17.

Joseph Darby, presiding elder of Beaufort's AME district, says Simmons was "dependable . . . and an excellent administrator," adding, "he had a very good sense of humor."[34] Simmons's nephew, Al Miller, says the bishop would send his uncle to a church to clean it up. "He obeyed the AME rules. He went by the book."[35] Miller also says, "When Dan was not in the pulpit, he was genuinely a good-hearted person. But when he left a church, members still called on him to visit a sick loved one or give them communion."[36] Miller also commented on the fact that his uncle had a gun license, and he carried a gun in his car to protect himself. Sometimes Simmons would visit rough neighborhoods while visiting the sick and bereaved in his capacity as minister, and he felt safer having a gun. The gun was in his car the evening of June 17; Simmons was shot but died later at the Medical University Hospital in Charleston. Since his death, his granddaughter Alana and her family have started the #HateWontWin movement to spread tolerance and encourage children and teenagers to connect with people from different backgrounds.

※

Malcolm Graham has said that he will spend the rest of his life honoring his sister Cynthia Graham Hurd and "pushing for justice at all levels."[37] One of six children, Cynthia was the oldest daughter. Her father was a truck driver, and her mother was a domestic worker for two families on Church Street. Cynthia became the matriarch of the family after her parents died more than twenty years ago, living in the house on Benson Street where they were raised in downtown Charleston. Cynthia called it "the family compound." A math major in college, she eventually commuted to the University of South Carolina to get her master's in library science. According to Malcolm, as a child she loved books so much that she read every volume of the *World Book Encyclopedia*.[38]

The Graham children grew up at Mother Emanuel Church, where their mother sang in the choir. Their parents are buried at Emanuel cemetery. Cynthia Graham Hurd was on a number of committees at Emanuel, and she served on the usher board. "If she wasn't at the library, she was at Emanuel AME," Malcolm told reporter Schuyler Kropf. [39]

Like all the Emanuel Nine, Cynthia Graham Hurd felt strongly about her neighborhood and its residents. According to her brother Malcolm, "She was community focused. She always had an interest in improving the community by delivering constituent services every day at the library, whether people were doing a job search in the computer or looking for answers to questions in a book . . . she was serving the public."[40]

Not only did Cynthia work thirty-one years, full-time, in the Charleston County library system; she also worked evenings for sixteen years at the College of Charleston Library. At the CCPL Dart Branch on Charleston's east side, she helped children with reading assignments and papers, as well as job searches. Sometimes she had to run off vagrants who were loitering in front of the library. She used to say, "You can't wait for folks to come into the library," so she would go out and draw people to it by working with schools in the area. She saw it as a ministry and a way to provide a unique public service for the community.[41]

Kim Odom, manager of the Dart branch, spoke at Cynthia Graham Hurd's funeral. When Odom joined the Dart staff fifteen years ago, Hurd took her to a desk, introduced her to the staff, and said, "Let's go." Odom asked, "Where?" Hurd answered, "To drive around the community. Before you can know what to do, you've got to know who we serve."[42]

Hurd's desire to serve was not limited to her work at the library. Her friend and library colleague Marvin Stewart, with whom she shared a brother-sister relationship, is reminded daily of her talents with a hammer and saw. The first floor of Stewart's two-story home in Charleston reflects Hurd's creativity and ability to imagine an interior design, then craft it with her hands. Hurd made the drapes and valences in Stewart's living room and painted the walls. She gutted the den; made new walls; hung a ceiling fan; measured, cut, and installed crown molding; then added a special touch: books, but not real books. The wallpaper pattern resembles books on bookshelves. Stewart and Hurd are librarians. That is how they met three decades ago when Hurd, fresh out of college, took her first job as a librarian assistant in a library where Stewart was a manager. From that moment they realized what they had in common: Mother Emanuel and parents who wanted their children to be better than themselves. They both grew up in the church but at different times.

Both of their mothers were domestic workers who made sacrifices to send their children to college.

As a divorced father of two girls, Stewart called on Hurd when he needed help getting one of his daughters ready for a high school prom. "She gave a shawl to match the dress, and she never asked for it back," Stewart says. When the daughter of Stewart's former spouse needed a math tutor, he turned to Hurd, who majored in math in college. Hurd and the student huddled together at the library for after-hours tutoring. It helped her pass her math course, and soon after Hurd hired her for a summer youth program job.[43]

Cynthia Graham Hurd was a member of the City of Charleston Housing Authority, which gave her another opportunity to serve the community surrounding the library. Like the Rev. Hilda Scott, Hurd had no children of her own, but any child that she came in contact with became one of her children. Before her death, Hurd was transferred from the Dart branch, in a predominantly African American community, to a branch in a Charleston suburb with a more diverse population. She was torn about leaving Dart but made the change nonetheless.

Stewart unexpectedly discovered another one of Hurd's talents. In Emanuel, many members sit in the same pews; over the years Hurd and Stewart had staked out seats not far from each other. One Sunday they sat together, and during the service, he discovered she had a lovely voice. Because he knew Hurd so well, Stewart did not imagine Hurd was at Bible study on June 17, because of her Wednesday night part-time job in the library at the College of Charleston. They had seen each other earlier that day during a county library staff meeting, but they didn't have time to "shoot the breeze," he said. "That was the last time I saw her."[44]

How can anyone ever know the last time he or she will see a loved one or how a seemingly ordinary Wednesday in June can turn into one's last day on earth? We can't know such things, and this is what makes the smallest of details matter—because it's these small moments and details that compose and illuminate a life.

※

Sen. Clementa Pinckney's day began routinely at the statehouse in Columbia with small and large details that signified family, legislative duties, and fashion. His office refrigerator has a "Yes! I Love My Library" sticker from his wife, Jennifer, a librarian. He attended a senate committee meeting where he advocated against Republican opposition for money to repair roads in his impoverished district. Then he joined a caucus with fellow Democrats and a lighter moment with a political adviser with whom he shared a newfound passion for colorful socks.[45] When the business of the state ended, there was no reason for Jennifer, Malana, and Clementa to travel together to Charleston that day, other than they wanted to spend quality time together.[46]

June 17 was also a busy day for Emanuel steward pro tempore Leon Alston, who saw the Pinckneys in Charleston at the church, first at an elevator committee meeting then at the Quarterly Conference, where he purposely sat behind Daniel Simmons so the minister would not see him and possibly entice him to stay for Bible study. Simmons often reminded Alston that to be a better steward, he needed to come to Bible study on Wednesdays. When the quarterly meeting ended, Simmons commented that it had been a long night and everyone was hungry. But Myra Thompson spoke up and said it was her night to teach Bible study and she wanted to proceed. After all, that night she'd had her license to preach renewed.

Alston had another reason to be at the church that night. As a general contractor he was commissioned to renovate the pastor's office and update the restroom. At 12:50 p.m. on June 17, Pinckney had texted a picture of the floor tile he wanted to use in the restroom to Alston.

Following the Quarterly Conference, Alston knocked on the door to the pastor's office, but to his surprise he found Jennifer Pinckney and her daughter, Malana, there. Alston had planned to start the work the following day, and that Wednesday the Pinckneys had selected the flooring for the office. Now they were in the office, picking paint colors for the walls. Alston told the pastor he was leaving, and Pinckney promised to call him after Bible study. "I am still waiting for that call," Alston says.[47]

After the Quarterly Conference, Pinckney helped Ruby Martin down the stairs fronting Calhoun Street. During a lighthearted moment, she complimented the pastor on his multicolored plaid socks, saying he looked "cool" on that hot summer night. The socks were a gift from his daughters, and as a dutiful father he was obligated to wear them. She went home, and the pastor went to Bible study. Less than an hour later, Emanuel member Willi Glee called Alston to say he heard there had been a shooting at the church. "I didn't believe it," Alston says. "I said, 'You mean outside the church?' He said, 'Polly Sheppard called me from the scene, hysterical, saying someone had shot up the church and killed the pastor.'"[48]

Rev. Pinckney undoubtedly affected his flock in a myriad of ways— from enticing Alston to become a more active member of the church to sharing his vision of Emanuel's future with Dudley Gregorie. Pinckney asked Alston to be a steward, but Alston replied that he needed to pray about it. "A week later he came to me and asked for my decision," Alston says. "I said, 'I am still praying.' He said, 'I was praying about it, and God told me to tell you to get off your knees and become a steward.' That was three years ago. Since that day I have not missed a Sunday in church, and I have become very active in the church."[49]

Gregorie praised the pastor as a modern-day minister who adeptly used technology, his smartphone and iPad, to juggle the demands of church and state. They shared a friendship and late-night phone calls to discuss the politics of the church and their shared experiences as elected officials. "I treated him like a son," said sixty-six-year-old Gregorie of the pastor who was twenty years his junior, noting Pinckney possessed a keen sense of big projects that would produce income for the church. One involved the proposed relocation of the two buildings adjacent to the church to make room for a boutique hotel that would not only serve the church's short-term housing needs but also would be open to tourists. The black-owned funeral home across the street had already been sold and converted to a boutique hotel.[50]

We can only imagine what Jennifer Pinckney has battled with since June 17, 2015. A Charleston psychiatrist speculates she is dealing with survivor's guilt, the trauma of hearing the gunfire and not knowing what was going on, and feelings of helplessness. "Through post-traumatic stress she is reliving the event, and then overlaid on that is anger that [her husband] left her alone to rear two children," the psychiatrist says. "So she has a lot of emotions, and she has the emotion of being abandoned, and then she has the emotion of being overwhelmed. She has the role to take over the family, and people are expecting her to carry on [Clementa's] legacy."[51]

A lasting and meaningful marriage is built between two loving people who are not merely husband and wife but share a deeper relationship built on friendship and strengthened by mutual pursuits. In a touching letter to her husband, which was included in his eulogistic service program, Jennifer referred to her spouse as "Ta." She spoke from her heart to not only her husband but also to Clementa, her "soul mate, confidant and friend."[52]

Earlier that day they had spent quality time together before the unthinkable occurred. Upon reflection Jennifer is grateful to God that he gave her and Clementa time together. "I do not know how to think about moving forward, but I know I must! I have tried to be strong for the girls, but this is so hard for all of us!"[53] In her final letter she wrote of her husband's promises to never leave her; that they'd be together for years;

together they would watch their children grow, marry, and have children; and in Jennifer's and Clementa's latter years, they would be together without the demands of the church or the state. Now she feels "robbed, cheated, and cut short" and angry that their children will mature without their father, and he will not see them grow. Clementa, their hero, is now their angel. Jennifer is thankful, however, that his life was not in vain. Through his example he taught his family to trust God. "We will believe that God will make a way for us! We believe that God used you to be a beacon of hope to transform our family, the Church, the State and our world."[54] That is Pinckney's mission. "I want him to smile down on us. I want him to be proud. I want to carry on his work," she said. Pinckney has formed a foundation in her husband's name to continue his campaign to upgrade public education and access to health care.[55]

When Jennifer and her girls look skyward, maybe they will see a rainbow through which their angel will inspire them that hope still lives and hear a songbird's melody that love will never die.[56]

TWELVE

WHAT IS FORGIVENESS?

All of the seats in the courtroom were taken by the time *Post and Courier* reporter Andrew Knapp stood in the doorway to observe a bond hearing for accused killer Dylann Roof. As a seasoned journalist who delves into public safety issues for Charleston's daily newspaper, Knapp has reported big stories before, but the words he was about to hear were shocking yet powerful—and for a moment unbelievable. Knapp checked himself to make sure that the words he was hearing were indeed being spoken. Family members of those who'd had their loved ones snatched from them just two days before spoke directly to Roof—who only heard their voices—as they said they forgave him for his alleged crime.[1]

Roof stood in front of two county sheriff's deputies in a nearby room at the county jail. On the television screen Roof could see the bond hearing judge but not the people in the packed courtroom. The courtroom audience could see Roof on a television screen, and Knapp watched Roof's face closely for any sign of emotion, but he showed none. Knapp felt certain that Roof must have felt something inside, but it will remain a mystery, perhaps, until Roof goes on trial for nine counts of murder. Knapp was in awe of what he witnessed as relatives of the victims called "for grace and mercy." Knapp says, "I can't imagine anyone not being affected by it in some way."[2]

There is virtually no precedent in America for what transpired at that bond hearing. The forgiveness expressed by some of the family members astounded everyone who heard them speak. The hearing was broadcast live on television, and almost as soon as the brief hearing was over, the video went viral, and people all over the world heard the trembling voice of Ethel Lance's daughter, Nadine Collier, who was the first person to say, "I forgive you." She was followed by soft-spoken minister Anthony Thompson, whose wife, Myra, had led the Bible study two nights before. He also expressed forgiveness, suggesting that Roof repent, confess, and give his life to Christ so he could change.

Felicia Sanders, who witnessed the massacre and miraculously survived with her granddaughter, followed Thompson. The pain in her voice was raw, but she still ended her statement with the words, "May God have mercy on you." In later statements she described the way she forgave immediately and said it was not a choice. "If you don't [forgive] you're letting evil into your heart. You're the one suffering. You're the one hating. You have to forgive. For you."[3]

Daniel Simmons's granddaughter, Alana, spoke next; her voice was clear and filled with conviction when she said, "Hate won't win." Since then, she has turned this idea into a powerful movement called Hate Won't Win.

DePayne Middleton-Doctor's sister, Bethane Middleton Brown, spoke last. Her voice was trembling yet defiant when she admitted that she was angry, but that her sister had taught the family that love came first—so she forgave Roof and prayed for his soul. In keeping with her sister's belief that theirs was a family that love built, she is now raising DePayne's four beautiful daughters. Since the cameras were on Roof, who remained expressionless throughout the proceedings, the disembodied voices were even more powerful to viewers. The sounds of anguish and the pain seemed even more acute.

There are cynics who assume these extraordinary expressions of forgiveness were only a trip of the tongue when these family members were put on the spot—but if that's true they would have recanted their statements or qualified them somehow. And that is not what has happened. In fact, there seemed to be a higher power at work that Friday morning in June, and it was for all of them a moment of revelation from which they continue to gather strength. Each of them said something distinctly different at the bond hearing, and all the complexities and contradictions that weave their anger and grief into the notion of forgiveness must be considered. This forgiveness is not easy; it is quite the opposite.

But not every family had a representative at the bond hearing, and not all the family members feel the same way about forgiveness. Forgiveness itself is as complex as any human action. These extraordinary expressions of forgiveness do not suggest acceptance, nor do they imply forgive and forget. Although no one spoke from Sharonda Coleman-Singleton's family at the bond hearing, her son, Chris, publicly expressed forgiveness. Chris, a baseball player for Charleston Southern University, spoke on ESPN with journalist Bob Woodward soon after the church massacre. His younger sister, Camryn, told Woodward that she was initially shocked that her brother responded with forgiveness, but she prayed about it and realized that being consumed with hatred was worse.[4]

Does this mean forgiveness is a choice one makes in order to survive the grief? If so, when is that acceptable? According to Cynthia Graham Hurd's brother, Malcolm Graham, forgiveness is possible under certain circumstances. Malcolm was driving to Charleston from his home in Charlotte when he heard the bond hearing unfolding on National Public Radio. "When I heard the first person and second person say, 'I forgive,' I said 'That's the sound bite. The media jumped on it and spread that forgive thing across nine families,' which is not true," he says. "If my sister was walking down the street and she was hit by a distracted driver who was texting and driving and she got killed and the person immediately said, 'Please forgive me; that was not my intent when I woke up this morning' . . . I would be very upset, but forgiveness would come a lot easier."[5]

Nadine Collier's sister, Sharon Risher, is "not there yet." As a pastor, she acknowledges the need for forgiveness as a practice in our society, but she considers it a process with no time limit: "The God I believe in is patting me on the back, saying, 'You take your time.'"[6] Forgiveness for some is a journey, and for everyone affected by this tragedy, this journey is indeterminate and unique. Built into this equation is the fact that we all grieve differently, and no two people experience loss in exactly the same way. Murder may be the hardest kind of death to process, and the emotional response is much more complicated because this unfathomable grief is coupled with anger. In Charleston the media attention has exacerbated the situation; something private became public immediately, in ways that were unexpected and out of one's control.

Ashland Magwood Temoney, DePayne Middleton-Doctor's niece, said as a Christian it is expected of her to forgive, and if she does not do so, it could prevent her from being blessed. "But it is really hard, and at times I am very angry. I am sick of hearing the news or seeing anything about the trial. It reminds me of that night all over again. It infuriates me that she had so much to live for and she had four girls who depended on her."[7]

Some family members who do not forgive readily admit their loved one embodied the principles of forgiveness attributed to Christianity. Nadine Collier stated that she heard her mother's voice when she spoke at the bond hearing, but when Susie Jackson's son, Walter, was asked about forgiveness he said, "Right now all in my heart is anger for him. I doubt if I'll ever forgive him."[8]

Polly Sheppard found that the teachings in the Bible require one to forgive although it took some time for her to forgive Dylann Roof: "With me, forgiveness is a process. I have to think about it. Sometimes I have to have a prodding from God to forgive people for small things. When it comes to something this magnificent, it would be a whole process for me."[9]

What did Jesus say about forgiveness, and what can that teach us about this extraordinary practice? In Matthew 18, Peter asks Jesus how often he should forgive if a member of the church sins against him. "'As many as seven times?' Jesus said to him, 'Not seven times, but, I tell you, seventy-seven times'" (vv. 21–22 NRSV). The response is clearly not about how often one forgives, but the number itself is haunting since Roof fired exactly seventy-seven bullets in the Emanuel Church basement. Christ's words from the cross at Calvary, "Father, forgive them; for they know not what they do" (Luke 23:34 KJV), reverberate across the centuries and have been used by countless people as an example: "Father Forgive" is inscribed on the wall behind the altar at the Coventry Cathedral in England, bombed by the Germans in 1940. It produced the International Centre for Reconciliation, which continues to address conflicts in societies around the world. In 1964, Dr. Martin Luther King Jr., in a sermon he titled "Love and Forgiveness," said, "These sublime words from the lips of our Lord and Master on the cross of Calvary represent love at its best. They represent the magnificent example of the courage to love."[10]

Clementa Pinckney echoed the teachings of King—only two months before Pinckney was killed—during a prayer he offered at a community event called Requiem on Racism, which was held in the sanctuary of Mother Emanuel Church in the wake of the police shooting of the unarmed Walter Scott in North Charleston. His words are particularly haunting when you consider the racist nature of Pinckney's murder: "We know that only love can conquer hate, that only love can bring all together in your name. . . . Together we come to bury racism, to bury bigotry, and to resurrect and revive love, compassion and tenderness. We pray that you would bless and empower all of us who are here to reach and to feel the love and to share the love." [11] Many community leaders spoke that day, including US Representative James Clyburn, and at the end of the event, Pinckney referred to it as a funeral in which they were metaphorically burying racism.

During the weeks following the murder of African American Walter Scott by white policeman Michael Slager, Senator Pinckney worked with his colleagues in the state senate to adopt a bill requiring police to wear body cameras. He gave a short, very moving speech on the Senate floor in May 2015, which ended with an expression of empathy and compassion that foreshadowed the statements of forgiveness made at Roof's bond hearing only one month later: "We have a great opportunity to allow sunshine into this process. . . . Our hearts go out to the Scott family, and our hearts go out to the Slager family because the Lord teaches us to love all, and we pray that over time, that justice be done."[12] (The body cameras bill was passed by the South Carolina General Assembly on June 4, 2015.)

Pinckney's expressions of love and empathy have a long tradition in the AME Church, going back to its founder, Richard Allen, when Allen asked the judge to release the Southern slaveholder who had tried to kidnap him in Philadelphia. At an Emancipation Day Program in the late 1950s, Benjamin Glover, who was severely beaten by the Ku Klux Klan as a young man when he tried to register to vote, stated publicly that despite that incident he had no hatred in his heart for white people, telling his African American audience that they should love the white man.[13] Where does this extraordinary capacity for love and forgiveness come from? South Carolina NAACP leader and AME minister Joseph Darby describes this capacity for forgiveness as a survival or coping skill to survive the horrific conditions during slavery times: "If you have no prospects to escape, you try to figure out how to forgive so that you can move on for your own psychological well-being. I think that's baked into the Southern African American experience. That doesn't mean I absolve you of all responsibilities; it just means I forgive you."[14] "Forgiveness, therefore, is a deep spiritual practice that helps people to survive as they refuse to give in to the anger and hate that they might rightfully feel toward those who have brutalized them for so long. So when the families forgave, they were taking the moral high ground," Dr. Jeremy Rutledge explained in a sermon on the subject at Charleston's Circular Congregational Church. He quoted Dr. Martin Luther King Jr., who once said, "We already have enough burden," and praised the families for turning a legal proceeding into a spiritual teaching.[15]

Renowned theologian James Cone has written extensively about the origins and implications of forgiveness within the African American community. Cone, the father of black liberation theology, was raised in the AME church in Arkansas, and he interprets the African American capacity for forgiveness as a form of resilience and resistance, a way to maintain one's humanity when one's social and political power has been stripped away: "One forgives the oppressor in order to transform anger into something that nourishes the soul."[16] Perhaps this is what Camryn Singleton meant when she spoke with Bob Woodward soon after her mother's murder, when she told him that being consumed with hatred was a worse choice. Perhaps it is what the family members were articulating at the bond hearing. That morning, Bethane Middleton Brown publicly spoke about her anger and her conscious decision to honor her sister's focus on choosing love rather than hate.

Darby explains that everyone who calls himself a Christian should practice forgiveness: "It ought to be hardwired into folks. If you say you're a follower of a Messiah who not only sacrificed his life, but forgave those who killed him, then that means forgiveness, as difficult as it is, has to be hardwired into the proposition."[17]

This approach to adversity brings us back to the story of the crucifixion, so central to all Christian thought. Cone explains the gospel as the way we move beyond the crucifixion by reminding us that God promised to be with us during a tragedy. Forgiveness, according to Cone, comes from this promise and the fact that "tragedy is not the last word."[18] Considered in this light, forgiveness becomes a powerful tool, particularly for the oppressed. It is a deeply spiritual practice and harkens back to the long history of struggle and resistance in the African American community. Cone's book *The Cross and the Lynching Tree* deepens the connection between the suffering experienced by African Americans, particularly in terms of lynching during the Jim Crow years, and the suffering of Christ on the cross. "In the mystery of God's revelation, black Christians believed that just knowing that Jesus went through an experience of suffering in a manner similar to theirs gave them faith that God was with them, even in suffering on lynching trees, just as God was present with Jesus in suffering on the cross."[19] This deep historical connection through suffering is critical in our understanding of forgiveness expressed at the bond hearing. The racist ideology inspired by the white supremacist beliefs that motivated Dylann Roof was no different from the racist ideology avowed by the Ku Klux Klan and others who participated in the lynchings that took place across the United States in the twentieth century.

Cone explores the connection between salvation and the cross and describes the cross as an "opening to the transcendent," particularly for the oppressed, "that transcendence of the spirit that no one can take away, no matter what they do."[20] The cross reminds us that "there is a dimension to life beyond the reach of the oppressor."[21] It takes enormous Christian faith to believe in transcendence, and this is what the world witnessed at the bond hearing—faith in the divine and the love that comes from that faith. With this faith also comes hope and the strength to go on. This hope has nurtured African Americans and provided strength, joy, and solace within the walls of the church for generations. Music, the blues in particular, also provided solace and hope and reminded people that "there was more to life than what one encountered daily in the white man's world."[22] Because the cross is a symbol of salvation, Cone explains, the focus has been on this positive aspect of the story while becoming disconnected from human suffering. This disconnect has led to what some call "cheap grace,"[23] and it has implications for Charleston.

Joseph Darby dislikes the "raging politeness" that characterizes the attitudes in Charleston and claims that it stems from a long-standing need for acceptance by "folks who will do anything but offend the status quo . . . it's about wanting to please people and get along at all costs." Others call it "go along to get along," and Darby says this attitude is worse in Charleston than anywhere else he has seen.[24] Malcolm Graham echoes Darby's sentiments and says the passivity in Charleston's black community is one of the reasons he left the city and never came back. He also explains that this passivity is why there were no riots or anger in the streets after the church killings.[25]

Darby often refers to the dangers of the *kumbaya* moment in Charleston. Many community leaders share his concern. This is not to discount the relief experienced throughout the city and beyond that there were no violent repercussions after the shooting; the unity and peace in Charleston have gone a long way toward healing. The fact that the Confederate flag is off the statehouse grounds is most certainly a hopeful sign, but institutional racism is still blamed for underfunded, poor-performing segregated schools; higher rates of unemployment and imprisonment in the African American population; housing and gentrification issues; unjust voter-ID laws that disproportionately affect African Americans; and so on.

Malcolm Graham agrees with Darby and reminds us that the Confederate flag would still be flying beside the statehouse if not for the murder of his sister and eight other beautiful souls. Mr. Graham worries that "the oversimplification of *I forgive* demonstrates a lack of under-standing of the significance of the incident." Graham admits that he does not fault or challenge anyone's "spiritual walk" or their capacity to forgive within that context. He has said numerous times that he is a forgiving man, but he does not forgive what happened to his sister Cynthia Graham Hurd, which was "premeditated, calculated, cold-blooded murder." He also says, "It was an attack on a race of people and an attack on humanity; it was an attack on the Christian church. Whether you're Baptist, Jewish, or Muslim, you should be extremely upset. There's no forgiveness for racism . . . it's just stupid. It's hate, pure hate. I don't forgive . . . That doesn't mean I'm not a forgiving spirit."[26]

A week after the church shooting, African American writer Roxane Gay began her op-ed piece in the *New York Times* saying, "I do not forgive Dylann Roof, a racist terrorist whose name I hate saying or knowing. I have no immediate connection to what happened in Charleston, S.C., last week beyond my humanity and my blackness, but I do not foresee ever forgiving his crimes, and I am wholly at ease with that choice."[27] Gay repeated the line of the Lord's Prayer: "Forgive us our trespasses as we forgive those who trespass against us," and she wondered if there are limits to this forgiveness, especially for those sins that fall outside of our own behavior. Her question, which most certainly is one many were asking at the time, is in keeping with Senator Graham's feelings about the nature of the crime committed at Emanuel Church. Gay also bemoaned the fact that African Americans are expected to forgive "in order to survive" the litany of racist practices that continue in America: "We forgive and forgive and forgive and those who trespass against us continue to trespass against us."[28]

Malcolm Graham is not alone among family members in his inability to forgive, and the facile way it has been interpreted by some members of the press is disturbing. There's a way that it seems to wash over the excruciating grief Senator Graham and other relatives and friends are enduring. DePayne Middleton-Doctor's cousin, Waltrina Middleton, is upset about the way the statements of forgiveness were immediately used to interpret the larger meaning of what happened at Emanuel Church: it "took away our narrative to be rightfully hurt. I can't turn off my pain."[29]

The grief among these families is bottomless, and within the small Emanuel family there are some who attended every funeral. It is difficult for most of us to imagine losing a loved one in this manner, and it is equally difficult to imagine losing nine friends in one day. And every mass shooting brings up memories of what happened to their loved ones. Both Nadine Collier and Malcolm Graham expressed anguish when they heard about the terrorist attacks in Paris five months after losing their loved ones. It brought the horror of their experience back into their lives in an immediate way. Ms. Collier commented, "I don't want to be remembering back. I don't even want to go back."[30] But mass shootings and terrorist attacks have become an inescapable part of our lives, and it is a cruel reality that Ms. Collier and too many others have to relive over and over again.

Less than one month after Paris, when fourteen people were killed at a holiday party in San Bernardino, California, Felicia Sanders told the *Post and Courier* that coping with these mass killings was the hardest part of coping with her own grief over losing her son and aunt under similar circumstances. She told reporters she prayed for all victims and their families. "My heart bleeds," she said in her Gullah accent. "I can relate, because not that long ago I been that person."[31]

Despite the implications of the expressions of forgiveness expressed at the bond hearing, the power of the words transcends the negative connotations. Those who spoke at the hearing did not plan what they would say, nor did they coordinate their efforts among themselves. It is simply what happened. Anthony Thompson didn't even want to go the bond hearing, but "the kids" (Kevin, Denise, and Anthony) talked him into attending. Before he became a minister in the Reformed Episcopal Church in 1995, Thompson worked for twenty-seven years as a probation officer for the state of South Carolina. During that time, he never carried a gun. He'd always had a thing about guns and didn't see the need for one. "I was more effective than if I had carried a gun," he explains. "My clients respected me so much more."[32]

He had been to many bond hearings in his lifetime, and he assumed this one would be procedural like the others. He didn't know he would have the opportunity to speak—and he even told his family that none of them should say a thing. But when the judge asked him if he would like to speak, Thompson heard a voice speaking to him—the same voice he had heard when he was only five years old, chasing and kicking at leaves in the Piggly Wiggly parking lot in downtown Charleston; the voice that told him he would preach one day. "The same voice said, 'I've got something to say, and this is what I want you to tell them.' And he told me exactly what to tell them. God told me exactly what to say because I didn't even want to be there. I wasn't even thinking about Dylann Roof. I'm still thinking about my wife and what had happened. Did she suffer? I said exactly what he told me—no more and no less. I knew where to begin, and I knew where to end. Because he told me. That was it."[33]

Thompson was calm throughout; he never raised his voice during the bond hearing, and he spoke in complete sentences: "I forgive you, and my family forgives you, but we would like you to take this opportunity to repent. Repent, and pass, give your life to the one who matters most, Christ. So he can change it, and change your ways, no matter what happens to you."[34]

Whatever we may believe, the power of the families' statements is larger than them. Their strength seemed to come from somewhere else, and who can say where faith resides? Their words touched something deep inside each of us. Thompson says that as soon as he spoke, he began to experience peace: "When I sat down, I was a different person. I wasn't that person thinking like when I came in there, 'What happened to my wife?' No more. I said, 'God, you've got her; you gave me my peace this morning.' I knew where to go from there. I still just don't know exactly what to do, but I knew not to dwell on the tragedy anymore. And I never dwell on Dylann Roof for one minute, for one second."[35]

According to Dr. Don Flowers Jr., pastor of Providence Baptist

Church on Daniel Island, South Carolina, Thompson's extraordinary statement embodies the connection between forgiveness and healing. He reminded us of the Lord's Prayer and its instructions about forgiving our trespasses the same way "we forgive those who trespass against us."[36] He explained this practice in the words of renowned theologian Lewis Smedes, whose book *Forgive and Forget* explores the spiritual dimensions of forgiveness in great depth: "'When you forgive someone, you slice away the wrong from the person who did it. You disengage the person from his harmful act. You re-create him. At one moment, you change that identity. He is remade in your memory.'"[37] This process is exactly what Thompson expressed about his experience after speaking at the bond hearing. Flowers also explained that the forgiveness expressed by the families "wasn't a sign of weakness, a sign of resignation. Rather it may be the most powerful thing they could do as they remake the future."[38] And remaking the future is exactly what they are doing.

Thompson says his statement was "a God thing. He had a bigger plan, and I was just a small portion of his plan."[39] He couldn't know at the time that the peace he felt would be experienced by others. Some call it grace, and this is what President Obama emphasized in his moving eulogy for Clementa Pinckney, which some say is his greatest speech. The president reminded us that grace comes unbidden: "We don't earn grace. We're all sinners. We don't deserve it. But God gives it to us anyway. And we choose how to receive it. It's our decision how to honor it. . . . Amazing grace."[40] The president went on to refer to the power of grace, the goodness at its root, and its power to effect change. And then he did something that surprised and delighted everyone: he sang the hymn "Amazing Grace." How powerful and how fitting, given the song's origins. Ironically, this hymn was written by an English former slave trader named John Newton; even more ironic is the fact that his slave ships brought captured Africans to Charleston, South Carolina. According to legend, Newton found his faith during a particularly rough storm in

1748. Fourteen years later he was ordained as an Anglican priest, and he wrote the words for "Amazing Grace" in 1772. It is worth noting that Newton also wrote a widely circulated pamphlet called "Thoughts upon a Slave Trade," which outlines the horrific conditions on the slave ships and publicly apologizes for his work as a slave trader.

President Obama focused on grace itself, and that is what most people consider when they hear or sing the famous hymn. But the idea of redemption and finding salvation—which permeates the later life of John Newton and the words to the hymn—is the part of Anthony Thompson's statement at the bond hearing that deepens our understanding of forgiveness in terms of Christianity. Daniel Simmons's daughter, Rose, says she speaks on behalf of her family when she says that she believes in the possibility of salvation for her father's killer, and she is against seeking the death penalty for Dylann Roof. She thinks that he has the "'opportunity for repentance . . . so that he can change other people's lives. And what a great ending to this story that would be—for him to know beyond a shadow of a doubt the impact of what he did, and to know and see God himself.'"[41]

President Obama's emphasis on grace and the words from the beloved hymn—"amazing grace . . . that saved a wretch like me," words written by a man hundreds of years ago whose early ideology probably didn't differ from Dylann Roof's racist beliefs—reinforces the hopes of Anthony Thompson and Rose Simmons. The president reminded us of the Christian definition of grace: "the free and benevolent favor of God as manifested in the salvation of sinners and the bestowal of blessings. Grace. . . . If we can find that grace, anything is possible. If we can tap that grace, everything can change. Amazing grace. Amazing grace . . .

"Clementa Pinckney found that grace.

"Cynthia Hurd found that grace.

"Susie Jackson found that grace.

"Ethel Lance found that grace.

"DePayne Middleton-Doctor found that grace.

"Tywanza Sanders found that grace.

"Daniel L. Simmons Sr. found that grace.

"Sharonda Coleman-Singleton found that grace.

"Myra Thompson found that grace.

"Through the example of their lives, they've now passed it on to us. May we find ourselves worthy of that precious and extraordinary gift as long as our lives endure. May grace now lead them home. May God continue to shed His grace on the United States of America."[42]

Amen.

THIRTEEN

THE UNFINISHED STORY

In his eulogy for Clementa Pinckney, President Obama addressed the challenges that lay ahead for Charleston, South Carolina, and the rest of the nation. He reminded us of our conflicted past in terms of race relations and the moral choices we must make to honor Pinckney's memory and life's work. He said, "That is how we express God's grace," and added, "it would be a betrayal of everything Pinckney stood for" if we do not follow through. The president warned that the country should not slip into a comfortable silence again. "That's what we so often do to avoid uncomfortable truths about the prejudice that still infects our society," he said. "To settle for symbolic gestures without following up with the hard work of more lasting change—that's how we lose our way again."[1]

President Obama described the deplorable conditions that characterize large sections of the "Corridor of Shame"—that part of the state that Pinckney represented in the South Carolina Senate. Poverty undermines a myriad of problems in Jasper County, from failing, dilapidated schools and limited employment opportunities to high rates of incarceration and infant mortality. Senator Pinckney fought hard to improve conditions for the people who lived there. President Obama also spoke about voting rights, gun violence, and poor police practices—all of these issues disproportionately affecting African Americans. Racism, which permeates our history, clearly continues to flow through America's infrastructure, infiltrating every aspect of daily life. Dylann Roof was a by-product of a racist ideology that seeped out of institutional practices into the mainstream culture and cyberspace with deadly results. The president's eulogy reminded us that Roof's actions meant to create a race war, but it led to the opposite. The unity in the Lowcountry, coupled with the forgiving words spoken at the bond hearing, coalesced into something more powerful and meaningful than anyone could have imagined. The president called it "the power of God's grace."[2] And for those who witnessed it and experienced it, it was an example of "that transcendence of the spirit that no one can take away, no matter what they do."[3]

With this grace comes enormous responsibility, especially when the eyes of the world are watching. President Obama described the "light of love that shone"[4] when Emanuel members opened the side door of their church to let Dylann Roof enter their space for Bible study on June 17, 2015. What a beautiful image and metaphor for these good people who welcomed a stranger into their midst without question, and now people are left holding on to that light. They still feel it every day in Charleston when strangers come to Emanuel Church to offer gifts and condolences and pay tribute to the fallen. They feel it when they gather and march for better wages and an end to the gentrification on the Charleston peninsula that has driven almost a quarter of the African American population to live elsewhere. They feel it when they pray in private or in their houses of worship. And they most certainly felt it when the good people of Thornton Township, Illinois, traveled to Charleston to announce their decision to nominate Mother Emanuel for the 2016 Nobel Peace Prize.

⁂

On Wednesday, September 16, 2015, a delegation of township officials, pastors, and citizens traveled to Charleston to meet with city officials and the leadership at Mother Emanuel to formally announce the nomination. It was part of their "Faith, Dignity, and Respect Initiative." Their goal is to learn about healing from the Charleston community and the church. They also hoped to create a safety plan for the seventeen municipalities in their township in case they ever experience a similar crisis. Frank Zuccarelli, president of the board of Thornton Township, said the nomination was inspired by the events in Charleston in the aftermath of the church shooting. It was something that deserved international acclaim and recognition. He said the community support and the strength of Mother Emanuel's church members embodies the idea behind the Nobel Peace Prize.[5] Their hope was to gather at least one million signatures on a petition in order to make the nomination possible.[6] It was also a way for the group to get permission from the church to move forward with the nomination. The gesture was publicly supported by Rev. Dr. Norvel Goff, Emanuel's interim pastor and presiding elder of the AME Edisto District. "We embrace the idea of moving forward with the Nobel Peace Prize, because it's not one that is sought by just a few," Goff said. "It's an acknowledgment that only God could have moved in such a miraculous way to allow us to stand on solid ground."[7]

The light that President Obama described is most certainly embodied by the citizens of Thornton Township. But light itself is intangible and unquantifiable. And how is it maintained and transformed into something tangible and lasting? A Nobel Peace Prize would most certainly help spread that light, but countless numbers of African Americans are looking for more immediate changes in their lives. Although the church shootings brought the horrors of racism to the surface in ways no one

could have imagined, it's not as if people were unaware of the racist ideology that flourished in the underbelly of America. People like Clementa
Pinckney, in Charleston and elsewhere, are working hard to correct
the systemic wrongs that disproportionately affect the lives of African
Americans. Many of them are members of the clergy. And it was the
clergy, along with city and state leaders, who held Charleston together
during its hour of greatest need.

When President Obama eulogized Rev. Pinckney, he reminded us
that Pinckney "was the progeny of a long line of the faithful—a family
of preachers who spread God's word, a family of protesters who sowed
change to expand voting rights and desegregate the South." The president
went on to quote Pinckney about his approach to his ministry, which
is intrinsic to the AME Church: "Our calling . . . is not just within the
walls of the congregation, but . . . the life of the community in which our
congregation resides."[8]

Pinckney's friend and colleague, Sen. Marlon Kimpson, explains
that "Clementa Pinckney's legislative duties were really second to his
pastoral obligations. He did a lot of his work through the church, which
included helping his constituents. This was first and foremost."[9]

Putting faith into action is the mission of the Charleston Area Justice
Ministry (CAJM), a multiracial interfaith organization composed of
many different congregations committed to social justice in the community. Through its focus on empowering marginalized people and
alleviating poverty and injustice in targeted ways, CAJM holds public
officials accountable for helping to solve the socioeconomic issues that
disproportionately affect minority populations. The central figures in
terms of leadership are Dr. Jeremy Rutledge of Circular Congregational
Church, which has a largely white congregation and was first established
in the 1600s; Rabbi Stephanie Alexander at Charleston's Kahal Kadosh
Beth Elohim Synagogue, which is the fourth oldest Jewish congregation
in the country; and Nelson B. Rivers III, pastor of Charity Missionary

Baptist Church, a predominantly African American church in North Charleston. Rivers is also a leader in Al Sharpton's National Action Network. These three extraordinary people became friends through their work in the Justice Ministry, and they, with members of their congregations, traveled together during the third week of June on the "Freedom Road Tour," a civil rights road trip through the South sponsored by Charity Missionary Baptist Church.

Starting in Atlanta, the group visited Ebenezer Baptist Church, where Martin Luther King Jr. delivered his first sermon in 1947, and afterward visited the iconic Edmund Pettus Bridge, site of the 1960s voting rights movement in Selma, Alabama. The group moved on to Jackson, Mississippi, home to civil rights activist Medgar Evers, who was shot to death in his driveway by white supremacist Byron de la Beckwith in 1963; they then proceeded to Philadelphia, Mississippi, where civil rights activists James Chaney, Andrew Goodman, and Michael Schwerner were murdered by the Ku Klux Klan in 1964.

They spent Wednesday, June 17, in Memphis, touring the National Civil Rights Museum. After supper the group's two buses headed out. Rivers was in one of the buses with the teenagers. On the second bus, Rutledge and Alexander were sitting near each other toward the front of the dimly lit coach. It was late, after ten o'clock, as they talked about visiting the Lorraine Motel, where Martin Luther King was assassinated. "All of that history seemed so recent; it's so close, you can feel it," Rutledge later explained. "And there was a lot of talk already on the bus about the blurring of the lines between that story and our story and the old black-and-white photos and the in-color experience of all being together and trying to be part of this story."[10]

Then the news of the shootings in Charleston pierced their reality through the cell phone of one of the travelers seated at the rear of the bus carrying Rivers and the teenagers. A stunning and chilling announcement was made, followed by prayers. After someone saw a Facebook post, Rivers called his wife, who was on the other bus. She had been on the phone to her sister, who had called Polly Sheppard, who said, "They're gone." At first Mrs. Rivers didn't understand the meaning of Sheppard's words, and then the terrible truth sank in.

Cell phones began to light up with calls and texts, especially Nelson Rivers's phone. His wife grew up in Emanuel Church, and the couple was married there. Their daughter was also married there on June 17, 2000. Like many on the bus that night, Rivers had a lot of friends at that church, and calls began coming directly from Mother Emanuel members. Soon they heard that Pinckney was one of the victims. They stopped at a rest area, and the three friends booked airplane tickets from their phones and iPads for a quick return to Charleston. The buses arrived at Jackson, Mississippi, a few hours after midnight, and hours later the ministers flew home.[11]

Less than a day after visiting the Lorraine Motel, they were leading others in prayer vigils on the streets of Charleston. Rutledge described the emotion that "it really did feel like this is just one story, and there was no difference between what happened in Memphis decades ago and what was happening in Charleston. Do people always not know that they're the story, that they're in it? Do they understand the present quality of history?"[12] Rutledge certainly does, and so do his friends Rabbi Alexander and Rev. Rivers. Through their existing relationships with the CAJM, it wasn't difficult for them to jointly arrange a prayer vigil at the College of Charleston's TD Arena two days after the shooting. In fact, everyone on the stage that night knew one another. Rivers and Charleston mayor Joseph Riley had been friends for thirty years. They were able to quickly organize an event that brought the community together for prayer and solace.

The future of Charleston depends on the strength of these critical relationships among the clergy because leadership is always required at critical moments. Rutledge, Rivers, and Alexander have emerged as strong leaders and have been seen at almost every event of importance that has occurred in the months following the church shooting. Their ability to lead is a much-needed blessing for this wounded community called the Holy City. Rutledge, Rivers, and Alexander have spoken at many events ranging from a press conference at Mother Emanuel for Gun Sense South Carolina, to joining the initiative of the Conference of Black Churches to foster racial reconciliation, an initiative that includes white churches.

The list of events and activities is seemingly endless, but there's a list, and that is what truly matters. And with all this activity comes the hope that Charleston could become a model of racial reconciliation. With each positive event, starting with the early vigils on Calhoun Street and the walk across the Ravenel Bridge, one or another asks how to keep the unity and love flowing across the divide of race and money. The more pressing question for many African Americans and citizens of goodwill is how to turn the removal of the Confederate flag from the statehouse grounds into action. The flag was a symbol of racist policies that remained in place after its removal.

Senator Kimpson's plan is to begin with the folks in the South Carolina House and Senate who voted in favor of the body-camera bill as well as the removal of the Confederate flag, because he believes this group of legislators were sensitive to the murders of the Emanuel Nine and the murder of Walter Scott. Many of them come from very conservative districts, and some of them received vicious hate mail from their constituents when they cast their votes. "They put aside in their hearts any preconceived notions to move this state forward. That coalition is the blueprint for a vote on expanding Medicaid, a vote for fully funded early childhood education, and Pinckney's passion was about children and education," Senator Kimpson says. He also believes economic empowerment needs to be the cornerstone of future action, and his goal is to keep pushing for "procurement opportunities" for African Americans in Charleston and the rest of the state.[13]

In early August 2015, the AME national leadership and NAACP national president Cornell William Brooks organized an 860-mile march from Selma, Alabama, to Washington, DC, called the Journey for Justice. The organizers sought to educate Americans about legislative issues, such as voting rights, education, jobs, and gun reform.[14] In each state along the way, they focused on a different issue of particular relevance there. The church shooting in Charleston created a sense of palpable urgency in both organizations.

In South Carolina some of the most pressing issues were on Senator Pinckney's agenda, as he fought hard for Medicaid expansion for uninsured South Carolinians. He was particularly concerned about the state's refusal to accept federal funding under the Affordable Care Act because so many South Carolinians are without medical insurance. In Jasper County, which was his home district, about one in four people did not have coverage in 2013.[15] Pinckney cared deeply about the issue and spoke often about it, trying to persuade others in the community and the state legislature to accept the much-needed funding. US Representative James Clyburn spoke to Pinckney about this issue repeatedly: "[He] knew what the [political] realities were, but that didn't mean he didn't have passion to get health care for his constituents."[16] Less than a month after Pinckney was murdered, Clyburn called for expanding Medicaid funding in South Carolina. He said that it would be more meaningful than removing the Confederate flag from the statehouse grounds, and it would be the best way to memorialize the senator. Clyburn also suggested a Clementa Pinckney Health Care Law, saying, "It's a simple expansion of Medicaid—that's all it is."[17]

About a month after the shootings, Cynthia Graham Hurd's brother published a moving editorial in the *Washington Post*, headlined "My Sister Was Killed in the Charleston Shooting. Removing the Confederate Flag Isn't Nearly Enough." A former North Carolina state senator, Malcolm Graham chastised the hypocrisy of politicians, particularly South

Carolina governor Nikki Haley and US senator Tim Scott, for being part of the political party that supports many of the policies that negatively affect African Americans. "What are they going to do about it?" he questioned. "Are they willing to put their seats on the line to challenge members of their own party and lose standing with many conservative voters they once courted?"[18] More pointedly, he wondered if they would be willing to expand Medicaid funding and support the Affordable Care Act, oppose restrictive voting laws, confront a judicial system in which African Americans are disproportionately imprisoned, and fund predominantly African American schools that go underfunded. "Anybody can be a popular politician," Graham continued. "You just say nothing and do nothing. It's when you speak truth to power—that's when you rise above rhetoric and become a true leader."[19] He ended the editorial with a rallying cry for everyone who was listening: "We can't simply move on. We've got work to do."[20]

Malcolm Graham's concerns are repeated again and again at events in Charleston and in editorials and articles published nationally. Pastor Joseph Darby questions the ability of politicians to change policy, and he describes the aftermath of the shooting as an "opportunity for something else to happen. You've got this vast store of good will, a bunch of folks who want to do something. Some of it is sincere, some of it is guilt driven—people who say, 'I'm not Dylann Roof. He doesn't represent me,' but you have all that, and the time is right to put together some serious conversation that leads, hopefully, to new relationships that open the door to new solutions, hopefully, stuff that influences public policy."[21] So people, such as Darby and Graham, continue to write editorials and show up at events, such as the Public Broadcasting Service's taping of "America After Charleston" or the town hall—subsequently broadcast on the A&E network—hosted by Mother Emanuel Church and moderated by singer Pharrell Williams and journalist Soledad O'Brien, called "Shining a Light, Conversations on Race in America." During the taping, emotions ran high; many had stories to share about run-ins with law enforcement and the ways African Americans are perceived no matter who they are or what they've accomplished.

A&E and PBS were not the only media outlets focused on the aftermath of the church shootings. Numerous feature articles have appeared in the *New Yorker* magazine and the *New York Times*; around Thanksgiving *Time* magazine featured a lengthy cover story headlined "Murder, Race, and Mercy." Almost daily a story appears about the church or the pending trial of the accused murderer, Dylann Roof. Noted documentary filmmaker Ken Burns and historian Henry Louis Gates Jr. traveled to Charleston in December for an evening called "American Fault Line: Race and the American Ideal." Proceeds from it benefited the International African American Museum planned for Charleston. In October, *Glamour* magazine named two shooting survivors, Polly Sheppard and Felicia Sanders, and three relatives of the victims, Nadine Collier, Alana Simmons, and Bethane Middleton-Brown, in its Women of the Year awards.

In Charleston, groups such as Gun Sense South Carolina have been organized around the need for gun safety laws. In January 2016, more than twelve hundred congregations throughout the state joined in a Stand Up Sunday event to honor victims of gun violence and work to reduce the numbers. Myra Thompson's husband, Anthony Thompson, released nine doves in front of Emanuel Church at the group's press conference in early December. State Senator Marlon Kimpson of Charleston, a close friend of Senator Pinckney's, proposed comprehensive gun-control legislation. One of its goals is to close a three-day waiting period that allows some people to purchase a gun before a background check has been completed. Since the tragedy, that waiting period has come to be known as "the Charleston loophole." That rule and mistakes in the background-check system at the federal level allowed Dylann Roof to purchase a gun. Senator Kimpson also called for an assault weapon ban and a permit requirement for all guns.[22] Both Polly Sheppard and Felicia Sanders also made public statements regarding gun control.

The Black Lives Matter organization in Charleston has been active on many fronts. They helped pull together Charleston's Days of Grace march, rally, and conference during the 2015 Labor Day weekend. Hundreds participated, including some of the Emanuel Nine relatives. Many fund-raisers and events have filled Charleston's vibrant arts community with numerous art shows, jazz and classical concerts, and poetry readings. A portrait of Pinckney, commissioned for the Charleston history wall in the hotel lobby at Charleston Place, was unveiled October 12, 2015. The pastor's family and Mayor Riley were present.

Creative input came from around the country. Singers Peter Mulvey, Patty Larkin, Jeff Daniels, Vince Gilbert, and Paula Cole collaborated on a song titled "Take Down Your Flag." A Presbyterian minister from Delaware wrote a hymn, "They Met to Read the Bible," which Presbyterian congregations sang throughout the United States. And the band Coldplay has included a sample of President Obama's rendition of "Amazing Grace" on their album, "A Head Full of Dreams." Chris Martin, Coldplay's lead singer, decided to include it and received permission from the White House "because of the historical significance of what he did and also that song being about, 'I'm lost but now I'm found.'"[23]

The role of history and how it is perceived has come under intense scrutiny. A conference, "Remembering Charleston: Using Historic Sites to Facilitate Dialogue & Racial Healing," was held November 4 and 5, 2015, in Charleston. Since it was widely known that the alleged killer visited many local historic sites—such as Fort Moultrie on Sullivan's Island and Fort Sumter National Monument in Charleston Harbor—the conference was designed to provide knowledge, tools, and resources to facilitate dialogues around race and racism, heritage, and healing, both at the workplace and with visitors. National Park Service employees, local historic sites staff, and members of Emanuel Church were invited.

Speakers included noted historian and coauthor Dr. Bernard Powers Jr., National Book Award–winner Edward Ball, and Michael Allen of the National Park Service, among others.

Allen has been revising interpretations at a number of historical sites in the Charleston area for decades, particularly those that exclude the critical role African Americans have played in the development of Lowcountry culture. He had just started a project coordinating the public's understanding of the Reconstruction period after the Civil War when the church shootings occurred. Now those deaths have amplified the importance of his work.

Fellow Charlestonian Joseph McGill, a descendant of slaves and now a tour guide of restored slave cabins at Magnolia Plantation and Gardens, received national attention for the slave-dwelling project he launched in 2010. The goal of the project is filling what he calls "'a void in preservation' at Southern plantations and beyond."[24] As of late 2015, McGill had slept in more than seventy slave dwellings throughout the country to bring attention to the need to preserve the structures.

Joe Riley, who left office as Charleston's mayor in January after forty years at city hall, remains committed to raising funds to build an International African American Museum in Charleston. His focus on education and historical accuracy is passionate.

※

What has happened at Mother Emanuel AME Church, a place that is now a pilgrimage site visited by people from all over the world? It has changed in many ways, from the police officer at the door every Wednesday night for Bible study and the dozens of people in attendance, to the white faces in the pews on Sundays. What do these kind of changes mean for a congregation still traumatized by the June 17 shooting? According to Darby, "some of the congregation haven't come back. They're going elsewhere.

They say it doesn't feel like home. There's diversity etc., but it's like when you have a death in the family you get visitors; then when the visitors go you get that one-on-one time to heal. They haven't had time to heal; somebody's been hovering over whatever goes on."[25]

The numbers in attendance diminished by autumn 2015, but the church was still a different place in multiple ways. Emanuel has always been a traditional church, and before June 17 they were down to one service on Sunday, often with fewer than one hundred people in attendance. Many members had joined some of the new megachurches in town that have a less traditional approach to worship. According to Emanuel congregant Evelyn Sinkler, "The church has always been a family church—the Rose family, Jacksons, Bennetts—people whose parents and grandparents have been members of the church for as long as they can remember." Sinkler says despite all the new faces in the crowd, few new members have actually joined the church, and in mid-October the crowds had diminished to the point where she could finally sit in her family's pew again.[26] There was some comfort in that ritual though, in general, church leaders and congregants have tried to celebrate the strangers in their midst. Evelyn's brother, Thomas Rose, described it as a blessing. Interim pastor Norvel Goff saw a "cross-generational, cross-racial future for a church that is no longer restricted to its former self."[27]

Goff is known for his inner strength, eloquence, and ability to step in and lead at a time of great need. In June 2015, he was presiding elder with the responsibility of managing thirty different churches in Charleston and areas south of the city. The additional responsibility for the pastoral care of Mother Emanuel was suddenly thrust on his shoulders. Given the circumstances, it was a daunting task. Despite the unprecedented challenges he faced, there were critics.

The two adults who survived the June 17 shooting, Felicia Sanders and Polly Sheppard, no longer attend Emanuel. It is extremely painful for either of them to be in the space where they experienced such horror. Sanders contacted Cress Darwin, pastor of neighboring Second Presbyterian Church, which had graciously broadcast the funeral for her son Tywanza and her aunt Susie Jackson on closed circuit television, since Mother Emanuel could not accommodate the huge crowds for their combined funerals in its sanctuary. Soon they were speaking on the phone daily and meeting once a week. Sanders joined the women's Bible study, and she and her granddaughter attend on Wednesday nights and share a light supper. Sometimes one of her sisters joins her, and sometimes Sheppard comes too. According to Darwin, "This is what she looks forward to all week. It's become a port."[28]

Donations across the board have been extremely generous. The first fund to be established—within days of the shooting—was the City of Charleston's Mother Emanuel Hope Fund, but there are many more, including scholarship and community funds. There is even a GoFundMe project that originated in New York to raise funds to deliver counseling to residents through art therapy. This kind of outpouring of attention and millions of dollars is not something any institution would be prepared for. According to attorney Wilbur Johnson, who represents the church, "It's an unprecedented situation, and when it happens to a church like Emanuel, which doesn't have a large staff, handling all of the mail that's coming in every day can be overwhelming. The church is keenly interested in doing the right thing."[29]

Cynthia Graham Hurd's husband, Arthur Hurd, filed a lawsuit in early October 2015, requesting a complete accounting of all donations made to the church since June 17. On Thanksgiving Day, Emanuel announced plans to begin distribution of the monies that have poured in since the incident: of the $3.4 million donated to the church, $1.5 million would go to the families of the nine victims, as well as the five survivors. The church would keep $1.9 million. Funds will be released as soon as the lawsuit with Arthur Hurd is settled.

Feelings run high when it comes to the issue of these funds. Ethel

Lance's daughter, Nadine Collier, the first to offer forgiveness at Roof's bond hearing, summed up the troubles brewing at Mother Emanuel best in an interview with the *Post and Courier* newspaper three months after her mother's murder. She had returned to the church on August 30, 2015—the first time she had been there since her mother's funeral. Inside the church, she said, "It wasn't the same. Everything was different. I didn't feel that warm welcome, that warm sensation, that happy-go-lucky sense I used to feel," adding, "Emanuel AME Church has prospered from these nine victims. They don't care about the families. That's my opinion."[30]

Others believe there is no wrongdoing on anyone's part. Leon Alston, Emanuel steward pro tempore, said he had no problem with Rev. Goff. Alston has not missed a Bible study session since June 17, and Goff began leading those sessions June 25—as he led the church. Alston offers the following summary of the state of the church in the aftermath of the shootings: "The mission of the church is to become whole again, and in due time it will. Moving forward the church needs to address the issues of the survivors, and comfort and counsel, if possible, the families of the fallen nine members. The church needs a lot of restoration inside and outside. We have structural problems. The visitation is more diverse. People are coming out of curiosity, and they are coming for other reasons, to see where this horrific event happened on June 17. Is it healthy? It is human nature to be curious, to come to worship with the survivors. Because we all are survivors; the entire congregation are survivors." Those who died "were our family," he remembers. "We looked forward to seeing them every Sunday, and they took a Wednesday out of their lives to go and hear and learn about God. So whatever reason it brings [visitors] into the church is good because when they come they have to get something out of it because the same people are coming back."[31]

The city of Charleston has taken steps to memorialize the fallen and remember the survivors. Emanuel trustee and Charleston city councilman

William Dudley Gregorie introduced a resolution in late 2015, to name fifteen elm trees planted in a green space at the newly renovated Gailliard Center as a tribute to the Emanuel Nine, the five survivors, and the Emanuel congregation. A previous resolution introduced by Gregorie was approved—to rename a portion of Calhoun Street the "Mother Emanuel Way Memorial District" between Meeting Street and the Cooper River. "It will always be a visible reminder of the tragedy as long as the building stands," Gregorie says. After the tragedy Gregorie suspended his effort to become Charleston's next mayor to get personally involved in organizing nine funerals and select a site for Pinckney's eulogistic service. Months later, Gregorie held back emotion when he reflected on Charleston's and his church's response to the massacre. It gave Charleston an opportunity to react "in a positive way; for the world to see how little old Mother Emanuel [was] not going to burn and pillage our city [but] protect the Holy City," he says. Gregorie admits that black Charlestonians easily utter the words *Holy City* in the face of slavery's legacy. "It was the Emanuel way that the city didn't react violently," he says.[32]

And the goodness that is brought each day to Emanuel AME Church far outweighs the troubles that have beset it. Volunteers have helped catalog the thousands of letters, cards, paintings, and prayer shawls. More than five hundred teddy bears have been received. "The correspondence alone is enough to fill thirty bankers boxes, and it's growing every day," notes the *Post and Courier*.[33] An entire building on the church property is filled with materials that have been sent or dropped at the church's door. It is a massive archiving project, but volunteers are getting help from the Smithsonian Institution; Charleston Archives, Libraries and Museums Council; and others. Deciding what to save was an issue only two months after the shooting. At that point only dying flowers were thrown away. It turns out sorting and storing artifacts is not unique to Emanuel Church, but the sheer magnitude is a new phenomenon. The *Post and Courier* reports, "While people have left flowers, stones and other personal mementos on graves for centuries, these sorts of public displays of mourning are relatively new. They appeared after the bombings at the Alfred P. Murrah Federal Building in Oklahoma City and at the Boston Marathon, after the massacre at Virginia Tech and the bonfire collapse at Texas A&M University. And some of the largest ones of all sprouted around lower Manhattan in the wake of 9/11."[34]

The church itself has become a sort of tourist destination and a site of pilgrimage. Norvel Goff told the paper that visitors have "energized" the congregation, and that all who visit are welcome. "It's become a touchstone for Charleston. People from around the world are coming to share how their communities have come together in their own way because of how this community came together."[35] Church historian and archivist Liz Alston (Leon Alston's sister-in-law) is continually astounded by the generosity of complete strangers. Whether it's Denzel Washington's wife, members of the Democratic National Committee, or a visiting Egyptian family, the sheer good in people astounds her. Working from home one Saturday in December, organizing various visits to the church that weekend, Alston confessed, "My cynicism is at a standstill; my humility is growing."[36] Alston's job is never ending, but she is unflappable. Years of serving on the contentious Charleston County School Board and, prior to that, as a high school principal prepared her for this role at this time.[37] This is the church that Emanuel's new pastor will lead.

On the fourth Sunday in January 2016, Mother Emanuel entered a new era of leadership when the Rev. Dr. Betty Deas Clark was appointed pastor. The Awendaw, South Carolina, native is the first female pastor in Mother Emanuel's history. She had been pastor of the historic Mount Pisgah AME Church in Sumter, South Carolina, founded in 1866.[38] As she looks toward building upon the healing that has begun at Emanuel, Dr. Clark told the congregation, "It's going to take me some time to sit with the people, cry with the people, talk to the people, then talk to God and ask him where do we go from here."[39] During the morning prayer, a female church member thanked God that he had sent a woman to heal the church and repair the brokenness.

In her sermon, "In Times Like These," Dr. Clark admonished the congregation to embrace the changes that have occurred at Emanuel, and that although "the storms of life" will come, "you have to be very sure that you grip the rock" of God's saving grace. The new pastor also encouraged church members to take advantage of Emanuel's free grief counseling services as necessary steps toward healing.[40] Emanuel is a busy place. The crowds at Bible study, however, have thinned, and fire marshals are no longer needed to block the doors on Sundays.

At Christmas 2015, the large basement room where nine beloved parishioners lost their lives was decorated with festive wreaths and garlands. A large, brightly lit tree filled a corner. On Saturday night the women's ministry met for a Christmas dinner. Toward the front of the room was an arrangement of empty chairs covered in white cloth with a rose on each seat—one for each of the women who died there. This is still the church home of Emanuel's congregational family—despite the new faces and the ones they will never see again—and they carry on and find strength in the faith that has brought them through all of life's tribulations. They have witnessed the worst of human behavior, counteracted by the goodwill of thousands of strangers, in a small city by the sea, whose citizens have loved them fiercely and continually. Time has shifted here, and what happens next may be uncertain, but the long history of this church, the slave trade that built Charleston, and the continuing struggle to overcome the shackles of the past is the story of all of us. As President Obama reminded Americans on the day of Clementa Pinckney's eulogistic service, "History can't be a sword to justify injustice, or a shield against progress, but must be a roadway toward a better world."[41] A better world can come from this battered church in the heart of the Holy City.

EPILOGUE

Our time spent with the Emanuel Nine families and those who survived this tragedy has given us an appreciation and deeper respect for their losses. As we have delved into the history of the church and Charleston, we have also marveled at the strength and courage of those who fought to seek social justice in the Holy City. During our research and interviews, we have also paused to reflect on our lives during that time of America's racial history that influenced each of us in different ways and in different regions of this country.

HERB FRAZIER

I was oblivious to the dangers that existed for colored people when my family lived at the Ansonborough Homes and worshiped at Emanuel AME Church. This time spent with my colleagues has reminded me of that and also reinforced my belief that our next generation should not be so naive to think South Carolina has substantially changed for the better just because the Confederate flag is gone from the statehouse.

I have a few fleeting images of a segregated Charleston in the early 1960s, but my grandmother Mable McNeil Frazier and father, Benjamin

Frazier, overly protected me from it and never warned me of the dangers and hatred that existed in the city. If they had done so, I would have understood why the people in the movie theater's balcony were black and why white people did not sunbathe at Atlantic Beach.

I remember a night Emanuel was filled with people dressed in black. Their arms were locked together as one body from the floor to the balcony, swaying side to side and with one voice singing "We Shall Overcome." I knew the gathering was important, but my grandmother did not tell me the reason for it, or maybe she did, and I have forgotten her lesson. Was Martin Luther King Jr. there that night? If so, I witnessed history, but I was too young to know.

My father may have chosen not to tell me much about segregation because of where we lived and shopped and the hospital that served us. The sturdy dwellings with indoor plumbing at Ansonborough Homes was a safe haven where white faces were rarely seen. Daddy was in the navy, so we shopped at the naval base, sat in an integrated waiting area to see a navy doctor, and ate in an integrated cafeteria on the base. My grandchildren enjoy similar situations and even more so. They have a much wider range of experiences with whites, to the extent that I worry they will be vulnerable to bigotry. It is an imperative that I teach them the history of people of African descent and warn them appropriately of the lingering racial hatred in South Carolina.

DR. BERNARD EDWARD POWERS JR.

Many years ago a professor of mine compared the role of the historian to that of the detective. His point was that both had to uncover evidence and assemble a case to demonstrate a point convincingly. As a nineteenth-century historian, my research, writing, and pursuit of evidence heretofore has typically involved people who are long deceased. Even so, after spending so much time reading their letters, personal diaries, and newspaper accounts about them, I begin to develop a feeling of kinship.

This project has been different because of the immediacy of the subject and my own personal immersion in the story as a participant observer. As a lifelong African Methodist, I have long been an admirer of Richard Allen, the denominational founder, for his deep religiosity, commitment to the church, and promotion of the social gospel. I found Allen's living counterpart at Emanuel Church in the person of Reverend Clementa Pinckney, whom I got to know personally and professionally. We shared a common love for history. I remember almost two months to the day before his murder, Rev. Pinckney delivered a speech at Hampton Park to a group of people who had gathered for an ecumenical ceremony commemorating the sesquicentennial of the end of the Civil War. I remember being struck by how generous his remarks were to the Confederate soldiers, but quickly upon reflection I realized this was because of his personality and his Christian witness. There was a level of forgiveness and understanding that few African Americans could have displayed in that situation.

Then several weeks later he was gone. However, his extraordinary display of magnanimity in the park and in other situations where I observed him motivated me to do all that I could to faithfully tell his story and the stories of the other families and the historic church that has been their spiritual sanctuary. Theirs is a most compelling story and as a guardian of at least aspects of that story, I have sometimes felt the special weight of responsibility for its proper telling. I hope I have been true to their story.

MARJORY WENTWORTH

The day we turned in the first draft of our manuscript, I ran into Myra Thompson's husband, Anthony, at the Harris Teeter grocery store downtown. We spoke for a long time and made plans to meet for dinner soon. Charleston is like that; it's really a small town, and when the shootings happened at Emanuel Church in June, everyone here was devastated. Reverend Thompson is one of the most extraordinary human beings I have ever met. And during our interview when he told me that God spoke to him and told him what to say at the bond hearing for his wife's murderer, I felt like God was there in the room with us. Even writing about it now brings me to tears. And there have been a lot of days like that as we wrote this book because of the range of emotions that are part of this story.

After writing these pages, I felt as though I knew them all because I learned so much about their lives and their habits. And I am left with a deeper understanding of what it means to practice one's faith. Lifelong Emanuel Church member Evelyn Sinkler told me that the people in Bible study at her church on June 17 were trying to strengthen their relationship with God, adding, like so many people we have spoken to during this process, "If I had been on the board, I would have been there, too, that night." I now carry her words in my heart. Her statement reminds me how quickly life can change and how so much is out of our control, but our relationship with God is in our hands.

I strongly believe that to be a writer in South Carolina and not write about the African American experience is to be not really here at all. As a poet, my job is to speak for those without a voice. As poet laureate of the state, my ultimate responsibility is to articulate what it means to be a South Carolinian. *We Are Charleston* embodies all these aspects of my writing life, and I hope I have done this story justice.

ACKNOWLEDGMENTS

We wish to thank the friends, family members, and survivors of the church shootings at Mother Emanuel AME Church. They have been generous with their time, and we are forever grateful: former North Carolina state senator Malcolm Graham, Rev. Anthony Thompson, Kim Odom, Michel Hammes, Douglas Henderson, Marvin Stewart, Evelyn Sinkler, Liz Alston, Leon Alston, Willi Glee, Maxine Smith, Rev. Dr. Norvel Goff, Charleston city councilman William Dudley Gregorie, Al Miller, and Charlene Spearen. We also thank Raphael James, Andrew Knapp, Rev. Nelson Rivers III, Rev. Jeremy Rutledge, Rev. Cress Darwin, Rev. Joseph Darby, state senator Marlon Kimpson, Muhiyidin d'Baha, and Phil Noble. The assistance of Lily Birkhimer of the Ohio History Connection and Nicole Joniec of the Library Company of Philadelphia were also indispensable to this project.

We are indebted to our agent, Jeff Kleinman, and his team at Folio Literary Management. He believed in the project from day one and has worked tirelessly on our behalf. We are grateful to our publisher, Matt Baugher; his support and enthusiasm for this project are infectious. Thanks also to our editor, Paula Major, and the marketing team led by Lori Cloud: the marketing manager, Kristi Smith; publicity director, Judy McDonough; and social media guru, Marissa Pellegrino.

ACKNOWLEDGMENTS

Marjory Wentworth wishes to thank Kathie Bennett at Magic Time Literary Publicity for her brilliance and encouragement. The idea for this book started with her. Marjory also wishes to thank Sam Francis, Chad Treado, Todd Harrison, Andy Brack, and Congressman James Clyburn. Special thanks to her dear husband, Peter Wentworth, whose support and faith in her is constant; his love lifts her and holds her through every hour of every day.

Herb Frazier thanks his soul mate and best friend, Adrienne Troy Frazier, for her love and support; and his children, Angela Thomas, Amanda Frazier, and Adrienne Frazier, for their love and understanding that Daddy was "busy." A special thanks goes to mother-in-law Brenda Turner; colleagues Tom and Mary Ann Johnson, Marlene Gray, and the rest of the staff at Magnolia Plantation and Gardens; Dorothy "Dot" Glover, Lish Thompson, and Nic Butler at the Charleston County Library; Christina Butler at the College of Charleston; Georgette Mayo, Curtis Franks, Tori Shaw, Barrye Brown, and Brendan Reardon at the Avery Research Center at the College of Charleston; Kerry Taylor at the Citadel; Gail Glover Faust and Oveta Glover at Mother Emanuel; Charles Francis at the Charleston Police Department; Nancy Wagner at the Charleston County Register of Mesne Conveyance Office; and Tolbert Smalls at the *Charleston Chronicle*.

Dr. Bernard Edward Powers Jr. thanks his parents, Bernard Sr. and Mildred, extraordinary human beings by any measure, whose wonderful examples of lives well-lived are responsible for the man he envisions becoming given time. He could not wish for a better brother than Brian, who always provides a "reality check," frequently alloyed with good humor and encouragement. Lou, Ron, Jordan, and Amari have positively shaped the direction of his life. Finally, through it all, Lorraine, his wife, has tolerated the clutter, stacks of books, and papers that accompany the writing process. She has been a source of inspiration and support; her love keeps him going and aspiring always to become something more.

NOTES

Introduction

1. Henry Louis Gates Jr., "Henry Louis Gates: If Clementa Pinckney Had Lived," Opinion Pages, *New York Times*, June 18, 2015, http://www.nytimes .com/2015/06/19/opinion/henry-louis-gates-if-clementa-pinckney-had -lived.html?_r=1.

2. See CNTraveler.com, "Everybody Loves Charleston: Voted USA's No. 1 City for Third Consecutive Year," *Conde Nast Traveler*, October 15, 2013, http://www.cntraveler.com/stories/2013-10-15/charleston-south-carolina -number-one-city-in-the-united-states; and Sam Spence, "Charleston Ranked #1 by *Travel+Leisure* Readers, Again," *Battery*, July 2, 2014, http:// www.charlestoncitypaper.com/TheBattery/archives/2014/07/02/charleston -ranked-1-by-travelleisure-readers-again.

3. The King Center, "The King Philosophy," http://www.thekingcenter.org /king-philosophy#sub4.

Chapter One: Wrong Church, Wrong People, Wrong Day

1. Allen G. Breed and Tamara Lush, "They Welcomed Him in Fellowship, He Turned on Them in Hate: The Tragedy at Mother Emanuel," Associated Press, June 20, 2015; Fox News, http://www.foxnews.com /us/2015/06/20/welcomed-him-in-fellowship-turned-on-them-in-hate -tragedy-at-mother-emanuel.html.

2. Jennifer Berry Hawes and Doug Pardue, "In an Hour, a Church Changes Forever," *Post and Courier*, June 19, 2015, www.postandcourier.com/article /20150619/PC16/150619306.

3. Jesse James DeConto, "Charleston shooting survivor Jennifer Pinckney: 'I want to carry on (Clementa's) work,'" Religion News Service, February 10, 2016, http://www.religionnews.com/2016/02/10/charleston-shooting -survivor-jennifer-pinckney-want-carry-clementas-work/.

4. Jennifer Berry Hawes, "Emanuel AME Survivors Feel Forgotten as Life Moves Forward," *Post and Courier*, September 8, 2015, http://www .postandcourier.com/article/20150908/PC16/150909382.

5. Andrew Knapp, interview by Herb Frazier, September 17, 2015.

6. Raphael James, interview by Herb Frazier, September 16, 2015.

7. Ibid.

8. Ibid

9. Ibid.

10. Joy Hunter, "Crisis Chaplains Respond Following Emanuel Shootings," Protestant Episcopal Church, Diocese of South Carolina, accessed December 22, 2015, http://www.diosc.com/sys/news-events/reflections -on-emanuel-ame-shootings/680-crisis-chaplains-respond-following -emanuel-shootings.

11. Muhiyidin d'Baha, interview by Marjory Wentworth, August 6, 2015.

12. Steve Reed, "Florist Helps Catch Suspect," Associated Press; *Post and Courier*, June 20, 2015, http://www.postandcourier.com/Assets/pdf /emanuelAme/June20A1.pdf, A8.

13. Nelson Rivers, interview by Marjory Wentworth, December 12, 2015.

14. Notes on the mayor's speech taken and transcribed by Marjory Wentworth.

15. Peter Baker, "After Charleston Shooting, a Sense at the White House of Horror, Loss and Resolve," *New York Times*, June 19, 2015, http://www .nytimes.com/2015/06/19/us/politics/obama-charleston-shooting.html.

16. Rob Groce, "Thomas Ravenel: Politics to Prison to Television—and Back to Politics?" Examiner.com, June 27, 2014, http://www.examiner.com/article /thomas-ravenel-politics-to-prison-to-television-and-back-to-politics.

Chapter Two: Forgiveness

1. Abigail Darlington, "Ethel Lance Remembered as Strong Woman, Mother," *Post and Courier*, June 18, 2015, http://www.postandcourier.com/article /20150618/PC16/150619365.

2. Ibid.

3. Abigail Darlington, "At Funeral for Ethel Lance, Family Says She Is 'Symbol of Love,'" *Post and Courier*, June 25, 2015, http://www .postandcourier.com/article/20150625/PC16/150629585.

4. Adam Parker, "Susie Jackson Remembered for Energy, Faith and Love of Family," *Post and Courier*, June 18, 2015, http://www.postandcourier.com /article/20150618/PC16/150619336/1177/susie-jackson-remembered-for -energy-faith-and-love-of-family.

5. Al Black, interview by Marjory Wentworth, September 15, 2015.

6. Bo Peterson, "Ty Sanders' Dry Humor Made Friends Think, Laugh," *Post and Courier*, June 18, 2015, http://www.postandcourier.com/article/2015 0618/PC16/150619364.

7. Alex Sanz and Russ Bynum, "The Latest on Charleston Shootings: Victims Identified," Associated Press, June 18, 2015, http://kwqc.com/2015/06/18 /the-latest-on-charleston-shooting-suspect-in-church-meeting/.

8. Doug Pardue, "Shooting Victim Depayne Middleton-Doctor Remembered as an Angel," *Post and Courier*, June 18, 2015, http://www.postandcourier .com/article/20150618/PC16/150619356/depayne-middleton-doctor.

9. Nate Scott, "College Baseball Player Gives Inspirational Talk After Mother Killed in Charleston Church Attack," *USA Today*, June 19, 2015, http:// ftw.usatoday.com/2015/06/charleston-church-chris-singleton-sharonda -coleman-singleton.

10. Elizabeth Leland, "Through Tears, Former NC Sen. Malcolm Graham Remembers Loving, 'Beautiful' Sister Killed in Charleston Shooting," *Charlotte Observer*, June 18, 2015, http://www.charlotteobserver.com /news/local/article24842785.html.

11. Mary Catherine Adams, interview by Herb Frazier, November 25, 2015.

12. Jennifer Berry Hawes, "The Rev. Clementa Pinckney," *Post and Courier*, June 21, 2015, http://www.postandcourier.com/article/20150621/PC16 /150629932/1005/null.

13. The *Monitor*'s Editorial Board, "A Black Church's Road to Recovery," *Christian Science Monitor*, June 18, 2015, http://www.csmonitor.com /Commentary/the-monitors-view/2015/0618/A-black-church-s-road-to -recovery.

14. Jennifer Berry Hawes, "Emanuel AME Survivors Feel Forgotten as Life Moves Forward," *Post and Courier*, September 8, 2015, http://www .postandcourier.com/article/20150908/PC16/150909382.

15. In South Carolina only a judge in a higher court, the Circuit Court, can set bond for a defendant charged with murder.

16. Melissa Boughton, "S.C. Supreme Court Replaces Charleston County Chief Magistrate Gosnell," *Post and Courier*, June 24, 2015, http://www .postandcourier.com/article/20150624/PC16/150629644.

17. "Bond Court Hearing for Dylann Roof 6-19-15," YouTube video, 1:04, posted by Charleston County Government, June 19, 2015, https://www .youtube.com/watch?v=3LwqtqdDaO8.

18. Young was later replaced on Roof's defense team by Bill McGuire of Columbia. Pennington is the Ninth Circuit public defender, and McGuire is the chief capital lawyer at the SC Commission on Indigent Defense.

19. "Bond Court Hearing for Dylann Roof 6-19-15," YouTube video, 6:44.

20. David Von Drehle, Jay Newton-Small, and Maya Rhodan, "Murder, Race and Mercy," *Time*, November 23, 2015, 62.

21. Richard Pérez-Peña, and Nikita Stewart, "I Will Never Be Able to Hold Her Again. But I Forgive You," *New York Times*, June 20, 2015, http:// www.nytimes.com/images/2015/06/20/nytfrontpage/scan.pdf.

22. "Bond Court Hearing for Dylann Roof 6-19-15," YouTube video, 10:10.

23. Ibid., 11:25.

24. Marguerite Michel, interview by Herb Frazier, September 9, 2015.

25. Ferrel Greene, interview by Herb Frazier, September 9, 2015.

26. Three congregations, formed in 1818, later became Emanuel Church. An early version of the current church building was erected in 1891.

27. Dr. King was in Charleston in 1963 for marches on King Street. This recollection could possibly be from that summer when he was at the church.

28. Michel, interview.

29. Joseph Tanfani, Timothy M. Phelps, and Richard A. Serrano, "Online Manifesto Linked to Charleston Suspect Dylann Roof Shows Evolving Views on Race," *Los Angeles Times*, June 20, 2015, http://www.latimes .com/nation/la-na-dylann-roof-manifesto-20150620-story.html.

30. Frances Robles and Nikita Stewart, "Dylann Roof's Past Reveals Trouble at Home and School," *New York Times*, July 16, 2015, http://www.nytimes .com/2015/07/17/us/charleston-shooting-dylann-roof-troubled-past.html.

31. Ibid.

32. Barry Paddock and Larry McShane, "Dylann Roof's Affection One Month Before Charleston Shooting Signaled Something Was Wrong to Stepmother: 'Like He Was Telling Me Goodbye,'" *New York Daily News*, June 22, 2015, http://www.nydailynews.com/news/national/dylann-roof -stepmother-hug-signaled-wrong-article-1.2265193.

33. Robles and Stewart, "Dylann Roof's Past Reveals Trouble at Home and School."

34. Ibid.

35. Ibid.

36. Ibid.

37. Ibid.

38. Rob Crilly and Raf Sanchez, "Dylann Roof: The Charleston Shooter's Racist Manifesto," *Telegraph* (UK), June 20, 2015, http://www.telegraph.co.uk/news/worldnews/northamerica/usa/11688675/Dylann-Roof-The-Charleston-killers-racist-manifesto.html; and Francis Robles, "Dylann Roof Photos and a Manifesto Are Posted on Website," *New York Times*, June 20 2015, http://www.nytimes.com/2015/06/21/us/dylann-storm-roof-photos-website-charleston-church-shooting.html.

39. Robles and Stewart, "Dylann Roof's Past Reveals Trouble at Home and School."

40. Ralph Ellis, Greg Botelho, and Ed Payne, "Charleston Church Shooter Hears Victim's Kin Say, 'I Forgive You,'" CNN, June 19, 2015, http://www.cnn.com/2015/06/19/us/charleston-church-shooting-main.

41. Frances Robles, Jason Horowitz, and Shaila Dewan, "Dylann Roof, Suspect in Charleston Shooting, Flew the Flags of White Power," *New York Times*, June 18, 2015, http://www.nytimes.com/2015/06/19/us/on-facebook-dylann-roof-charleston-suspect-wears-symbols-of-white-supremacy.html.

42. Jeremy Borden, Sari Horwitz, and Jerry Markon, "For Accused Killer Dylann Roof, a Life That Had Quietly Drifted off Track," *Washington Post*, June 18, 2015, https://www.washingtonpost.com/politics/accused-killer-in-sc-slayings-described-as-a-quiet-loner/2015/06/18/a4127390-15d0-11e5-89f3-61410da94eb1_story.html.

43. Ryan Parker, "Dylann Roof's Uncle: 'He'll Get No Sympathy from Us,'" *Los Angeles Times*, June 18, 2015, http://www.latimes.com/nation/nationnow/la-na-nn-dylann-roof-uncle-20150618-story.html.

Chapter Three: The Flag Comes Down

1. David Wren and Doug Pardue, "Manifesto Attributed to Dylann Roof Drew Inspiration from Hate Group with Local Tie," *Post and Courier*, June 20, 2015, http://www.postandcourier.com/article/20150620/PC16/150629910.

2. Cynthia Roldan and Schuyler Kropf, "Gov. Nikki Haley Joins Call to Remove Confederate Flag," *Post and Courier*, June 22, 2015, http://www.postandcourier.com/article/20150622/PC1603/150629833.

3. Amy Chozik, "Hillary Clinton Says Confederate Flag 'Shouldn't Fly Anywhere,'" *New York Times*, June 23, 2015, http://www.nytimes.com /2015/06/24/us/politics/hillary-clinton-says-confederate-flag-shouldnt -fly-anywhere.html.

4. Jonathan Martin, "Republicans Tread Carefully in Fight over Confederate Flag," *New York Times*, June 21, 2015, http://www.nytimes.com/2015/06/22 /us/politics/republicans-tread-carefully-in-criticism-of-confederate-flag .html?action=click&pgtype=Homepage&module=a-lede-package-region &region=top-news&WT.nav=top-news.

5. Ibid.

6. Russell Moore, "The Cross and the Confederate Flag," RussellMoore.com, June 19, 2015, http://www.russellmoore.com/2015/06/19/the-cross-and -the-confederate-flag/.

7. Roldan and Kropf, "Gov. Nikki Haley Joins Call to Remove Confederate Flag."

8. Brenda Rindge, "Jenny Horne: She Needed to Get the Flag Debate Back on Track," *Post and Courier*, July 9, 2015, http://www.postandcourier.com /article/20150709/PC16/150709417/1006/horne-x2019-s-emotional-plea -pivotal-to-flag-debate.

9. Nikky Finney, "A New Day Dawns," *State* (Columbia, SC), July 11, 2015, http://www.thestate.com/living/article26928424.html.

Chapter Four: The Sin of Slavery

1. Francis Robles, "Dylann Roof Photos and a Manifesto Are Posted on Website," *New York Times*, June 20 2015, http://www.nytimes.com/2015 /06/21/us/dylann-storm-roof-photos-website-charleston-church-shooting .html.

2. John Smith, *The Generall Historie of Virginia, New England and the Summer Isles* (London: Michael Sparkes, 1624), 126; Charles Hatch, *America's Oldest Legislative Assembly and Its Jamestown Statehouses* (Washington DC: Department of the Interior, 1956).

3. "Slaves and Thralls in the Viking Age," Historical knowledge, National Museum of Denmark, http://en.natmus.dk/historical-knowledge /denmark/prehistoric-period-until-1050-ad/the-viking-age/power-and -aristocracy/slaves-and-thralls/; David Eltis and Stanley L. Engerman eds., *The Cambridge World History of Slavery Volume 3 AD 1420–AD 1804* (Cambridge, UK: Cambridge University, 2011), 275–85.

4. David Brion Davis, *Inhuman Bondage: The Rise and Fall of Slavery in the New World* (New York: Oxford, 2006), 80.

5. David Eltis, "A Brief Overview of the Trans-Atlantic Slave Trade," http://www.slavevoyages.org/assessment/essays#, "The Middle Passage" (accessed January 25, 2016).

6. Timothy Breen and Stephen Innes, *Thyne Owne Ground: Race and Freedom on Virginia's Eastern Shore 1640–1676* (New York: Oxford University, 2004), 4–5; Winthrop Jordan, *White Over Black: American Attitudes toward the Negro 1550–1812* (Chapel Hill, NC: University of North Carolina, 2012), 49–52.

7. Jordan, *White Over Black*, 5–7.

8. Ibid., 20–24.

9. Jennifer Morgan, "Some Could Suckle over Their Shoulder: Male Travelers, Female Bodies, and the Gendering of Racial Ideology, 1500–1770," *William and Mary Quarterly*, 3rd ser., 1 (1997): 183.

10. Ibid., 181, 183, 189.

11. Breen and Innes, *Thyne Owne Ground*, 28, 30.

12. Edmund S. Morgan, *American Slavery American Freedom: The Ordeal of Colonial Virginia* (New York: W. W. Norton, 1975), 329.

13. Ibid., 312.

14. T. H. Breen, "A Changing Labor Force and Race Relations in Virginia 1660–1710," *Journal of Social History*, 1 (1973): 17–18.

15. Peter H. Wood, *Black Majority: Negroes in Colonial South Carolina 1670–1740* (New York: Knopf, 1974), 15–20.

16. Daniel Littlefield, *Rice and Slaves: Ethnicity and the Slave Trade in Colonial South Carolina* (Urbana, IL: University of Illinois, 1991), 76–78, 113; Davis, *Inhuman Bondage*, 137; Ira Berlin, *Many Thousands Gone: The First Two Centuries of Slavery in North America* (Cambridge, MA: Belknap, 1998), 143; Wood, *Black Majority*, 143.

17. Wood, *Black Majority*, 21; Philip Morgan, *Slave Counterpoint: Black Culture in the Eighteenth-Century Chesapeake and Lowcountry* (Chapel Hill, NC: University of North Carolina, 1998), 61; Walter Fraser, *Charleston! Charleston!: The History of a Southern City* (Columbia: University of South Carolina, 1989), 6; James McMillin, *The Final Victims: Foreign Slave Trade to North America, 1783–1810* (Columbia: University of South Carolina, 2004), 110–14.

18. Morgan, *Slave Counterpoint*, 59–61; Wood, *Black Majority*, xiv; Walter Edgar, *South Carolina: A History* (Columbia, SC: University of South Carolina, 1998), 32, 78.

19. A. Leon Higginbotham Jr., *In the Matter of Color: Race & The American Legal Process: The Colonial Period* (New York: Oxford, 1978), 171.

20. Berlin, *Many Thousands Gone*, 55, 181; Ira Berlin, "Time, Space and the Evolution of Afro-American Society on British Mainland North America," *American Historical Review* 1 (1980): 46.

21. William D. Piersen, *Black Yankees: The Development of an Afro-American Subculture in Eighteenth-Century New England* (Amherst, MA: University of Massachusetts, 1988), 18; Berlin, *Many Thousands Gone*, 49.

22. Berlin, "Time, Space and the Evolution," 54, 74–78.

23. Piersen, *Black Yankees*, 122.

24. Ibid., 128–29.

25. Higginbotham, *In the Matter of Color*, 62, 72.

26. Ibid., 124–25.

Chapter Five: Revolutionary Ideas and the Rise of African Methodism

1. "From George Washington to Bryan Fairfax, 20 July 1774," Founders Online, National Archives, last updated December 30, 2015, http://founders.archives.gov/GEWN-02-10-02-0281; "Liberty or Death" speech (text), Patrick Henry Center for Individual Liberty, accessed January 25, 2016, http://www.patrickhenrycenter.com/Speeches.aspx#LIBERTY; "George Washington to George William Fairfax, May 31, 1775," Library of Congress, accessed January 25, 2016, http://www.loc.gov/teachers/classroommaterials/presentationsandactivities/presentations/timeline/amrev/shots/fair.html.

2. John H. Franklin, *From Slavery to Freedom: A History of African Americans* (New York: McGraw-Hill, 1994), 79–81.

3. Carol George, *Segregated Sabbaths: Richard Allen and the Emergence of Independent Black Churches 1760–1840* (New York: Oxford University Press, 1973), 24–25.

4. Richard Allen, *The Life, Experience, and Gospel Labours of the Rt. Rev. Richard Allen* (Philadelphia: Martin & Boden, 1833), 6–7.

5. Richard Newman, *Freedom's Prophet: Bishop Richard Allen, the AME Church, and the Black Founding Fathers* (New York: New York University, 2009), 37; Allen, *The Life, Experience*, 5.

6. Gary Nash, *Forging Freedom: The Formation of Philadelphia's Black Community, 1720–1840* (Cambridge, MA: Harvard, 1991), 110–11.

7. George, *Segregated Sabbaths*, 42.

8. Allen, *The Life, Experience*, 7–8; Dee E. Andrews, *The Methodists and Revolutionary America, 1760–1800* (Princeton, NJ: Princeton University Press, 2000), 127–28; Newman, *Freedom's Prophet*, 42–44.

9. Allen, *The Life, Experience*, 8–12; George, *Segregated Sabbaths*, 30–31.

10. Nash, *Forging Freedom*, 42–43; Andrews, *The Methodists*, 46; "The Pennsylvania Abolition Society," accessed January 25, 2016, http://www .paabolition.org.

11. Allen, *The Life, Experience*, 12–13.

12. Ibid.; Newman, *Freedom's Prophet*, 63–68.

13. George, *Segregated Sabbaths*, 51, 56; Rev. William Douglass, *Annals of the First African Church, in the United States of America* (Philadelphia: King & Baird, 1862), 15, 18–19.

14. Allen, *The Life, Experience*, 16; "About Us," African Episcopal Church of St. Thomas, accessed January 25, 2016, http://www.aecst.org/about.htm; George, *Segregated Sabbaths*, 63.

15. Allen, *The Life, Experience*, 16–18.

16. Ibid., 14, 18–21.

17. Douglass, *Annals of the First African Church*, 12.

18. Christopher Phillips, *Freedom's Port: The African American Community of Baltimore, 1790–1860* (Urbana, IL: University of Illinois, 1997), 117, 125, 128; George, *Segregated Sabbaths*, 56.

19. Phillips, *Freedom's Port*, 129–31.

20. Ibid., 133, 135, 138; "Bethel African Methodist Episcopal Church, Baltimore, Maryland, (1785–)," BlackPast.org, accessed January 25, 2016, http://blackpast.org/aah/bethel-african-methodist-episcopal-church -baltimore-maryland-1785.

21. Phillips, *Freedom's Port*, 134–35.

22. Ibid. At first there were two bishops elected (Allen and Coker), but upon his return Allen, who had been away, objected, thinking it pretentious. They voted again for a single bishop, and Allen was elected. George, *Segregated Sabbaths*, 86; James A. Handy, *Scraps of African Methodist Episcopal History* (Philadelphia: A.M.E. Book Concern, 1902), 32.

23. Allen, *The Life, Experience*, 21.

24. Daniel A. Payne, *History of the African Methodist Episcopal Church* (Nashville: A.M.E. Sunday School Union, 1891), 84; Martha Simmons and Frank A. Thomas eds., *Preaching with Sacred Fire: An Anthology of*

African American Sermons 1750–Present (New York: W. W. Norton, 2010), 109–10; George, *Segregated Sabbaths*, 126.

25. Allen, *The Life, Experience*, 29–42; Newman, *Freedom's Prophet*, 87–88, 94–95.

26. Julie Winch, *Philadelphia's Black Elite: Activism, Accommodation, and the Struggle for Autonomy, 1787–1848* (Philadelphia: Temple University, 1988), 34–35.

27. Paul Finkelman, ed., *Encyclopedia of African American History 1619–1895: From the Colonial Period to the Age of Frederick Douglass*, 3 vols. (New York: Oxford University, 2006), 1:237.

28. Payne, *History of the African Methodist Episcopal Church*, 84, 87.

29. Bernard Powers, "'The Worst of All Barbarisms': Racial Anxiety and the Approach of Secession in the Palmetto State," *South Carolina Historical Magazine* 112 (2011): 139–56.

30. F. A. Mood, *Methodism in Charleston* (Nashville: E. Stevenson & J. E. Evans, 1856), 23, 28, 73, 86–90; Andrews, *The Methodists and Revolutionary America*, 126–27.

31. Mood, *Methodism in Charleston*, 116, 123.

32. Ibid., 130–32; Bernard Powers, *Black Charlestonians: A Social History 1822–1885* (Fayetteville, AR: University of Arkansas, 1994), 20–21.

33. Mood, *Methodism in Charleston*, 132–33; Douglas R. Egerton, *He Shall Go Out Free: The Lives of Denmark Vesey* (Lanham, MD: Rowman & Littlefield, 2005), 110.

34. Powers, *Black Charlestonians*, 21; Peter Hinks, *To Awaken My Afflicted Brethren: David Walker and the Problem of Antebellum Slave Resistance* (University Park, PA: Pennsylvania University, 1997), 26.

35. Vincent Harding, *There Is a River: The Black Struggle for Freedom in America* (New York: Harcourt Brace, 1981), 67.

Chapter Six: The Slave Conspiracy

1. "African Church," *Essex Patriot*, June 27, 1818; *Charleston Courier*, June 9 and 11, 1818.

2. Lionel H. Kennedy and Thomas Parker, *An Official Report of the Trials of Sundry Negroes, Charged with an Attempt to Raise an Insurrection* (Charleston: James R. Schenck, 1822), 42–43; Douglas R. Egerton, *He Shall Go Out Free: The Lives of Denmark Vesey* (Lanham, MD: Rowman & Littlefield, 2005), 77–81.

3. Marina Wikramanayake, *A World in Shadow: The Free Black in Antebellum South Carolina* (Columbia, SC: University of South Carolina, 1989), 60, 63–67.

4. Egerton, *He Shall Go Out Free*, 77; Kennedy and Parker, *An Official Report of the Trials of Sundry Negroes*, 43.

5. Kennedy and Parker, *An Official Report of the Trials of Sundry Negroes*, 19.

6. Ibid., 86.

7. Bernard Powers, *Black Charlestonians: A Social History 1822–1885* (Fayetteville, AR: University of Arkansas, 1994), 30; Kennedy and Parker, *An Official Report*, 17–18, 67.

8. Kennedy and Parker, *An Official Report*, 67, 81–82; David Brion Davis, *Inhuman Bondage: The Rise and Fall of Slavery in the New World* (New York: Oxford University, 2006), 168–69.

9. Kennedy and Parker, *An Official Report*, 18, 82.

10. Ibid., 23.

11. Jennifer Berry Hawes and Doug Pardue, "In an Hour, A Church Changes Forever," *Charleston Post and Courier*, June 19, 2015, http://www .postandcourier.com/article/20150619/PC16/150619306; Alexis Stevens, "Report: Roof Almost Didn't Go Through with Killing S.C. Churchgoers," AJC.com (Atlanta), June 19, 2015, http://ajc.com/news/news/national /report-dylann-roof-confesses-says-he-wanted-to-sta/nmggX/.

12. Egerton, *He Shall Go Out Free*, 139.

13. Ibid., 135.

14. Powers, *Black Charlestonians*, 28; Kennedy and Parker, *An Official Report*, 64, 83, 96.

15. Kennedy and Parker, *An Official Report*, 34–35, 47, 50, 95, 97–98; Powers, *Black Charlestonians*, 32.

16. Hinks, *To Awaken My Afflicted Brethren*, 38; Egerton, *He Shall Go Out Free*, 221.

17. Joseph E. Lowndes, Julie Novkov, and Dorian Warren eds., *Race and American Political Development* (New York: Routledge, 2008), 167–68.

18. Lowndes, Novkov, and Warren, *Race and American Political Development*, 167–68; Walter Fraser, *Charleston! Charleston!: The History of a Southern City* (Columbia: University of South Carolina, 1989), 202–03; Wikramanayake, *A World in Shadow*, 58.

19. W. Jeffrey Bolster, *Black Jacks: African American Seamen in the Age of Sail* (Cambridge, MA: Harvard University, 2009), 194–96.

20. Fraser, *Charleston! Charleston!*, 203–4; Powers, *Black Charlestonians*, 33.

21. "Brief History of the Citadel," the Citadel, accessed January 26, 2016, http://www.citadel.edu/root/brief-history.

22. Ibid.; "History of the Monument," Charleston County Public Library, accessed January 26, 2016, http://ccpl.org/content.asp?id=16261&action =detail&catID=6179&parentID=5908.

23. Robles, "Dylann Roof Photos;" Nick Corasaniti, Richard Pérez-Peña, and Lizette Alvarez, "Church Massacre Suspect Held as Charleston Grieves," *New York Times,* June 19, 2015, http://www.nytimes.com/2015/06/19/us /charleston-church-shooting.html.

24. Jack Hitt, "History Returns to Charleston," *New Yorker,* June 19, 2015, http://www.newyorker.com/news/news-desk/history-returns-to -charleston; for an example of a disparaging characterization of Vesey in the local press, see Jack Leland, "Portrait of a Man: Denmark Vesey," *Charleston Post and Courier,* August 9, 1976.

25. "Denmark Vesey: Freedom Fighter or Terrorist?," *Atlanta Journal- Constitution,* July 11, 2006, History News Network, http://history newsnetwork.org/article/28013; "Deed Prohibits Marion Square Use for Parking," *Charleston News and Courier,* November 20, 1945.

26. Hitt, "History Returns to Charleston;" *Atlanta Journal-Constitution,* "Denmark Vesey;" David Blight, *Race and Reunion: The Civil War in American Memory* (Cambridge, MA: Belknap Press, 2002), 67–71.

27. Hitt, "History Returns to Charleston;" Adam Parker, "Denmark Vesey Monument Unveiled in Hampton Park Before Hundreds," *Post and Courier,* February 15, 2014, http://www.postandcourier.com/article /20140215/PC16/140219534/1177/denmark-vesey-monument-unveiled-in -hampton-park-before-hundreds.

28. Barney Blakeney, "Vesey Monument Unveiled as First to Honor an African American in the Lowcountry," *Chronicle,* February 19, 2014, http://www .charlestonchronicle.net/78500/2152/vesey-monument-unveiled-as-first-to -honor-an-african-american-in-the-lowcountry.

29. Melissa Boughton, "Comfort in the Valley of the Shadow of Death," *Charleston Post and Courier,* July 6, 2015.

30. Howard Bell, *Minutes of the Proceedings of the National Negro Conventions 1830–1864* (New York: Arno Press, 1969), i; Richard Newman, *Freedom's Prophet: Bishop Richard Allen, the AME Church, and the Black Founding Fathers* (New York: New York University, 2009), 264.

31. Earl Ofari, *Let Your Motto Be Resistance: The Life and Thought of Henry Highland Garnet* (Boston: Beacon, 1972), emphasis in the original, 150–51.

32. Steven A. Channing, *Crisis of Fear: Secession in South Carolina* (New York: W. W. Norton, 1970), 39.

33. Edgar, *South Carolina: A History*, 311; Simon Henderson, *Aspects of American History* (London: Routledge, 2009), 66.

Chapter Seven: Resurrection

1. James M. McPherson, *Ordeal by Fire: The Civil War and Reconstruction* (New York: McGraw-Hill, 1992), 624–25.

2. William E. Gienapp ed., *This Fiery Trial: The Speeches and Writings of Abraham Lincoln* (New York: Oxford University, 2002), 150, 184.

3. W. E. B. DuBois, *Black Reconstruction in America 1860–1880* (New York: Atheneum, 1971), 122.

4. Ibid., 122.

5. Charles Joyner, *Down by the Riverside: A South Carolina Slave Community* (Urbana, IL: University of Illinois, 1984), 225; Elizabeth H. Botume, *First Days Amongst the Contrabands* (New York: Arno Press, 1968), 11.

6. "Freedmen's Jubilee," *Charleston Courier*, March 22, 1865.

7. "Fort Sumter: Restoration of the Stars and Stripes," *New York Times*, April 18, 1865, http://www.nytimes.com/1865/04/18/news/fort-sumter-restoration-stars-stripes-solemn-impressive-ceremonies-gen-anderson.html.

8. Drew G. Faust, *This Republic of Suffering: Death and the American Civil War* (New York: Knopf, 2008), xi; Walter Edgar, *South Carolina: A History* (Columbia, SC: University of South Carolina, 1998), 375.

9. John Rhodehamel and Louise Taper, *"Right or Wrong, God Judge Me": The Writings of John Wilkes Booth* (Urbana, IL: University of Illinois, 2000), 9, 15; Eric Foner, *Reconstruction: America's Unfinished Revolution 1863–77* (New York: Harper & Row, 1988), 74–75.

10. Rob Crilly and Raf Sanchez, "Dylann Roof: The Charleston Shooter's Racist Manifesto," *Telegraph* (UK), June 20, 2015, http://www.telegraph.co.uk/news/worldnews/northamerica/usa/11688675/Dylann-Roof-The-Charleston-killers-racist-manifesto.html.

11. "The First Missionaries to the South, from the A.M.E. Church," *Christian Recorder*, May 30, 1863.

12. "Charleston Correspondence," *Christian Recorder*, June 3, 1865.

13. Ibid.

14. "Meeting of the South Carolina Conference," *Christian Recorder*, June 3, 1865.

15. Ibid.; Daniel A. Payne, *History of the African Methodist Episcopal Church* (Nashville: A.M.E. Sunday School Union, 1891), 470.

16. Bernard Powers, "'I Go to Set the Captives Free': The Activism of Richard Harvey Cain, Nationalist Churchman and Reconstruction-Era Leader," in *The Southern Elite and Social Change*, eds. Randy Finley and Thomas A. DeBlack (Fayetteville, AR: University of Arkansas, 2002), 35–36.

17. "The African M.E. Church," *Charleston Courier*, May 31, 1865.

18. Ibid.; John O. Wilson, *Sketch of the Methodist Church in Charleston, S. C., 1785–1887* (Charleston: Lucas, Richardson, 1888), 23.

19. "Charleston Correspondence," *Christian Recorder*, October 14, 1865; Alada Shinault-Small, "Emanuel African Methodist Episcopal Church: Abridged History" (pamphlet, in Dr. Bernard Powers Jr.'s possession).

20. Reginald Hildebrand, *The Times Were Strange and Stirring: Methodist Preachers and the Crisis of Emancipation* (Durham, NC: Duke University, 1995), 59. Additionally, this definition of black nationalism is found in Sterling Stuckey, *The Ideological Origins of Black Nationalism* (Boston: Beacon Press, 1972), 1–2.

21. "Charleston Correspondence," *Christian Recorder*, October 14, 1865.

22. Ibid., "Emanuel Chapel," *Christian Recorder*, April 15, 1875; Shinault-Small, "Emanuel African Methodist Episcopal Church."

23. For examples, see "Information Wanted," *Christian Recorder*, December 9, 1865, April 14, 1866, and April 27, 1867; "Temperance and Religion," *Christian Recorder*, June 8, 1882.

24. Ibid., "Meeting of the South Carolina Conference."

25. Ibid., "Charleston Correspondence," October 14, 1865; "Remember Now Thy Creator in the Days of Thy Youth," *Christian Recorder*, June 29, 1867.

26. "Charleston Correspondence," February 11, 1871; "Emanuel Chapel;" Joel Williamson, *After Slavery: The Negro in South Carolina During Reconstruction, 1861–1877* (Chapel Hill, NC: University of North Carolina, 1965), 190–91; James L. Underwood and W. Lewis Burke, *At Freedom's Door: African American Founding Fathers and Lawyers in Reconstruction South Carolina* (Columbia, SC: University of South Carolina, 2000), 118.

27. "Programme of the Funeral Services of Bishop Richard H. Cain, January 21, '87," *Christian Recorder*, February 3, 1887.

28. Powers, "I Go to Set the Captives Free," 47.

29. Thomas Holt, *Black over White: Negro Political Leadership in South Carolina during Reconstruction* (Urbana, IL: University of Illinois, 1977), 96.

30. Powers, "I Go to Set the Captives Free," 46–47, 50–51.

31. "The General Conference," *Christian Recorder*, May 24, 1888; Powers, *Black Charlestonians*, 123–24.

32. "Civil Rights Ride 2013—Clementa C. Pinckney, SC Senate, Pastor Mother Emanuel A.M.E.," YouTube video, 3:08, from a public address given at Emanuel, posted by Mullikin Law Firm, February 20, 2015, http://www.youtube.com/watch?v=XP35_JVnP6g.

33. Ibid., 11:52.

34. Suzy Khimm, "Clementa Pinckney's Political Ministry: 'Righteous Indignation in the Face of Injustices,'" *New Republic*, June 18, 2015, https://newrepublic.com/article/122077/clementa-pinckneys-faith-fueled-his-politics; Kevin Sack and Gardiner Harris, "President Obama Eulogizes Charleston Pastor as One Who Understood Grace," *New York Times*, June 26, 2015, http://www.nytimes.com/2015/06/27/us/thousands-gather-for-funeral-of-clementa-pinckney-in-charleston.html; Scott Calvert, "Slain Pastor Clementa Pinckney's Mission Suited His Storied Church," *Wall Street Journal*, June 18, 2015, http://www.wsj.com/articles/pastor-state-sen-clementa-pinckney-among-dead-in-charleston-shooting-1434638129; Andy Shain, "Pinckney 'Was The Moral Conscience of the General Assembly,'" *The Buzz (blog)*, June 18, 2015, http://www.thestate.com/news/politics-government/politics-columns-blogs/the-buzz/article24839449.html.

35. "Civil Rights Ride 2013," 1:57.

36. Ibid., 10:31.

37. Susan Millar Williams and Stephen G. Hoffius, *Upheaval in Charleston: Earthquake and Murder on the Eve of Jim Crow* (Athens, GA: University of Georgia, 2011), ix, 127.

38. "The Earthquake," *Christian Recorder*, September 30, 1886.

39. "Charleston in Ruins," *New York Freeman*, September 18, 1886; "The Charleston Disaster," *Christian Recorder*, September 16, 1886.

40. "On the Wing," *Christian Recorder*, September 30 and October 7, 1886.

41. "The Man and the Hour," *Charleston News and Courier*, September 8, 1886; "Charleston Earthquake and Cyclones Collection of Pictures and Clippings 1886–87 (CECCPC)," W. A. Courtney Collection, Charleston Library Society (CLS).

42. "The City Out of Doors," *Charleston News and Courier*, September 7, 1886; "Wiping Out the Traces," *Charleston News and Courier*, September 8, 1886; "Life in the Camps," *Charleston News and Courier*, September 10, 1886; "An Appeal, *Christian Recorder*, October 21, 1886; Williams and Hoffius, *Upheaval*, 110.

43. "The City Out of Doors," *Charleston News and Courier*, September 7, 1886.

44. Williams and Hoffius, *Upheaval*, 92, 105–6, 110; "Suffering Charleston," *New York Freeman*, September 25, 1886.

45. "The Colored Clergy," *Charleston News and Courier*, September 7, 1886; CECCPC, W. A. Courtney Collection.

46. CECCPC, W. A. Courtney Collection; Williams and Hoffius, *Upheaval*, 115.

Chapter Eight: Jim Crow

1. "Mr. Rind Talks," *Charleston Evening Post*, June 10, 1896, NewsLibrary.com, accessed June 30, 2015, transcribed by Dr. Bernard Powers Jr.

2. Ibid.; "'Racist' Spray Painted on John C. Calhoun Statue," WLTX News 19, June 23, 2015, http://www.wltx.com/story/news/2015/06/23 /john-c-calhoun-statue-vandalized/29162911/.

3. Michael Johnson and James Roark, *No Chariot Let Down: Charleston's Free People of Color on the Eve of the Civil War* (Chapel Hill: University of North Carolina, 1984), 7, 128.

4. "Calhoun Unveiled," *Manning Times*, May 4, 1887, Newspapers.com, https://www.newspapers.com/image/68237180/?terms=calhoun; "Sold as Old Metal," *Charleston Evening Post*, August 8, 1896, NewsLibrary.com, accessed June 30, 2015, transcribed by Dr. Bernard Powers Jr.

5. Works Projects Administration, *Slave Narratives: South Carolina Narratives*, vol. 1 of *Slave Narratives: A Folk History of Slavery in the United States, From Interviews with Former Slaves* (Washington, DC: Scholarly Press, 1976), 196.

6. Mamie G. Fields, *Lemon Swamp and Other Places: A Carolina Memoir* (New York: Free Press, 1983), 57.

7. George Tindall, *South Carolina Negroes 1877–1900* (Columbia, SC: University of South Carolina, 2003), 58.

8. Walter Edgar, *South Carolina Encyclopedia* (Columbia, SC: University of South Carolina, 2006), 217; Edmund Drago, *Initiative, Paternalism, and Race Relations: Charleston's Avery Normal Institute* (Athens, GA: University of Georgia, 1990), 116.

9. William Archer, *Through Afro-America: An English Reading of the Race Problem* (New York: E. P. Dutton, 1910), 172–73; Tindall, *South Carolina Negroes*, 88.

10. Tindall, *South Carolina Negroes,* 263–64.

11. "Who was Jim Crow," Jim Crow Museum of Racist Memorabilia, Ferris State University, accessed January 3, 2016, http://www.ferris.edu/news/jimcrow /who.htm; Robert C. Toll, *Blacking Up: The Minstrel Show in Nineteenth Century America* (New York: Oxford University Press, 1974), 75, 88.

12. Tindall, *South Carolina Negroes,* 293.

13. Bernard Powers, *Black Charlestonians: A Social History 1822–1885* (Fayetteville, AR: University of Arkansas, 1994), 264–65.

14. William Archer, *Through Afro-America,* 176; Fields, *Lemon Swamp,* 64–65; Powers, *Black Charlestonians,* 265.

15. Fields, *Lemon Swamp,* 52, 55–58.

16. R. Scott Baker, *Paradoxes of Desegregation: African American Struggles for Educational Equity in Charleston, South Carolina, 1926–1972* (Columbia, SC: University of South Carolina, 2006), 4, 14.

17. Sherman Pyatt, *Burke High School 1894–2006* (Charleston: Arcadia, 2007), 7–8; "Oral History Interview with Eugene C. Hunt, 1980," August 28 and November 4, 1980, http://lcdl.library.cofc.edu/lcdl/catalog/lcdl:23399; and "Oral History Interview with Eugene C. Hunt, 1985," December 4, 1985, http://lcdl.library.cofc.edu/lcdl/catalog/lcdl:23400, Avery Research Center Oral Histories Collection, Lowcountry Digital Library, College of Charleston Addlestone Library.

18. Drago, *Initiative, Paternalism, and Race Relations,* 175–76.

19. Louise Allen, *A Bluestocking in Charleston: The Life and Career of Laura Bragg* (Columbia, SC: University of South Carolina, 2001), 63, 80.

20. Fields, *Lemon Swamp,* 47–48.

21. Tindall, *South Carolina Negroes,* 238–39.

22. Gloria J. Browne-Marshall, *Race, Law, and American Society: 1607–Present* (New York: Routledge, 2013), xxix.

23. Peter Lau, *Democracy Rising: South Carolina and the Fight for Black Equality Since 1865* (Lexington: University of Kentucky, 2006), 50–51.

24. Ibid., 52–53.

25. Ibid., 52.

26. "Negro Teachers Are in Earnest," *State,* March 11, 1910, GenealogyBank .com, accessed July 27, 2015, transcribed by Herb Frazier.

27. Elizabeth R. Bethel, *Promiseland: A Century of Life in a Negro Community* (Philadelphia: Temple University, 1981), 214–18.

28. Ibid.

29. Ibid.

30. Ibid.

31. Ibid.

32. "A.M.E. Conference Here," *News and Courier*, December 20, 1919; "Hundreds Here from All Parts of Country for A.M.E. Councils," *News and Courier*, February 25, 1937.

33. "Negroes Plan Program," *News and Courier*, January 20, 1934.

34. "'Heaven-Bound,' Sunday Night," *News and Courier*, April 15, 1936; "Azalea Festival Events Listed by Steering Committee," *News and Courier*, March 16, 1940.

35. "Mass Meeting at Emanuel Church," *News and Courier*, March 7, 1919; "To Sing 'Heaven Bound,' *News and Courier*, April 23, 1936; "Race Relations Sunday," *News and Courier*, February 9, 1935.

Chapter Nine: Life in the Borough

1. Dr. Frank R. Veal, "Charleston Negro Congregation Believed About 160 Years Old," *News and Courier*, July 17, 1950.

2. Al Dunmore, "Annie and Her Church," *Courier* magazine, February, 23, 1952.

3. Walter Brown, interview by Herb Frazier, October, 8, 2015.

4. Ibid.

5. Ibid.

6. Bernard Powers, *Black Charlestonians: A Social History 1822–1885* (Fayetteville, AR: University of Arkansas, 1994), 127–33.

7. "The Charleston Steam Cotton Mill Now in Operation," *Charleston News and Courier*, December 29, 1882.

8. Ibid.

9. Walter Hill, *Family, Life, and Work Culture: Black Charleston, South Carolina, 1880 to 1910* (doctoral dissertation, University of Maryland College Park, 1989), 82.

10. Ibid.

11. Rev. M. W. Gilbert, "The Negro and the Vesta Mill," *News and Courier*, February 2, 1901.

12. National Register of Historic Places Inventory—Nomination Form, Cigar Factory, http://www.nationalregister.sc.gov/charleston/S10817710113 /S10817710113.pdf, accessed January 21, 2016.

13. "Local Cigar Factory Hires 25 New Workers Each Week," *News and Courier*, June 27, 1931.

14. Marguerite Michel, interview by Herb Frazier, September 9, 2015.

15. William Black, interview by Herb Frazier, October 13, 2015.

16. Lillie Mae Marsh Doster, interviewee, Southern Oral History Program, University of North Carolina Libraries, accessed January 26, 2016, dc.lib .unc.edu/cdm/compoundobject/collection/sohp/id/5770/rec/1.

17. Ibid.

18. Brown, interview.

19. Doster, interviewee, Southern Oral History Program.

20. Richard Field, interview by Herb Frazier, October 28, 2015.

21. Doster, interviewee, Southern Oral History Program.

22. Bo Petersen, "'We Shall Overcome': Civil Rights Anthem Rose to Prominence in Charleston Strike," *Post and Courier*, September 21, 2003.

23. Black, interview.

24. Ibid.

25. Alissa Clare Keller, "'Turning Shambles into Showcases': Herbert A. DeCosta, Jr.'s Role in the Ansonborough Rehabilitation Project in Charleston, South Carolina" (graduate thesis, Clemson University, May 2011), 36–42, http://tigerprints.clemson.edu/cgi/viewcontent.cgi?article =2133&context=all_theses.

26. Historic Charleston Foundation, unpub. notes; Leland, DYKYC, October 21, 1983, Charleston County Public Library, Business District, accessed January 26, 2016, http://www.ccpl.org/content.asp?action=detail&catID =6024&id.

27. Philip Simmons Foundation, Inc., About Philip Simmons, accessed January 26, 2016, http://www.philipsimmons.us/aboutsimmons.html.

28. Keller, "'Turning Shambles into Showcases.'"

29. Ibid., 37.

30. James M. Hutchisson, *DuBose Heyward: A Charleston Gentleman and the World of Porgy and Bess* (Jackson, MS: University Press of Mississippi, 2000), 169.

Chapter Ten: Civil Rights

1. William Roger Witherspoon, *Martin Luther King, Jr.: To the Mountaintop* (Garden City, NY: Doubleday, 1985), 109.

2. "The Charleston Movement," NAACP Report to the Community, undated, Emanuel AME Church archive.

3. John H. Wrighten, speaker at Emancipation Day program, Palmetto Voters Association, Progressive Club, Johns Island, South Carolina, January 3, 1959, tape-recorded program provided by Gail Glover Faust and Oveta Glover, transcribed by Herb Frazier.

4. In 1967, Thurgood Marshall became the first black person appointed to the United States Supreme Court.

5. Walter Fraser, *Charleston! Charleston!: The History of a Southern City* (Columbia: University of South Carolina, 1989), 394.

6. Benjamin Glover, speaker at Emancipation Day program, Palmetto Voters Association, Progressive Club, Johns Island, South Carolina, January 3, 1959, tape-recorded program provided by Gail Glover Faust and Oveta Glover, transcribed by Herb Frazier.

7. Ibid.

8. Robert E. Botsch, "*Briggs v. Elliott* (1954)," University of South Carolina Aiken, accessed January 17, 2016, http://polisci.usca.edu/aasc /briggsvelliott.htm.

9. Walter Edgar, *South Carolina: A History* (Columbia, SC: University of South Carolina, 1998), 523.

10. Ibid., 524.

11. Ibid., 528.

12. Undated petition from the Emanuel AME Church archive.

13. Edgar, *South Carolina: A History*, 527.

14. Fraser, *Charleston! Charleston!*, 405.

15. Ibid., 401.

16. Edmund L. Drago with Marvin Dulaney, *Charleston's Avery Center: From Education and Civil Rights to Preserving the African American Experience* (Charleston, SC: History Press, 2006), 243.

17. Charles Foster in 1966 was the first black student enrolled in the Citadel's Corps of Cadets. Foster graduated from Charles A. Brown High School, which had opened in 1962 across the street from the American Tobacco Company's cigar factory.

18. J. Arthur Brown, presentation on November 5–6, 1982, South Carolina Voices of the Civil Rights Movement (document of video transcript), Avery Research Center for African American History and Culture archive, College of Charleston, transcribed by Herb Frazier.

19. "Negroes Denied School Transfer," *News and Courier*, October 10, 1960.

20. Oveta Glover Faust, interview by Herb Frazier, November 9, 2015.

21. In January 1963, Charleston resident Harvey Gantt, a Burke High School graduate, was the first black student enrolled in Clemson University in Clemson, South Carolina.

22. The eleven students were Millicent Brown, Cassandra Alexander, Eddie Alexander, Gerald Alexander, Ralph Dawson, Jacqueline Ford, Barbara Ford, Gale Ford, Oveta Glover, Clarisse Hines, and Valerie Wright.

23. Faust, interview.

24. Millicent Brown, presentation on November 5–6, 1982, South Carolina Voices of the Civil Rights Movement (document of video transcript), Avery Research Center for African American History and Culture archive, College of Charleston, transcribed by Herb Frazier.

25. Ibid.

26. Faust, interview.

27. Millicent Brown is project director of Somebody Had to Do It: First Children in School Desegregation, established in 2008.

28. James Blake, presentation on November 5–6, 1982, South Carolina Voices of the Civil Rights Movement (document of video transcript), Avery Research Center for African American History and Culture archive, College of Charleston, transcribed by Herb Frazier.

29. Associated Press, "Police Remove Three Negroes from Lunch Counter in Shelby," *Greensboro Record*, February 19, 1960.

30. Associated Press, "14 Negroes Arrested in Charleston Sit-in," *Greensboro Record*, February 12, 1961.

31. Associated Press, "46 Lawyers Ask Wallace to Obey Law" *Evening Star* (Washington DC), June 10, 1963.

32. Associated Press, "Negroes Added to Sales Forces," *Times-Picayune* (New Orleans, LA), May 22, 1962.

33. Harvey Jones, interview by Herb Frazier, October 8, 2015.

34. Ibid.

35. Associated Press, "Speedy Civil Rights Solution Predicted by Vice President," *Evening Star* (Washington, DC), August 16, 1963.

36. Charles Dibble, "Negroes Attempt to Use Burges Pool, Hampton Park," *News and Courier*, July 13, 1963.

37. "Police Arrest Six for Trespassing," *News and Courier*, July 14, 1963.

38. Undated flyer from the Charleston civil rights movement, Emanuel AME Church archive.

39. James Blake, presentation on November 5–6, 1982, South Carolina Voices of the Civil Rights Movement (document of video transcript), Avery Research Center for African American History and Culture archive, College of Charleston, transcribed by Herb Frazier.
40. "5 Local Policemen Hurt in Near Riot," *Charleston Evening Post*, July, 17, 1963.
41. Associated Press, "Troops Sent to Charleston," *Virginian-Pilot* (Norfolk, VA), July 18, 1963.
42. United Press International, "800 Negroes Hold Rally in Charleston," *Marietta (GA) Journal*, July 18, 1963.
43. Associated Press, "Troops Sent to Charleston."
44. Jones, interview.
45. NAACP Report to the Community, undated, Emanuel AME Church archive.
46. Herb Frazier, "Minister, Parks Tied by Legacy," *Post and Courier*, October, 26, 2005.
47. William Black, interview by Herb Frazier, October 13, 2015.
48. Three black students, Robert G. Anderson, Henrie Dobbins Monteith, and James L. Solomon Jr., had been admitted to the University of South Carolina in September 1963: a first for USC.
49. Steve Estes, *Charleston in Black and White: Race and Power in the South after the Civil Rights Movement* (Chapel Hill, NC: University of North Carolina, 2015), 22–23.
50. Ibid., 23–24.
51. Reynard N. Blake Jr., "The Development of Black Leadership and Black Political Participation in Charleston, South Carolina from 1960–1990: Implications for Community Development" (master's thesis, Michigan State University, 1996), in numerous discussions with Herb Frazier.
52. Mary Moultrie, presentation on November 5–6, 1982, South Carolina Voices of the Civil Rights Movement (document of video transcript), Avery Research Center for African American History and Culture archive, College of Charleston, transcribed by Herb Frazier.
53. Herb Frazier, "Workers Fought for Respect," *Post and Courier*, April 17, 1994.
54. Ibid.

Chapter Eleven: People in Service to the Church

1. Andrew Billingsley, *Mighty Like a River: The Black Church and Social Reform* (New York: Oxford University Press, 1999), 135.

2. Ibid., 136.

3. Eric Frazier, "Mama Hilda, Her Interest Made the Difference for Youngsters," *Post and Courier*, December 18, 1994.

4. Leon Alston, interview by Herb Frazier, November 20, 2015.

5. Ruby Martin, interview by Herb Frazier, November 30, 2015.

6. Anthony Thompson, interview by Marjory Wentworth, November 23, 2015.

7. Ibid.

8. Ibid.

9. Ibid.

10. Ibid.

11. Evelyn Sinkler, interview by Marjory Wentworth, September 30, 2015.

12. Ibid.

13. Carrie Kreiswirth, "New *E:60* Exclusive Delivers Powerful Message of Love and Forgiveness in Wake of Charleston Shootings," ESPN *Front Row* (blog), August 2015, http://www.espnfrontrow.com/2015/08/new-e60 -exclusive-delivers-powerful-message-of-love-and-forgiveness-in-wake -of-charleston-shootings/.

14. Lucy McCalmont, "Baseball Game May Have Saved Chris Singleton from Charleston Shooting," *HuffPost Sports*, August 4, 2015, http://www .huffingtonpost.com/entry/chris-singleton-charleston-espn _55c1183de4b0e716be076edb.

15. Interview with Linda Meggett Brown by Herb Frazier, January 16, 2016.

16. At this writing, Gracyn is 23; Kaylin, 18; Hali, 13; and Czana, 11.

17. Brown, interview.

18. Brenda Nelson, interview by Herb Frazier, December 13, 2015.

19. Alex Sanz and Russ Bynum, "The Latest on Charleston Shootings: Victims Identified," Associated Press, June 18, 2015, http://kwqc.com/2015/06/18 /the-latest-on-charleston-shooting-suspect-in-church-meeting/.

20. Ashland Magwood Temoney, interview by Herb Frazier, December 10, 2015.

21. William Dudley Gregorie, interview by Herb Frazier, November 21, 2015.

22. Ibid.

23. Adam Parker, "Susie Jackson Remembered as Family and Church Matriarch," *Post and Courier*, June 27, 2015, http://www.postandcourier.com /article/20150627/PC16/150629358.

24. Sinkler, interview.

25. Abigail Darlington, "Their Love Will Live On," *Post and Courier*, June 26, 2015.

26. Ibid.

27. Sinkler, interview.

28. Bo Peterson, "Poet, Hero Tywanza Sanders Laid to Rest," *Post and Courier*, June 28, 2015, http://www.postandcourier.com/article/20150627/PC16/150629386.

29. Ibid.

30. Charlene Spearen, interview by Marjory Wentworth, November 30, 2015.

31. Ibid.

32. Ibid.

33. Ibid.

34. Tony Bartelme, "In Remembrance, Daniel L. Simmons Sr." (supplement), *Post and Courier*, June 21, 2015, http://www.postandcourier.com/article/20150621/PC16/150629897/1177/daniel-l-simmons-sr.

35. Al Miller, interview by Herb Frazier, October 9, 2015.

36. Ibid.

37. Malcolm Graham, in a text message to Marjory Wentworth, December 4, 2015.

38. Malcolm Graham, "My Sister Was Killed in the Charleston Shooting, Removing the Confederate Flag Isn't Nearly Enough," *Washington Post*, August 12, 2015, https://www.washingtonpost.com/posteverything/wp/2015/08/12/my-sister-was-killed-in-the-charleston-church-shooting-removing-the-confederate-flag-isnt-nearly-enough/.

39. Schuyler Kropf, "In Remembrance, Cynthia Graham Hurd" (supplement), *The Post and Courier*, June 21, 2015.

40. Malcolm Graham, interview by Marjory Wentworth, October 9, 2015.

41. Ibid.

42. Kim Odom's remarks during Cynthia Graham Hurd's funeral, Mother Emanuel AME Church, June 27, 2015, a copy of her remarks given to authors with permission to use.

43. Marvin Stewart, interview by Herb Frazier, November, 17, 2015.

44. Ibid.

45. Jason Horowitz, "Clementa Pinckey's Last Day," *Matter*, June 21, 2015, https://medium.com/matter/clementa-pinckney-s-last-day-6744ba6b23d8#.9rbxwehq9.

46. From the printed eulogistic service program for the Honorable Reverend Clementa Carlos Pinckney, Friday, June 25, 2015, at the College of Charleston's TD Arena, and transcribed by the authors.

47. Alston, interview.

48. Ibid.
49. Ibid.
50. Gregorie, interview.
51. Anonymous Charleston psychiatrist, interview by Herb Frazier, December 10, 2015.
52. Jennifer Benjamin Pinckney's letter to her husband, printed in the program for his eulogistic service, Friday, June 25, 2015, at the College of Charleston's TD Arena, and transcribed by Herb Frazier.
53. Ibid.
54. Ibid.
55. Jesse James DeConto, "Charleston shooting survivor Jennifer Pinckney: 'I want to carry on (Clementa's) work,'" Religion News Service, February 10, 2016, http://www.religionnews.com/2016/02/10/charleston-shooting -survivor-jennifer-pinckney-want-carry-clementas-work/.
56. Jennifer Benjamin Pinckney's letter to her husband.

Chapter Twelve: What Is Forgiveness?

1. Andrew Knapp, interview by Herb Frazier, September 17, 2015.
2. Ibid.
3. David Von Drehle, Jay Newton-Small, and Maya Rhodam, "Murder, Race and Mercy," Time, November 23, 2015.
4. Carrie Kreiswirth, "New E:60 Exclusive Delivers Powerful Message of Love and Forgiveness in Wake of Charleston Shootings," ESPN Front Row (blog), August 2015, http://www.espnfrontrow.com/2015/08/new-e60 -exclusive-delivers-powerful-message-of-love-and-forgiveness-in-wake -of-charleston-shootings/.
5. Malcolm Graham, interview by Marjory Wentworth, October 9, 2015.
6. "Rev. Sharon Risher: I Don't Forgive Him Yet," CNN (video), September 10, 2015, http://www.cnn.com/videos/tv/2015/09/10/exp-the-loneliest -club-rev-risher-survivor-of-charleston-church-shooting.cnn.
7. Ashland Magwood Temoney, interview by Herb Frazier, December 6, 2015.
8. Anthea Butler, "Shooters of color are called 'terrorists' and 'thugs.' Why are white shooters called 'mentally ill'?," June 19, 2015, MaComb Daily, http://www.macombdaily.com/article/MD/20150619/NEWS/150619573.
9. Jennifer Berry Hawes, "Emanuel AME Survivors Feel Forgotten as Life Moves Forward," Post and Courier, September 8, 2015, http://www .postandcourier.com/article/20150908/PC16/150909382.

10. Dr. Martin Luther King Jr., "Love and Forgiveness," American Baptist Convention, Atlantic City, New Jersey, May 5, 1964, http://www .thekingcenter.org/archive/document/love-and-forgiveness.

11. Paul Bowers, "Charleston Shooting Victim Rev. Pinckney's Haunting Prayer at Anti-Racism Event: 'Only Love Can Conquer Hate,'" *Charleston City Paper*, June 18, 2015, http://www.charlestoncitypaper.com/TheBattery /archives/2015/06/18/rev-pinckneys-prayer-at-emanuel-ame-only-love -can-conquer-hate.

12. "Senator Clementa Pinckney," YouTube video, 5:52, from a speech to the South Carolina State Senate, posted by Michael Adams, June 18, 2015, http://www.youtube.com/watch?v=z0fDAKq9FDc.

13. Benjamin Glover was a guest speaker at the Palmetto Voters Association, Progressive Club, Emancipation Day program, January 3, 1959, Johns Island, South Carolina. An audiotape recording of the program was provided to Herb Frazier by Gail Glover Faust and Oveta Glover.

14. Joseph Darby, interview by the authors, November 19, 2015.

15. Jeremy Rutledge, "What Is Forgiveness?," Circular Congregational Church, Charleston, SC, November 8, 2015, transcript of sermon provided to Marjory Wentworth by Jeremy Rutledge.

16. Adam Parker, "Theologian James Cone to Visit Charleston Area," *Post and Courier*, November 11, 2015, http://www.postandcourier.com/article /20151107/PC1204/151109508/1177/theologian-james-cone-to-visit -charleston-area.

17. Darby, interview.

18. Parker, "Theologian James Cone to Visit Charleston Area."

19. James Cone, *The Cross and the Lynching Tree* (New York: Orbis, 2011), 21–22.

20. Ibid., 158.

21. Ibid., 161–62.

22. Ibid., 12.

23. Ibid., xiv–xv.

24. Darby, interview.

25. Graham, interview.

26. Ibid.

27. Roxane Gay, "Why I Can't Forgive Dylann Roof," Opinion Pages, *New York Times*, June 23, 2015, http://www.nytimes.com/2015/06/24/opinion/why-i -cant-forgive-dylann-roof.html.

28. Ibid.

29. Drehle, Newton-Small, and Rhodam, "Murder, Race and Mercy."

30. Jennifer Berry Hawes, "Sense of Loss, Grief Relived by Families," *Post and Courier*, November 21, 2015.

31. Jennifer Berry Hawes, Gavin Jackson, and Christina Elmore, "Charleston Relives Trauma of Gun Violence as S.C. Debate Heats Up," *Post and Courier*, December 4, 2015.

32. Anthony Thompson, interview by Marjory Wentworth, November 23, 2015.

33. Ibid.

34. David W. MacDougall, "I Forgive You," *Post and Courier*, July 4, 2015.

35. Thompson, interview.

36. David MacDougall, "Could You Forgive a Man Accused of Killing Someone You Loved?" *Post and Courier*, July 3, 2015, http://www.postandcourier.com/article/20150703/PC1204/150709816/could-you-forgive-a-man-accused-of-killing-someone-you-loved.

37. Ibid.

38. Ibid.

39. Thompson, interview.

40. "Remarks by the President in Eulogy for the Honorable Reverend Clementa Pinckney," transcription, White House, Office of the Press Secretary, June 26, 2015, https://www.whitehouse.gov/the-press-office/2015/06/26/remarks-president-eulogy-honorable-reverend-clementa-pinckney.

41. Drehle, Newton-Small, and Rhodam, "Murder, Race and Mercy."

42. "Remarks by the President," transcription.

Chapter Thirteen: The Unfinished Story

1. "Remarks by the President in Eulogy for the Honorable Reverend Clementa Pinckney," transcription, White House, Office of the Press Secretary, June 26, 2015, https://www.whitehouse.gov/the-press-office/2015/06/26/remarks-president-eulogy-honorable-reverend-clementa-pinckney.

2. Ibid.

3. James Cone, *The Cross and the Lynching Tree* (New York: Orbis, 2011), 158.

4. "Remarks by the President," transcription.

5. Karina Bolster, "Mother Emanuel Embraces Process for Nobel Peace Prize Nomination," Live 5 News, Frankly Media, September 16, 2015, http://www.live5news.com/story/30050125/mother-emanuel-embraces-process-for-nobel-peace-prize-nomination.

6. Ibid.

7. Ibid.

8. "Remarks by the President," transcription.

9. Marlon Kimpson, interview by Marjory Wentworth, December 17, 2015.

10. Jeremy Rutledge, interview by Marjory Wentworth, December 10, 2015.

11. Nelson Rivers, interview by Marjory Wentworth, December 12, 2015.

12. Rutledge, interview.

13. Kimpson, interview.

14. Melissa Boughton, "NAACP Leader: Join Journey for Justice," *Post and Courier*, August 6, 2015.

15. Lauren Sausser, "Clyburn: Lawmakers Should Remember Sen. Clementa Pinckney by Expanding Medicaid," *Post and Courier*, July 4, 2015, http://www.postandcourier.com/article/20150704/pc16/150709844/1177/clyburn-lawmakers-should-remember-sen-clementa-pinckney-by-expanding-medicaid.

16. Ibid.

17. Ibid.

18. Malcolm Graham, "My Sister was Killed in the Charleston Shooting, Removing the Confederate Flag Isn't Nearly Enough," *Washington Post*, August 12, 2015, http://www.charlotteobserver.com/opinion/op-ed/article30848886.html.

19. Ibid.

20. Ibid.

21. Joseph Darby, interview by the authors, November 19, 2015.

22. "Sen. Marlon Kimpson Pre-Files Comprehensive Gun Reform Package and $15 per hour Minimum Wage Legislation," press release, the website of Senator Marlon Kimpson, accessed January 27, 2016, http://marlonkimpson.com/pre-files/.

23. Abigail Darlington, "Coldplay's New Album Samples Obama Singing 'Amazing Grace' in Charleston," *Post and Courier*, November 23, 2015, http://www.charlestonscene.com/article/20151123/CS/151129732/1007/coldplay-x2019-s-new-album-samples-obama-singing-x201c-amazing-grace-x201d-in-charleston/.

24. Jennifer Schuessler, "A Journey to Enclaves of Slavery in the North," *New York Times*, C21, August 14, 2015; also see earlier version of this article at http://www.nytimes.com/2015/08/14/arts/confronting-slavery-at-long-islands-oldest-estates.html.

25. Darby, interview.

26. Evelyn Sinkler, interview by Marjory Wentworth, October 12, 2015.

27. Richard Fausset, "Open Doors and Lingering Pain at Charleston Church Where 9 Were Killed," *New York Times*, October 19, 2015, http://mobile .nytimes.com/2015/10/19/us/after-shootings-varying-shades-of-recovery -at-charleston-church.html?_r=0.

28. Cress Darwin, interview by Marjory Wentworth, October 15, 2015.

29. Wilbur Johnson, interview by Herb Frazier, December 5, 2015.

30. Jennifer Berry Hawes and Andrew Knapp, "Emanuel AME Victims' Families, Survivors Wait as Loose Ends Hang," *Post and Courier*, September 21, 2015, http://www.postandcourier.com/article/20150921 /PC16/150929951.

31. Leon Alston, interview by Herb Frazier, November 20, 2015.

32. William Dudley Gregorie, interview by Herb Frazier, November 21, 2015.

33. Robert Behre, "Emanuel's Massive, Makeshift Memorial Raises Preservation Questions," *Post and Courier*, August 29, 2015, http://www .postandcourier.com/article/20150829/PC16/150829327/1177/emanuel -x2019-s-massive-makeshift-memorial-raises-preservation-questions.

34. Ibid.

35. Andrew Knapp, "Visiting Emanuel AME, Leaving Expressions of Sympathy Seen as Rite of Passage in Charleston Tourism," *Post and Courier*, August 8, 2015, http://www.postandcourier.com/article/20150808/PC16/150809552 /1177/visiting-emanuel-ame-leaving-expressions-of-sympathy-seen-as-rite -of-passage-in-charleston-tourism.

36. Liz Alston, interview by Marjory Wentworth, December 12, 2015.

37. Ibid.

38. "Betty Deas Clark Named New Pastor and First Female Pastor of Mother Emanuel AME Church; Seeks to Bring Hope, Unity Following Church Massacre," Black Christian News Network One, January 24, 2016, http:// blackchristiannews.com/2016/01/betty-deas-clark-named-new-pastor-and -first-female-pastor-of-emanuel-ame-church-seeks-to-bring-hope-unity -following-church-massacre/.

39. Leonardo Blair, "Charleston AME Church Names Woman as New Pastor for First Time After Fatal Church Shooting," *Christian Post*, January 26, 2016, http://www.christianpost.com/news/charleston-ame-church-names -woman-as-new-pastor-for-first-time-after-fatal-church-shooting-155960/.

40. Notes on the January 31, 2016, service at Emanuel and Dr. Clark's sermon that day were taken by Dr. Bernard Powers Jr.

41. "Remarks by the President," transcription.

ABOUT THE AUTHORS

Herb Frazier has edited and reported for five daily newspapers in the South, including his hometown paper, the *Post and Courier*. In 1990, the South Carolina Press Association named him Journalist of the Year. He has taught news writing as a visiting lecturer at Rhodes University in South Africa. He is a former Michigan Journalism Fellow at the University of Michigan. He is the marketing and public relations manager at Magnolia Plantation and Gardens near Charleston, South Carolina. Frazier is the author of *Behind God's Back: Gullah Memories*. His upcoming book is *Crossing the Sea on a Sacred Song*, the story of the Mende funeral song.

Bernard E. Powers Jr. is professor of history at the College of Charleston, where he teaches United States and African American history. He has been a consultant to historic sites and served on the boards of history-oriented nonprofits, such as the Historic Charleston Foundation and Charleston's International African American Museum. Powers has been seen in PBS films, such as "The African Americans: Many Rivers to Cross" and "Slavery and the Making of America" and has served as manuscript referee for academic presses and journals. His work on African American social history has been published in book chapters, journals, and encyclopedias. One article was selected for republication by the *South Carolina Historical Magazine* in its *Articles from a Century of Excellence Centennial*, volume 1900–2000. He has been an associate editor for the *South Carolina Encyclopedia* and editor of "The Legacy of African American Leadership" for the Association for the Study of African American Life and History. Powers's major publication is *Black Charlestonians: A Social History 1822–1885*, which won a Choice Outstanding Academic Book Award. He is presently conducting research on African Methodism in South Carolina.

Marjory Wentworth's poems have been nominated for the Pushcart Prize five times. Her books of poetry include *Noticing Eden, Despite Gravity, The Endless Repetition of an Ordinary Miracle,* and *New and Selected Poems.* She is the cowriter with Juan Mendez of *Taking a Stand: The Evolution of Human Rights,* coeditor with Kwame Dawes of *Seeking: Poetry and Prose Inspired by the Art of Jonathan Green,* and the author of the prizewinning children's story *Shackles.* She is the cofounder and former president of the Lowcountry Initiative for the Literary Arts. She serves on the editorial board of the University of South Carolina's Palmetto Poetry Series, and she is the poetry editor for *Charleston Currents.* Her work is included in the South Carolina Poetry Archives at Furman University, and she is the poet laureate of South Carolina.